Resonant Gaps

The University of Georgia Press

ATHENS AND LONDON

RESONANT

GAPS {
Between

Baudelaire

& Wagner

Margaret Miner

© 1995 by the University of Georgia Press
Athens, Georgia 30602
All rights reserved
Designed by Louise OFarrell
Set in 10½/14 Fournier by Tseng Information Systems, Inc.

The paper in this book meets the guidelines for permanence
and durability of the Committee on Production Guidelines for
Book Longevity of the Council on Library Resources.

Printed in the United States of America

99 98 97 96 95   C   5   4   3   2   I

Library of Congress Cataloging in Publication Data
Miner, Margaret.
Resonant gaps : between Baudelaire and Wagner / Margaret Miner.
p.   cm.
Contains Baudelaire's essay Richard Wagner et Tannhäuser à
Paris, originally published: Paris : E. Dentu, 1861.
Includes bibliographical references (p.   ) and index.
ISBN 0-8203-1709-8 (alk. paper)
1. Baudelaire, Charles, 1821–1867—Knowledge—Music.
2. Wagner, Richard, 1813–1883—Influence.   3. Music and
literature.   4. French literature—History and criticism.
I. Baudelaire, Charles, 1821–1867. Richard Wagner et Tannhäuser
à Paris.   II. Title.
ML80.B35M5   1995
780'.084—dc20   94-28793

British Library Cataloging in Publication Data available

In memory of
Gerhard S. Ottersberg
1898–1993

CONTENTS

Acknowledgments   ix

1   *From an Unsafe Distance*   1

2   *Emphatic Music*   25

3   *Music in Person*   61

4   *Openings*   99

5   *Breach of Genius*   143

APPENDIX 1   *Richard Wagner et "Tannhäuser" à Paris*
by Charles Baudelaire   167

APPENDIX 2   Prelude to *Lohengrin*
by Richard Wagner   197

Notes   203

Bibliography   239

Index   249

ACKNOWLEDGMENTS

MY SINCERE THANKS go first to Vanderbilt University, which generously allowed me a semester of leave to work on this book. I owe a great deal of gratitude to all my colleagues in the Department of French and Italian, who were as continuously encouraging as they were tactful about not asking every two minutes how the manuscript was coming along. In particular, I offer my warmest thanks to Claude Pichois and Barbara Bowen for their good counsel and their faith in me; special thanks also to Vince Bowen, Virginia Scott, and Mary-Kay Miller, all of whom dispensed quantities of high-quality caffeine and moral support at crucial intervals.

This project could not have been completed without invaluable help of all sorts from Peter Brooks. Much-appreciated assistance has also come at various times from Susan Blood, Richard Goodkin, Frank Paul Bowman, and an anonymous reader of the manuscript. Many thanks to Susan Nicholson, of Vanderbilt University's W. T. Bandy Center for Baudelaire Studies, for help with Appendix 1; just as many thanks to John Schaffer and Edward Pearsall for help with Appendix 2. Thomas H. Goetz has kindly given permission to print a revised and expanded version of "Putting the Emphasis on Music: Baudelaire and the *Lohengrin* Prelude" (*Nineteenth-Century French Studies* 21, nos. 3–4 [1993]: 384–401) as chapter 2. I am deeply grateful to Kelly Caudle and Grace Buonocore, my editors at the University of Georgia Press; a particular word of gratitude goes to Karen K. Orchard, associate director and executive editor of the Press.

Heartfelt thanks to Ruth and Walt Miner, whose unblinking encouragement was as vital to me in this enterprise as in all others. A demure thank-you to Bud and Rose, who may be right to give book writing a very low priority in the general scheme of things. And my most profound thanks to Brian Hyer, who, despite the difficulties of our commute, has contrived never for a moment to be far away in any sense that matters.

1 { *From an Unsafe Distance*

THIS BOOK is about the literary project, as conceived and attempted by Charles Baudelaire, of writing on music. While examining this project, I reexplore some territory already mapped and inhabited at various times by Baudelaire specialists, theorists of romanticism and symbolism, students of Wagnerism, and a long line of music and literary critics. Although the present study by no means ignores the traces of all these previous expeditions, it nonetheless goes exploring on its own account and for its own purposes. Possibly the best way to give a preliminary overview of its aims is to emphasize that expressions such as "reexplore territory" and "inhabited" have not been chosen at random: I devote much attention to the effects produced and the questions raised by geographical metaphors, personifications, and images of both chronological ordering and mythological repetition. This book sets out, in other words, to study the ways in which Baudelaire and other authors whose work is at times bound up with his—mainly Liszt, Wagner, Nietzsche, Mallarmé, and Proust—exploit certain powers of figurative language while writing on music in general, and on Wagner's music in particular.

The central preposition in the phrase "writing on music" has also been chosen deliberately. Especially problematic with respect to Baudelaire, this "on" hints at the effort of all these authors to superimpose some of their writing so directly onto music that the two might become fused—inseparable, if not indistinguishable, from each other. In specific instances, that is, Baudelaire and the others try to make their readers take the preposition much more literally than usual. In addition to the relatively commonplace literary projects that consist of using language either to evoke or to imitate a piece of music, the authors studied here all attempt in one way or another to discover a common place where their writing about Wagner's music may somehow coincide with its referent, where their writing may be literal enough to erase the distinction between reading about Wagner's music and listening to it. Following Baudelaire, one might say, these authors try to use figurative language in such a manner that it inscribes itself literally on music.

The writing on music to be considered here, then, aims to put its figures at the service of the letter and thereby to render the letter profoundly, essentially musical; it is from these complex relations between the figures of language and their literal goals that this book draws its energy. I argue, ultimately, that the writing in question fails to reach its goal, that it fails to overcome the gap separating it from the music toward which it is directed. But as I also try to show, this failure is never complete: although music and letters remain in some ways distant from each other, all of the authors are nevertheless able to make that distance productive. Distance thus becomes the paradoxical means by which writing can draw closer to music, even if literal bonds between the two are always elusive. Figurative language, already vital to the project of superimposing letters on music, is also crucial to the exploitation of their irreducible distance. For this reason, figures of language and their polymorphic role in the project of writing on music dominate my critical narrative in the pages to follow.

PROVOCATIVE CIRCUMSTANCES

Charles Baudelaire's 1861 essay *Richard Wagner et "Tannhäuser" à Paris* is central to all chapters of this book. It does not occupy any of them entirely; sometimes it serves only as a point of departure or arrival or else as a means of passage between other texts. But I return to the essay repeatedly, and my argument frequently works its way outward—to varying distances—from detailed readings of quotations from the essay. It is therefore worth considering at the outset why the essay itself invites such excursions, how it promises to reward them, and what the worth of this promise might be.

From most points of view, Baudelaire's Wagner essay is an anomaly. It is the only piece of music criticism that Baudelaire ever attempted, despite the prominence of music as a theme and a metaphor throughout his writings. Baudelaire would probably have been the first to admit, moreover, that his essay did not fit very well under the heading of music criticism, except in the broadest sense given to the term by journalistic practices of his day: begun as a fan letter to Wagner, the essay eventually mixed the polemical tone of a position paper (aimed at the prejudiced few) with the exaggerated enthusiasm of an advertisement (aimed at the uninformed many).[1] By most standards, Baudelaire was not really qualified to write about Wagner at all; he had practically no musical education, a very limited acquaintance with Wagner's theoretical prose, and a notoriously inadequate experience of Wagner's operatic works. Yet since the late nineteenth century, his essay has been regarded by all sorts of people as an exemplary response to Wagner's art. Already in Baudelaire's own time, the essay was clearly the most eloquent and complex statement to come from among the French admirers of Wagner. If Baudelaire's essay is an anomaly, then, it is at any rate an outstanding and durable one.

Perhaps the most evident thing about the essay is its continual, slightly overdone effort to sidestep expectations and evade classification. Upon even a rapid skimming, it is hard to miss Baudelaire's heavy-handed presentation of his text as an exception, as discourse that counts on its unusual circumstances and peripheral status. His sudden, impassioned declarations, his equally sudden disclaimers of expertise, his sweeping generalizations followed by denials of the authority to make them—all these suggest that Baudelaire is out to exploit the seductive power inherent in the exceptional and the unprecedented. And Baudelaire has in fact succeeded: his essay has repeatedly been granted the impressive, if self-contradictory, status of an all-encompassing exception. It has been held up, for instance, as an unexpected demonstration of all the critical talents that Baudelaire usually lavished instead on the visual arts, as the unlikely occasion for a summary of all Baudelaire's major aesthetic principles, as the most extraordinary exposition of "all the recurring issues of the literary response to Wagner," and even as evidence that Baudelaire was "the most advanced consciousness" of Wagner's epoch.[2] Prolonging a paradox that Baudelaire apparently wanted to set in action, readers of *Richard Wagner et "Tann-häuser" à Paris* have gotten into the habit of enshrining it as a normative deviation, a standard-setting anomaly erected in the midst of Baudelaire studies, Wagner studies, comparative studies, and the history of ideas.

This habit is probably impossible to set aside all at once; the peculiar logic at work in the reception of the essay would no doubt overturn any quick effort to take away either the normative or the anomalous side of its perceived character. I would like instead to begin by studying some of the essay's methods of keeping the two sides of its character visible. If readers have on the whole perpetuated its paradoxical reputation, it is because they have found themselves encouraged to do so both by the essay's rhetoric and by the nature of its involvement in its cultural surroundings. In this first chapter, I concentrate on what I take to be the predominant metaphor with which the essay tries not only to represent its own situation at the time of its writing, but also to figure and—crucially—to limit the uses that can be made of it at any time, in any situation. More precisely, I try to show how *Richard Wagner et "Tannhäuser" à Paris* attempts to set itself up as a particular kind of landmark, as something unusual and obtrusive that nonetheless fades into the landscape when it is not serving to mark distances and directions—when it is not serving, that is, to draw one's gaze as much *away* from itself as toward itself. My fundamental argument is that Baudelaire's essay does in fact serve as such a landmark, that the essay effectively recognizes and figures its own inability to attract critical attention without also deflecting it elsewhere.

What the essay does not sufficiently recognize, on the other hand, is its corresponding inability to determine in any reliable way where and how critical attention, once deflected, will travel. As noted earlier, the essay is strategically placed at the periphery of several disciplines, so that readers approaching from the direction of, say, literary criticism may easily reorient themselves toward music history or aesthetics. But despite his various disclaimers and apologies, Baudelaire is not always inclined to leave the view open on all sides, or rather, to make clear that his essay is a marker, not a checkpoint. Put another way, the essay does not reflect very much on the possible differences between a landmark and a monument; it confuses the enabling visibility of the one with the view-blocking mass of the other.

Seen as a monument, the essay tends to slow the circulation of readers around it, imposing normal traffic patterns and fixed stopping points. Seen as a landmark, however, the essay does not so much regulate as it facilitates movement, pointing out a network of routes in and through the regions around itself. This book attempts to turn the obedient parade of tourists (pilgrims?) into a hiking adventure: it aims to discover what kinds of travel become possible when Baudelaire's essay is allowed to stand out as an exceptional text, but is denied its traditionally monumental, normative, definitive status. Taking Baudelaire's essay as a landmark that freely draws and deflects interpretation, this study is meant to suggest how remarkably varied the surrounding circulation might become and how wide a territory it might cover.

Baudelaire himself formulated his paradoxical ambitions for *Richard Wagner* when he called it a "long-meditated work of *circumstance.*"[3] This oxymoron, with its emphatic juxtaposition of ephemeral circumstance and sustained meditation, serves very well to evoke the tension later implicit in the essay's reputation as an exception. The circumstance in question actually involved two events, both of them brief and explosive. Baudelaire first considered writing his essay in early February 1860, on the occasion of three controversial concerts that Wagner presented in Paris at the Théâtre-Italien in order to promote excerpts from his operas. But Baudelaire did not finish the essay until late March 1861, during the uproar that followed three disastrous performances of *Tannhäuser* at the Paris Opéra. In between these events, Baudelaire reflected, hesitated, studied books by and about Wagner, and tried to hear more of Wagner's music; having been extraordinarily moved by his experience at the Théâtre-Italien, he prolonged and delayed the work of writing about it.[4] As a result, the publication of Baudelaire's essay was adroitly timed so as to profit both from scandals of the musical season and from leisurely, intimate meditation.

These two profit motives, however, remain somewhat at odds with each other in *Richard Wagner.* Although Baudelaire refers throughout his essay to various incidents surrounding Wagner's Paris performances, he does not always integrate them thoroughly with his personal reflections. Baudelaire in fact draws attention to this gap between event and contemplation by means of a postscript, "Encore quelques mots," which he appended to the essay when it appeared in book form a month after its initial publication in the *Revue européenne*.[5] In this postscript, he bitterly summarizes the combination of circumstances that led to the failure of *Tannhäuser:* the political involvement of Napoléon III in its production; the artistic inadequacies of the orchestra, the set designers, and most of the soloists; the omission of a ballet scene in the second act, to the fury of Jockey Club members whose mistresses were dancers at the Opéra; the general hostility of the Parisian press; and above all, the character of *Tannhäuser* as a serious and unfamiliar work that called for more "sustained attention" than Paris audiences were accustomed, in Baudelaire's opinion, to give operas.[6] But Baudelaire gives his own attention to all these matters of circumstance only in an addendum that stands well apart from the essay proper, and even then, it would appear, he gives it mainly at the prompting of his publisher.[7] In the four sections of the essay itself, most of his meditative concentration is directed elsewhere.

To discover the focus of Baudelaire's meditating, it is helpful to study those junctures at which, immersed in his intensely personal admiration for Wagner, he abruptly recalls that he must compete for the public's attention with a crowd of professional musicians and concert reviewers. Twice during the course of the essay, Baudelaire interrupts himself to declare his lack of musical expertise and to recommend that readers turn elsewhere for "an encomium in technical style" (¶6) or a "complete and technical review" (¶31). On the second occasion, however, Baudelaire nuances his apology and explains that he is not entirely sorry to keep his distance from such technical writing: "I must therefore limit myself to general views that, however rapid they may be, are nonetheless useful. Besides, is it not more convenient, for certain minds, to judge the beauty of a landscape by placing themselves on a height than by traveling successively over all the paths that furrow it?" (¶31). This question, with its imagery of paths and overviews, figures the distance between Baudelaire's essay and Wagner's music as something salutary and productive, but it also gives reasons to mistrust that distance. Interpreted rhetorically, the question reassures readers by claiming, first, that this music is as easy to appreciate as a pretty landscape and, second, that a good look over the musical scenery will serve just as well as a laborious march down every trail. Understood in this way, the question holds up Baudelaire's essay as an excellent telescope (or opera glass) for surveying Wagner's music from afar, or else it offers the essay as a means of traveling far enough away from the music to enjoy a panoramic view. Interpreted as a genuine inquiry, however, the question is less reassuring. Formulated negatively, it hints that a cliff-top view, no matter how spectacular, is simply a convenience for the lazy, the impatient, or the handicapped. It implies that the distance between the essay and the music must after all be crossed, and it raises the disquieting possibility that to cross with the eyes or the imagination is not as good as a journey on foot. Interpreted literally, then, the question obliges readers to wonder just how Baudelaire might help them move from his text to Wagner's music or, perhaps, just how far their reading may be from listening.[8]

While he thus leaves some doubt about its intent, Baudelaire nonetheless succeeds with his question in establishing distance as one of the fundamental concerns of his essay. This manner of problematizing critical and aesthetic distance by means of a spatial metaphor is already familiar to readers of Baudelaire's art criticism, in which his occasional references to music are overshadowed by no apologies for technical incompetence. In particular, Baudelaire raises questions of music and distance during two discussions of Delacroix as a colorist. The first is found in Baudelaire's *Salon de 1846*, the second in his *Exposition universelle (1855):*

> The best way of knowing whether a painting is melodious is to look at it from far enough away so as to understand neither the subject nor the lines. If it is melodious, it already has a meaning, and it has already taken its place in the repertory of memories.[9]

> [S]een from too great a distance to analyze or even to understand the subject, a painting by Delacroix has already produced a rich, happy or melancholy impression on the soul. One could say that this painting, like sorcerers or mesmerists, projects its thought from a distance. . . . Then its admirable color tones [accords de sa couleur] often make one dream of harmony and melody, and the impression one brings away from his paintings is often almost musical. (2:595)

In both these passages, Baudelaire encourages the observer to stand absurdly far away from the canvas so as to avoid taking the painting too literally. Exaggerated distance, that is, results in a closeness that has nothing to do with physical proximity, since it consists in the privilege of looking beyond the exactitude of lines and colors to the intimate, synesthetic blending of painted and musical figures. It is therefore possible for observers at an exposition to maintain distance and to overcome it at precisely the same time: by exploiting their measurable separation from the canvas, they may come immeasurably closer than those who stand too near to see the painting as it "projects its thought" into the distance. For art critics and their readers, however, this exploitation of distance depends less on the floor space of galleries than on the use of figurative language. Whatever his concrete vantage point, Baudelaire proves that the canvas is very far away by writing that the "painting is melodious" and that it gives him an "almost musical" impression; he uses the linguistic distance between "tableau" and "mélodieux" to suggest his extreme nearness to the painting and his consequent discovery of the painting's extreme nearness to music. Baudelaire doubly exploits the distance between literal and figurative description by making it stand, first, for the literal distance between the eye and the canvas or between the canvas and a musical score and, second, for the figurative lack of distance between the critical observer and the painting or between the painting and a melody.[10]

If the art critic must rely on language to place readers at the proper distance from a painting, then perhaps the music critic must do likewise: maybe the climber surveying Wagner's music from a high lookout point corresponds to the observer studying Delacroix's painting from too far away. It may therefore be possible to interpret Baudelaire's question both literally and figuratively, since his essay must place readers at an exaggerated distance from the musical landscape for the apparently contradictory purpose of bringing them much closer to it than would otherwise be conceivable. Elsewhere in his writing, Baudelaire makes similar connections between musical understanding, concrete or spatial distance, and the abstract or conceptual distance separating different arts; a celebrated example of this is his declaration in *Mon cœur mis à nu* that "music," like "all the arts, more or less," "gives the idea of space" (1:702). But Baudelaire also shows persistent ambivalence or indecisiveness where this particular group of related distances is concerned. Just after the passage from his *Exposition universelle (1855)* quoted above, for example, Baudelaire confusingly tries to argue further for the connections between musical, visual, and inter-pretive spaces while at the same time apologizing for the "subterfuges of language" that make his argument possible. He first quotes, from his own poem "Les Phares" (1:13), the quatrain in which Delacroix's work appears as a "lake of blood" where "strange fanfares / Pass like a stifled sigh from Weber," thus apparently reemphasizing that linguistic distance can serve to bring music and painting very close together. But he then proceeds to foreshorten this distance and to drain away much of its power by adding the following explanation: *"the fanfares and Weber:* ideas of romantic music awakened by the harmonies of his [Delacroix's] color" (2:595). Rather than literal closeness, Baudelaire now suggests, his writing effects only a figurative rapprochement between painting and music; like a lighthouse beacon, his poem allows the two arts to glimpse each other, but it keeps a safe interval between them.

For Baudelaire, then, it is difficult or impossible to assign a stable value to the distance that separates his writing from Wagner's music. Although determined to set his essay well apart from its musical topic, like a hilltop far removed from the lands it overlooks, he is unable to state the exact nature and consequences of the gap between them. From some points of view, this divide may be useful or even essential, paradoxically allowing Baudelaire and his readers to perceive the closeness of musical and textual composition, the synesthetic exchange of properties between music and letters. But from other points of view, this gap may function more simply as a hindrance, as an invisible barrier preventing any actual movement be-tween the domain of Baudelaire's essay and the region of Wagner's music. *Richard Wagner* is thus a locus of hesitation or indecision: it marks Baude-laire's inability either to establish the real proximity of writing to music or to admit their definitive separation from each other. One of the results of this wavering is a persistent, mutually exploitative rapport between the tone of Baudelaire's essay, which is frequently emphatic or declamatory, and its argumentation, which often proves upon scrutiny to be neither thorough nor convincing. Uncertain whether the various "subterfuges of language" he deploys will turn their distance from the music to good use or merely push the music further away, Baudelaire remains poised like a traveler stranded on a high cliff above a magnificent landscape.

MODES OF TRANSPORT

This poised uncertainty takes a starker, more condensed form in Baudelaire's much cited poem "La Musique." Baudelaire was perhaps more at ease figuring music as a seascape than as a landscape; allusions to the musical sound and movements of water permeate *Les Fleurs du Mal*.[11] But since this poem is partly a meditation on the difficulty of traveling over literal and figurative distances, it explores the same fundamental problem as the Wagner essay. And more concisely than the essay, the poem shows what is at stake when figurative writing attempts to voyage into literal proximity with music.

> La musique souvent me prend comme une mer!
>   Vers ma pâle étoile,
> Sous un plafond de brume ou dans un vaste éther,
>   Je mets à la voile;
>
> La poitrine en avant et les poumons gonflés
>   Comme de la toile,
> J'escalade le dos des flots amoncelés
>   Que la nuit me voile;
>
> Je sens vibrer en moi toutes les passions
>   D'un vaisseau qui souffre;
> Le bon vent, la tempête et ses convulsions
>
>   Sur l'immense gouffre
> Me bercent. D'autres fois, calme plat, grand miroir
>   De mon désespoir!
>
>   (1:68)

> [Music often takes me like a sea!
> Toward my pale star,
> Beneath a ceiling of fog or in a vast ether,
> I set sail;
>
> Breast forward and lungs swollen
> Like sails,

I climb the backs of piled-up waves
That the night veils from me;

I feel vibrating in me all the passions
Of a vessel that suffers;
The good wind, the tempest and its convulsions

On the immense abyss
Cradle me. At other times, flat calm, great mirror
Of my despair.]

At some levels, this poem insists on the visceral closeness between sea and sailor, or music and listener. The exclamation in the first line, together with the pronounced, uneven alternation between twelve-syllable and five-syllable lines, makes it clear that the narrating vessel does not observe from the far-off shore, but is tossed or cradled or becalmed in the intimacy of the water. As the first line also declares, however, this closeness is only occasional. The musical sea "often"—but not always—takes the narrator, and the ambiguous resonance of "takes" (sensual embrace or violent assault?) gives a doubtful cast to their intimacy. The quatrains both point to this separation between sea and narrator by evoking a scenario that is in some ways similar to the hilltop image from *Richard Wagner:* the narrator climbs to the crest of the waves and faces out over the expanse separating him from his "pale star." But whereas the climber in the Wagner essay gazes at the countryside below, the wave-mounting sailor here cannot even glimpse the seascape before him, since the sail (in French, *voile*) under which he might move forward is so closely bound up with the nighttime veil (also *voile*) that makes voyaging uncertain. More immediately and urgently than the Wagner essay, therefore, this poem identifies music with distance; the music/ocean is not so much the far-off destination of the narrator's travels as it is the still-uncrossed space that makes travel desirable and difficult, the equivocal distance that makes stars appear both excessively remote and attainably close. It might be tempting to suggest that this ink-dark stretch of sea ultimately represents the possibility of a perfect coincidence between music and writing, between the sonorous waves and currents rendered by musicians and the furrows traced on the page by star-gazing poets. But the final tercet of the sonnet confirms the impossibility of this ideal coincidence. Seen in daylight whenever the wind subsides, the music/ocean still reaches into the distance, but it now prevents the narrator from hoping either to move or to see across this distance. With its mirroring surface, this second seascape accentuates both the narrator's isolation and the endless, illusory reflections that make the spaces around him impossible to judge. The musical sea of this poem thus forces upon the writer/narrator a double, unpredictably alternating outlook on distance: it serves at some moments to bring the starry skyline enticingly close and at other moments to make vision dauntingly unreliable. But this mercurial distance refuses at all moments to let the poet cross definitively over it.[12]

It is important to notice that the distance placed in question by "La Musique," hospitable or not, is always horizontal. The narrator climbs up the waves for the purpose of looking or moving ahead rather than down, and the "abyss," or *gouffre,* of the last tercet—unlike most of Baudelaire's *gouffres*—does not inspire any acute fear of falling. However equivocal it may be in other regards, the poem is clearly about traveling, not about drowning; its transports do not involve any loss of self-awareness or of critical judgment. The musical sea is above all a surface whose changes in quality and texture continually remind the narrator that his relation to it is problematic and that his writing about it must be provisional. Whether it shakes him convulsively or confronts him brutally with his own reflection, the music/ocean divides the narrator both from itself and from himself. In consequence, his attention is never fully immersed in the musical sea; it is continually dispersed outward, either beyond the tossing waves to the "pale star" or along the reflecting surface that extends into infinity. The narrator's experience of the music is thus never immediate and never complete, so that his attempts to capture it in writing—whether hopefully or despairingly, whether with similes or metaphors or strange metrical patterns—could conceivably stretch on into vast temporal and spatial distances, spreading out over interminable pages.

"La Musique," which was first published in 1857, is often cited as evidence that Baudelaire was predisposed to sympathize with Wagner's musical aesthetics. But the poem in fact diverges strikingly from some of the uses Wagner made in the 1840s and 1850s of the sea as an extended metaphor for music. In *Das Kunstwerk der Zukunft,* for instance, Wagner figures music as a sea of harmony that touches, on one side, the shore of rhythm (dance, dramatic gesture) and, on the other, the shore of melody (sung to words). Dismissing its surface as insignificant, Wagner claims that "man dives into this sea in order to return to daylight refreshed and beautiful; his heart feels wonderfully expanded when he looks down into this depth, capable of all the most inconceivable possibilities, whose bottom his eye shall never fathom, whose unfathomableness thereby fills him with wonder and intimations of the infinite."[13] Unlike Baudelaire's infinitely changeable, infinitely extended ocean, this musical sea consists of a single, uniform element (harmony), and it is strictly delimited by the shores on either side. One purpose of the sea is to connect these two shores; in a preceding passage, Wagner half comically says that if the sea of music were to shrink, one would need railroads, or at the very least steamboats, to link the continents of dance and poetry.[14] The best thing to do in this musical sea, however, is to dive: the primary movement evoked is vertical. Wagner's diver is submerged in a total, unmediated experience of pure harmony, and even his occasional returns to the surface involve no anguishing separation from the music. On the contrary, the sunlight enables him to stare back downward, his heart "wonderfully expanded" in proportion to the immense vista below it. And while the depths provoke "intimations of the infinite," they do not bring any accompanying sense of frustration: although unable fully to explore the musical infinitude, the diver nonetheless belongs to it as completely as could be desired.

One might perhaps object that on a number of important occasions, Wagner also conjures up hostile seas and laborious, interminable attempts to cross them. The various sailing voyages of *Tristan und Isolde* might be understood, among other things, as a quest for absolute immersion in musical experience, a despairing quest whose goal alternately seems unattainably far-off and unbearably close. *Der fliegende Holländer* might provide a similar example; the Dutchman has repeatedly thrown himself "down into the sea's deepest maw," only to find himself back on his course over limitless distances.[15] But in both these instances, the travelers eventually reach their desired destination, taking a final dive into a musical sea much like the one evoked in *Das Kunstwerk der Zukunft.* As if gazing into the turbulent water that has brought Isolde's ship, Tristan invokes the sunlight that shines down on his flowing blood (act 3, scene 2), while Isolde explicitly compares her imminent death to a dive into harmonious waves (act 3, scene 3); the Dutchman's ship sinks at the moment of Senta's ecstatic dive from the cliff above her home into the ocean (act 3, scene 2). Unlike the unfinishable expedition of "La Musique," then, these operatic travels end in scenes of complete and comforting immersion. Baudelaire's tormented navigator must recount an endlessly interrupted voyage toward a deceptively distant star. Wagner's divers, arriving at familiar shores and delighted by the distant depths, have briefer, more satisfying journeys to narrate.

If "La Musique" excludes all hope for an ideal experience of music that would be both immediate and total, it is not because Baudelaire found such an ideal unattractive. On the contrary, his extensive summary of *Der fliegende Holländer* near the end of *Richard Wagner*, as well as his praise for the "supernatural grandeur" of Senta's transfiguring plunge into the sea (¶45), would suggest that he longs for submersion in music that could be instantly and entirely encompassed in writing. Thus divided between longing and resignation, Baudelaire's poem and essay both have much in common with "Höchst zerstreute Gedanken," a section of E. T. A. Hoffmann's *Kreisleriana*. It is here that the musician Johann Kreisler famously evokes the synesthetic mixture of "colors, sounds and perfumes" that he perceives upon listening to music.[16] Widely regarded as one of the more evident sources for Baudelaire's sonnet "Correspondances," Hoffmann's meditation on synesthesia is also quoted at length in *Salon de 1846*, shortly after the passage on melodious paintings discussed above. In the quotation, Kreisler evokes an "odor of brown and red marigolds" mingled with the far-off sounds of an oboe, suggesting that together they form one example of a completely enveloping, instantly accessible experience (2:425–26).[17] They seem to enable Kreisler, in other words, to exploit aesthetic distance consistently and successfully: the aromatic colors of oboe music, perceived from a sufficient mental and physical distance ("as if in the distance"), seem to cluster so closely around the perceiving subject that even the linguistic gaps involved in formulating the experience appear negligible; the literal incoherence separating "odor" and "oboe sounds" and "brown" would seem merely to strengthen the figurative bonds that hold them together. Yet for all its wholeness and immediacy when first encountered, Kreisler recalls and retells this experience in a way that emphasizes its sketchy, fragmentary character. Presented as a three-sentence snippet, unconnected to other fragments in a series whose title advertises its disjointed disorganization ("Extremely Scattered Thoughts"), Kreisler's brown-scented, red-flowered oboe tones do not seem to flow into an engulfing sea of unmediated experience. In the first fragment, Kreisler explains that the section's title is, much to his chagrin, appropriate: although he has for years felt driven to write about his impressions of various artworks, these writings have always remained "scattered"; they are bits of interpretation that do more to fracture and dissipate his experience than to keep him immersed in it. And although Kreisler ironically foresees that his future readers will look for some principle of wholeness hidden among the fragments, he also implies that the very act of looking will probably prevent them from finding such a principle: once dispersed throughout the fragments, he hints, their attention will always be drawn further and further outward. Even if readers literally ignore Kreisler's injunction to burn his "Thoughts," they will still obey it figuratively, scattering the ashes of his aesthetic experience as they pursue flickering interpretations into the distance.

As readers of Kreisler's scattered remarks, Baudelaire and his contemporaries must have considered the disquieting possibility that while listeners might feel themselves able to bathe in an absolutely immediate and engulfing experience of music, they would never be able to convey that experience adequately in writing. The wider one distends the gap between literal and figurative formulations, suggests Kreisler, the further music will retreat from one's text; his fragrantly musical marigolds—and maybe also Baudelaire's "melodious paintings"—will simply disperse readers' attention, separating them further and further from the music with which the text set out to unite them. It is unlikely, moreover, that this threat of textual dispersion was an idle abstraction for musical readers of the 1850s and 1860s: as a number of music enthusiasts and concert reviewers were well aware, most of the French writing on Wagner during this period had precisely the effect of rendering his music inaccessible, despite its perpetual claims to lead readers into direct proximity with this music. Even without the publication of Baudelaire's essay, that is, circumstances in the musical press would have given French readers an opportunity to meditate on the deceptive distances between writing and Wagner's music.

By the end of 1860, highlights from Wagner's larger prose works had been summarized several times in French journals. In 1852, J.-F. Fétis discussed *Eine Mitteilung an meine Freunde* in a series of articles, and various accounts of *Die Kunst und die Revolution, Das Kunstwerk der Zukunft,* and *Oper und Drama* appeared in France at other times; Wagner himself recapitulated the three latter books in his 1860 *Lettre sur la musique.*[18] Garbled and biased as many of these summaries were, they effectively turned not only the famous "music of the future" [la musique de l'avenir] but also such formulations as "the reuniting of the arts" [la réunion des arts] and "organic unity" [l'unité organique] into catchphrases that the French public routinely associated with Wagner. Haphazardly exploited by both Wagner's admirers and his adversaries, these slogans may have been essentially meaningless to casual readers of the latest Wagner news. Even so, a few music journalists apparently continued to take some of the catchphrases literally, using them not as mere formulas, but rather as evocations of the wholeness and immediacy that were supposed to characterize any experience of Wagner's music. The results of this were double: journalists writing against Wagner reacted by filling their columns with images intended to convey the remoteness or inaccessibility of his music; journalists in favor of Wagner's music determinedly figured it as a place of easy approach and rapid access.

In both cases, the writers nearly always chose images that had to do with traveling, often over an unusual landscape. One irate reviewer, for example, responded to a performance of the overture to *Die Meistersinger* by writing, "Its melody is beautiful, but the harmony that ought to sustain this melody only jostles and hampers it. Wagner strikes me as someone in good health with good legs who obstinately persists in walking with crutches."[19] Another hostile critic, limping through a review of Wagner's 1860 concerts in Paris, declared, "I'll admit it frankly: a long race over moors and marshes, beneath a heavy, black sky streaked with pallid lightning, would not have exhausted me more than the stubborn attention that it was my duty to devote to all these pieces."[20] Wagner's music thus appeared to the

Parisian public as a pitted and desolate territory, across which a crippled composer tried to drag stumbling listeners. Other critics found the journey across Wagner's music to be invigorating or even exhilarating; but like Tannhäuser describing the rigors of his pilgrimage to Rome, they also evoked landscapes that were somewhat harsh and bleak. As a favorable reviewer of the 1860 concerts put it, Wagner's "grandiose harmonies, his profoundly modulated melodies [chants], indeterminate in their form, his truncated and yet sublime accents are like the breath of wind that passes over a deserted beach."[21] The vista that opens before this listener is impressive, but it is not hospitable to travelers: the space to be crossed is eerily formless and entirely deserted; the windy "accents" sweeping over it are strangely and disturbingly "truncated," as if the musical panorama has the power to hinder or lame anything—even wind—that moves through it.

Still another traveler/reviewer of the 1860 concerts makes explicit the crippling relation between writing and the Wagnerian landscape. He does so, tellingly, in the midst of a lyrical passage on the freedom of movement that he hears above all else in Wagner's music. Claiming that Wagner has rejected the venerable, old-fashioned parallel between the punctuation of written discourse and the cadences of music, the reviewer declares that Wagner's music, like a stretch of unbroken terrain, allows for no pause, no "intermediate stop." As a paradoxical consequence, any listener thrust into this territory is disoriented and ultimately paralyzed: "Once one has entered this domain, where everything is unknown, there can be no rest: one is surrounded by immensity, one perceives in this space worlds that one is unable to reach; the vague uncertainty that seizes the soul leaves it only at the moment when, abandoning its search without result, it [the soul] returns to the positive [revient au positif] by setting foot once more in the world where it was created and where it understands things better."[22] Upon their escape from this music, listeners find that their wandering may have been no more than a vision—either a trick of the uncertain light or else an adventure of the imagination—and that it has certainly been a "search without result," a journey that ends up where it started out. Like Baudelaire's musical travelers, these listeners seem to stay rooted to the spot, whether that spot is figured as a mountainous lookout point or a becalmed sea; the music is for them an expanse that, in certain ways, they never cross. Writing, they discover, will offer them no safe paths, vehicles, or resting places: it may carry their gaze rapidly and recklessly across the music, but it gives them little hope of moving through the music palpably and in person. As a mode of transport over musical distance, writing would appear to be unreliable and inadequate.

IN CONCERT

In 1873 Charles Grandmougin published an opuscule entitled *Esquisse sur Richard Wagner*. More ambitious but less eloquent than Baudelaire, Grandmougin wanted to defend Wagner's music during the aftermath of the Franco-Prussian War, when French sentiment against the composer was running even higher than usual. In the second section of his treatise, Grandmougin attempts to rank Wagner with the classical German masters most admired in France, using geographical metaphors to suggest both Wagner's place and his prominence among them. Mozart's music, according to Grandmougin, leads listeners down "those little paths that run alongside the rivers, where the walker strays on beautiful spring days," a trek so charmingly uneventful that in the end "one moves without advancing, and one plunges into contemplative somnolence."[23] For listeners who would rather not find themselves stalled in such lowlands, Grandmougin recommends Beethoven instead, because "one feels, while listening, the same impression as when one climbs a mountain. The plain unfolds little by little below our feet; the horizon widens; . . . and when we reach the summit of the mountain, we hardly recognize the countryside, so thoroughly has the crescendo of the ascent metamorphosed the whole landscape."[24] A similarly thrilling climb awaits Wagner's listeners, claims Grandmougin, but the climb does not take place on a mountain, nor does it arrive at the same overview. To hear Wagner's operas is rather to scale "admirable monuments," superb but manmade, and the view from their summit is equally fabricated: looking down, one sees not open country, but rather a painted landscape, a handcrafted scene peopled with small figures that "are developed according to parallels and mutual contrasts like the different color values of a painting."[25] If Beethoven's music spreads out a natural vista, then Wagner's operas form an immense picture gallery;

both exploit the "metamorphosing" power of their distance from listeners, but Wagner encloses the Beethovenian panorama within visibly handmade frames. Or, to put this another way, "if Wagner is linked to Beethoven, . . . it is principally for having transported the symphony into the theater."[26]

It was not lost on Grandmougin, then, that any possibility of surveying the Wagnerian landscape was bound up not only with the space between listeners and the music, but also with the distance between the concert hall and the theater. Wagner was of course notorious, in France and elsewhere, for the demands he made on his audiences. In the postscript to his essay, Baudelaire dryly insisted that even had there been no other difficulties, *Tannhäuser* would have failed in Paris simply because Wagner tried so hard to elicit intelligent and imaginative attention from listeners, rather than letting them take their usual "digestive pleasure" at the Opéra (¶53). While French operagoers had never been noted for their rapt concentration, however, French concertgoers of the same era had set up somewhat different standards for audience behavior. From the 1830s onward, Parisians distinguished between numerous kinds of concerts with various forms of etiquette appropriate to them; charity concerts, salon concerts, and garden concerts all established their own codes for relations between audiences and performers, and some were much less severe than others.[27] At formal symphony orchestra concerts, however, listeners were increasingly expected to sit absorbed in meditation, projecting all their attention away from themselves and over the space that separated them from the music being made on stage.[28]

Even so, Wagner's orchestral concerts in 1860 fostered instead the kind of listener-centered uproar that was generally associated with the frivolous habitués of the Opéra. Most press accounts of those concerts, including Baudelaire's, give a more or less elaborate description of the tumult in the audience, as if all attention in the hall were irresistibly concentrated on listeners rather than spread out toward the stage and the controversial music produced there. Both hostile and favorable critics eagerly recount the open antagonism between "frenetic admirers" and "relentless detractors"; many of the articles drift away from the music altogether in order to evoke the noisy confrontations held outside in the foyer.[29] Well after the famous performances of 1860 and 1861, moreover, the antics of Wagner's hyperanimated audiences continued to fascinate the French press. Throughout the 1860s and early 1870s, for example, it was almost certain that "the applause of some and the whistles of others" would drown out part of the music whenever the conductor Jules Pasdeloup scheduled a Wagner overture for one of his Concerts Populaires de Musique Classique.[30] Held in the enormous Cirque Napoléon, Pasdeloup's concerts attracted up to four thousand listeners who perched on hard benches while straining to see the orchestra. In the turmoil surrounding any Wagner excerpts on the program, therefore, the sea of agitated listeners must have blocked all sight of the musicians and all sound of the music.

Such concerts, at which fragments of Wagner's music were barely perceptible amid the confusion they provoked, were far removed from the ideal performance conditions Wagner tried to create for himself at Bayreuth. Yet however ludicrous a comparison between the Bayreuth Festspielhaus and the Cirque Napoléon might seem, each raised the same problem with respect to Wagner's works: the problem of manipulating the audience's distance from—and therefore its vision of—the music. As Wagner was acutely aware, both the extent and the character of this distance were crucial; the Festspielhaus was, among other things, his most deliberate attempt to control the power of distance in all its aspects. Central to this attempt was Wagner's celebrated plan to hide the orchestra by sinking it well below the spectators' line of vision and by placing all seats in graduated rows that faced toward the stage, thus eliminating the traditional tiers of boxes around the walls of the theater. Such an arrangement, as Wagner and his architects discovered, left a blank gap between the proscenium and the first row of seats, a gap that Wagner grandiosely named "the 'mystic gulf,'" because it had to part reality from ideality."[31] In order to make sure that the audience's gaze would travel properly over it, this gap was framed by a second proscenium, wider than the one that framed the stage; Wagner's hope was that the relation between these two proscenia would create "the singular illusion of an apparent throwing-back of the scene itself, making the spectator imagine it quite far away, though he still beholds it in all the clearness of its actual proximity; while this in turn gives rise to the illusion that the persons figuring upon the stage are of larger, superhuman stature."[32] Wagner heavily and repeatedly emphasized that the sheer existence of a "gulf" just before the stage was not enough; what mattered was the particular, ambiguous quality of the space through which the audience directed its gaze. The "floating atmosphere of distance" between the two proscenia needed to push the stage away into "the unapproachable world of dreams," but it simultaneously needed to bring the listener close enough for the "spectral music" to induce "that clairvoyance in which the scenic picture melts into the truest effigy of life itself."[33] And in order to draw every listener more effectively toward and over this paradoxical distance, Wagner's architects went on to frame the double proscenium at the front of the Festspielhaus within an expanding series of proscenia that engulfed the whole theater: "[T]o do full justice to the idea of an auditorium narrowing in true perspective toward the stage, we must extend the process to the whole interior, adding proscenium after proscenium until they reached their climax in the crowning gallery, and thus enclosing the entire audience in the vista, no matter where it took its place."[34]

Given the startling way in which Baudelaire's essay figures (or prefigures) this design for the Bayreuth Festspielhaus, one might plausibly suppose that Baudelaire's brief experience of Wagner's music inspired him with even greater clairvoyance than Wagner might have expected. Equally startling, moreover, is the way in which Baudelaire's imagery corresponds to the opening of the *Ring* tetralogy for which Bayreuth was constructed. Like Baudelaire's climber, who looks from a cliff top over musical scenery, Wotan and Fricka stare far over the valley of the Rhine toward the newly built Walhalla (*Das Rheingold,* scene 2); in the same way, spectators at Bayreuth peer over a gulf toward a scene lighted and permeated with music from the orchestra below. For the gods, the valley will be magically bridged by a rainbow at the end of scene 4, so that the gaping distance between their rocky lookout point and the castle miraculously poses no obstacle. But for Baudelaire's climber as well as the Bayreuth spectators, exaggerated distance is precisely what seems to bring them within reach of the music; it is the equivocal means of transport that draws their gaze into the Wagnerian landscape, but keeps them from descending onto any of the paths there. Yet both Baudelaire's hilltop and the mountainous ledge across from Walhalla form part of the surrounding country, just as a landmark fits into the lands around it, and the seats of the Festspielhaus similarly belong to the continuous chain of proscenia leading back from the stage: in each instance, the vantage point is—as Wagner remarked—"enclosed within the vista" that opens away from it.

The claustrophobic implications of this last remark might well have disturbed Baudelaire had he lived long enough to see the building and flourishing of Wagner's theater. While his figurative overview of paths in the Wagner landscape was beautiful and seductive, a literal journey to Bayreuth would almost certainly have disheartened him. Already in 1876, at the opening of the Festspielhaus, the material conditions of the trip to Bayreuth often threatened to efface the spiritual transports that Wagner promised to his listeners. Typical of reports from the first Bayreuth festival were Tchaikovsky's comments on his trip to the obscure little town, which was largely unprepared for an influx of travelers: "The road [to the Festspielhaus] lies uphill, with absolutely no shade, so that one is exposed to the scorching rays of the sun. . . . From all sides one hears complaints of hunger and thirst, mingled with comments on present or past performances."[35] Considering that both the complaints and the comments came, in Tchaikovsky's opinion, from a "horde of false admirers" who cared very little for the music, his tone rings hollow when he finally declares that "anyone who believes in the civilising power of Art must take away from Bayreuth a very refreshing impression."[36] Even after the town's residents had learned to cope with annual tourist invasions, moreover, an excursion to Bayreuth was at least as much an earthbound trudge as it was a panoramic adventure. Albert Lavignac's *Voyage artistique à Bayreuth,* for example, begins as follows: "One goes to Bayreuth however one wishes, on foot, on horseback, by carriage, by bicycle, by train, and the true pilgrim ought to go there on his knees. But the most practical way, at least for the French, is by railroad."[37] Despite his ironic overtones and his half-humorous reluctance to "compete unfairly with the Baedeker Guide,"[38] Lavignac was earnestly convinced that practical information about restaurant cars and hotel prices, as well as detailed yearly lists of French travelers to Bayreuth, all formed an indispensable accompaniment to the opera analyses in the latter part of his book. Other commentators on Wagner, claimed Lavignac, mistakenly dealt only with elevated aesthetic visions of Bayreuth, writing "nebulosities" that simply blocked or obscured the practical path Wagner's admirers ought to follow: "[F]ar from smoothing out the road, they clutter it up with difficulties."[39]

In view of Lavignac's plodding tourist guide, it seems more than probable that Baudelaire would, like Nietzsche, have found the trip to Bayreuth difficult and profoundly disturbing. Even when he proposes only to use his essay as a vehicle for traveling figuratively over Wagnerian territory, Baudelaire hesitates: despite its emblematic significance, Baudelaire offers his landscape overview merely as an apology in the form of a question that slips discreetly into the middle of an argument. It is as if Baudelaire is instead searching for a way to bypass all need for a journey into Wagner's works, as if he would much prefer to avoid the dizzying and disorienting effects of any movement—whether by leaps of vision or by railway travel—toward the music. Throughout *Richard Wagner*, therefore, Baudelaire attempts again and again to lessen or suppress various distances that he discovers between his text and the music. His aim in doing so is not to freeze movement entirely; it is rather to inscribe his writing on Wagner's music so that the two might travel together over a landscape that shelters rather than separates them. To this end, Baudelaire makes use of fascinatingly diverse tactics: italicization, quotation, personification, digression, and an out-and-out hunt for metaphors all figure among his textual maneuvers. It is the variety and intricacy of these efforts to conquer distances between writing and music that form the point of departure for each of the remaining chapters in this book.

Ultimately, however, distances always reassert themselves, whether they are viewed as frustrating barriers or promising conditions for intimacy between Baudelaire's essay and the music on which he tries to write. No matter how far he pushes his numerous "subterfuges of language," they always continue to serve as rhetorical instruments for surveying the musical panorama rather than as vehicles for moving along its network of paths. This remains the case, moreover, when Mallarmé and Proust subsequently set out on their explorations of the Wagnerian landscape. Both take Baudelaire's essay as one of their guiding landmarks, and both venture into regions only tantalizingly glimpsed from *Richard Wagner:* most notably, they both pursue questions about Baudelaire's attempt to approach the music with a critical essay rather than with other kinds of writing. But neither Mallarmé nor Proust fully overcomes the mercurial distances they confront; however subtly or thoroughly they exploit its paradoxical possibilities, the gap between their writing and Wagner's music remains intact. Baudelaire therefore writes for them all when he declares, in closing the postscript to his essay, that "in the end the idea is launched, the breach [trouée] is made" (¶64). Defiantly foretelling that the *Tannhäuser* scandal of 1861 will open up broad and unexpected visions of Wagnerian territory, Baudelaire not only evokes the circumstances of Wagner's controversial reception in France, but also demands that his readers meditate on the breach or gap—the "trouée"—between music and writing.

2 } *Emphatic Music*

BAUDELAIRE'S most daring attempt to suppress the distance between writing and music takes place in the first part of *Richard Wagner et "Tannhäuser" à Paris*. The essay is divided into four sections plus its postscript, with the second, third, and fourth sections devoted respectively to a consideration of Wagner's theoretical positions, a discussion of three of his operas, and an effort to define the fundamental traits of his distinctive genius. In the first part of the essay, however, Baudelaire follows a less conventional and less predictable outline. After a preliminary attempt to locate his own aesthetics as a writer in relation to Wagner's aesthetics as a composer, Baudelaire undertakes to demonstrate in precise terms that a part of his text may literally coincide with a piece of Wagner's music. His demonstration focuses on three programs written for Wagner's prelude to *Lohengrin* and includes not only an inquiry into their various levels of meaning, but also an experiment carried out, typographically, on the level of the letter. The apparent thesis behind this demonstration is that rhetorical figuration and typographical inscription may effectively interact for the purpose of translating music straight onto the printed pages of literature or, conversely, of transporting those pages directly into the realm of music.

But this thesis is never made fully explicit: although Baudelaire is willing to state his views on artistic translation in general, he is strikingly reluctant to explain the specific reasoning involved in his *Lohengrin* prelude demonstration. The more concrete his argument appears to become, the more he avoids considering its foundations and its implications. What

Baudelaire *does* recognize explicitly is the interpretive burden that his reticence places on his readers. Already in the first paragraph of his essay, Baudelaire abruptly approaches readers with a double request for help in confronting two crucial types of distance. He does not openly link this request with his image of a climber gazing over a faraway landscape, which he evokes only in part 3. But it is nonetheless clear that the distances of part 1, like the vistas of part 3, are deceptive; although they can be explored and exploited, they can perhaps never be definitively crossed. Georges Poulet has remarked that "distance is not only an interval, it is an ambient milieu, a field of union."[1] This is in fact the view that Baudelaire adopts at the beginning of his essay: however much he may want to conquer distances, he lays as much stress on the movement required for coming over them as on the final moments when they are overcome. The opening paragraph of part 1 reads as follows:

> Let us climb back [Remontons], if you will, over the course of thirteen months, to the beginning of the question, and let me be permitted, in this assessment, to speak often in my own name [mon nom personnel]. This *I,* justly accused of impertinence in many cases, nevertheless implies great modesty; it encloses the writer within the strictest limits of sincerity. By reducing his task, it makes that task easier. After all, it is not necessary to be an expert in probability to become certain that this sincerity will find friends among impartial readers; there is obviously some chance that the artless and candid critic, by recounting only his own impressions, will also recount those of a few unknown supporters.[2]

Baudelaire's first concern is the temporal distance between the present moment and the recent past, specifically between the failure of *Tannhäuser* in March 1861 and the promotional concerts Wagner presented in February 1860. Baudelaire proposes to overcome this distance with a sort of narrative climb backward to 1860, as if the concerts were a promontory with a better view of Wagnerian territory than the opera. By recounting the story of the concerts, he hopes to deal with the Wagner question from its beginning in public controversy at the Théâtre-Italien to its outbreak in massive scandal at the Opéra. But this argumentative and historical intention is almost certainly not the only one to motivate Baudelaire's narrative:

the "beginning of the question" is broad and indefinite enough to include less obvious meanings, especially since its only antecedent is the essay's title. In addition to counting back a year and a month from *Tannhäuser*, for example, Baudelaire may want to measure the separation between hearing Wagner's music as a concertgoer and remembering it as a writer. He may also want to discover the limits of his ability to count or to measure, since he claims only to move toward the origin of an actual, continuing question and not to find an answer or a result. While retelling the story of the 1860 concerts, Baudelaire attempts to explore an ill-defined question, but not to travel beyond the uncertainties of questioning.

Whatever the purposes of this narrative traveling, Baudelaire insists that it should be a collective journey. After asking readers to join him on the trek back to 1860, Baudelaire pauses to consider the intersubjective distance that separates them from himself. The possibility of overcoming this distance, he decides, hinges on the pronoun *I*, which must be regarded as both indispensable and suspect. On one hand, *I* confers the advantages of "great modesty," "sincerity," and facility. Because it allows Baudelaire to "speak in [his] own name," *I* frees him from the responsibility of representing readers as well as from the risk of misrepresenting them; it keeps his subjective discourse at a safe distance from readers. On the other hand, Baudelaire also depends on *I* for means of escape from the restrictive bounds of these same advantages. The occasional "impertinence" of this pronoun comes not from its power to insulate the subjective writer, but from its simultaneous power to place him in instant, intimate contact with every reader. Baudelaire explicitly hopes for anonymous "friends" and "impartial readers" who will regard his essay as if it were their own, who will read the printed *I* as if it referred to them: he wishes to discover that when he writes *I*, he is at once expressing himself and quoting "unknown supporters." Throughout *Richard Wagner*, Baudelaire wants *I* to cover any gaps that might separate self-expression from quotation, so that writer and readers may proceed together toward Wagner's music.[3]

Baudelaire indicates, however, that his success with *I* is far from certain. Despite his confidence in friendly, unbiased readers, he admits that he is not an "expert in probability," that he has only "some chance" in his favor, and that his pronominal maneuver is nothing but a gamble. The authority of *I* in his essay remains in question: there is no assurance that *I* is at the same time stable enough to represent Baudelaire and mobile enough to travel among readers. When Walter Benjamin discusses gambling as a motif in Baudelaire's writing, he emphasizes that games of chance require the exact, unproductive repetition of beginnings. Gamblers endlessly initiate another round, place another bet, pick up another card, all without any hope of controlling or shaping what they begin with such gestures. Time spent gambling consists of tiny intervals devoid of accomplishment; like workers on a production line, gamblers are caught in the "hellish" time lived out by "those who are not allowed to complete anything they have tackled."[4] From this perspective, allusions to gambling in the first paragraph of *Richard Wagner* are particularly threatening, since Baudelaire intends to explore a question from its beginning and thematizes this intent with various images of purposeful movement and expansive intervals. Baudelaire plays for high stakes, placing both historical understanding of Wagner and intersubjective communication with readers at risk. While the odds may not be against him, neither are they clearly in his favor: his essay moves forward under a threat of failure.

PROGRAMS

This threat is veiled, however, by the slightly exaggerated panache with which Baudelaire turns, in his second paragraph, to the main arguments of part 1: "Thirteen months ago, then, Paris was abuzz with rumor" (¶2). Apparently confident that his readers will accompany him on a smooth narrative ascent to the 1860 concerts, he first gives a brief history of Wagner's uncertain reputation in Paris during the 1850s. This leads to a description of the chaotic publicity that preceded Wagner in 1860 to the Théâtre-Italien and turned music journals into the ground for "a veritable battle of doctrines" (¶3). After evoking a preliminary skirmish at one of Wagner's rehearsals, Baudelaire tells about the decisive confrontation that was fought during the three concerts themselves. Wagner's music, declares Baudelaire, emerged victorious from these evenings of violent combat: "Wagner had been audacious: the program for his concert included neither instrumental solos, nor vocal songs, nor any of those exhibitions so dear to a public in love with virtuosos and their tours de force. Nothing but ensemble pieces, choruses or symphonies. The fight was violent, it is true; but the public, abandoned to itself, caught fire from some of those irresistible pieces whose thought was most clearly expressed for it [i.e., the public], and Wagner's music triumphed by its own strength" (¶4). The word "program" draws attention to itself in this passage, because it seems to stand curiously apart from the music in question. Unlike other French critics of his day, Baudelaire does not say that Wagner's greatest daring lay in his revolutionary style of composition or even in his ambition to impose that style on audiences outside Germany. In Baudelaire's view, Wagner's particular audacity consisted rather in his choice of a concert program, in his manner of dividing up, arranging, and introducing—packaging—fragments of his music for Parisian listeners. Ignoring the French predilection for virtuoso soloists, Wagner extracted from his operas only instrumental overtures and ensemble works for chorus and orchestra.[5] His music therefore found itself at a double disadvantage, pitted against a skeptical audience and crippled—as if in a straitjacket—by a hostile program. Baudelaire recounts, however, that the music was equal to such a challenge: it "set fire" to its listeners, trapped in the theater and temporarily abandoned by their vanguard of sarcastic journalists, and it forced them to acknowledge the program as "irresistible." Fighting against both its audience and its program, Wagner's concert music "triumphed by its own strength."

With this bizarre struggle between the music and its program, Baudelaire's story of the concerts breaks off. The abrupt ending throws particular emphasis onto the strange menace of the program and also prompts readers to notice the ambiguity in Baudelaire's use of the word. While "program" serves at first in the passage quoted above as an abstract term for Wagner's selection and ordering of the works performed, the word subsequently comes to denote the list of titles printed in a booklet that was, as Baudelaire eventually confirms, "distributed at that time in the Théâtre-Italien" (¶7). Beneath each title in this booklet, Wagner furnished a brief text about the music in order that listeners such as Baudelaire, who lacked musical training, might still find the "thought" of every piece to be "clearly expressed" (¶4). Such texts, which like the booklet itself were called *programs,* were not something unfamiliar to audiences in Paris: they had been distributed occasionally at concerts there, at least since 1829, when patrons of the Société des Concerts du Conservatoire first read Beethoven's descriptive titles for the Pastoral Symphony in French translation, and certainly since 1830, when Berlioz shocked audiences with stories of love and opium in the program for his *Symphonie fantastique*.[6] Taken in its most general sense, program music had been cultivated in France well before the nineteenth century; at its broadest, the genre included instrumental compositions that were associated with a story or an event only by means of a title or by any means other than words sung in conjunction with the music.[7] But French concertgoers in 1860 had not yet fully accepted the genre in its narrowest definition, which called for purely instrumental music that the composer associated with a separate text, whether this text was written for the occasion or borrowed from some other author. After Wagner's concerts, therefore, several reviews attacked the issue much more directly than did Baudelaire's essay, claiming in general that the music could not possibly bear much relation to all the things mentioned in the programs and that music should not in any case need booklets in order to be properly appreciated. Even a favorable reviewer was obliged to write that Wagner's program was "a charming study, very well done, that did not fail to attract mockery."[8]

Wagner tried to defend himself from such mockery by protesting that as an opera composer reduced to giving concerts, he could make his music comprehensible *only* by means of a text: "In the impossibility of making his operas heard in their entirety, the author permits himself to offer the public a few lines of explanation, which will allow for better understanding of the meaning of the detached pieces that he offers today."[9] This protest applied even to the overtures, although these were less difficult to separate from the operas than other extracts; Wagner was convinced that their specific import would be misinterpreted in the absence of a program. He shared this conviction with other composers of program music, who similarly claimed that without a text listeners would find themselves misguided or handicapped. When Franz Liszt, for example, ventured a definition of the term *program* in an article on Berlioz, he characterized it largely in the negative, as a preventive measure: "[A program is] any preface in intelligible language added to purely instrumental music, by means of which the composer aims to preserve his listeners from an arbitrary poetic interpretation and to call their attention in advance to the poetic idea of the whole composition, or to a particular part of it."[10] But French listeners in 1860, especially those who wrote for journals, were not merely skeptical of program music in general; they were also unwilling to admit the specific authority of a composer's program. Despite resistance to programs distributed before concerts, it had long been fashionable for both reviewers and other members of the audience to respond to instrumental music by devising imaginative programs of their own. Composers might be condemned for relying on texts, but the musical press often encouraged listeners to invent programs for themselves.[11] Thus the same sympathetic reviewer who defended Wagner's program from mockery as the "genuine and irrevocable analysis of the master" also demanded on behalf of listeners: "Will it no longer be possible to dream over a sound? to assimilate it into a poetic and literary interpretation? to give it, even by means of words, an original development, while of course remaining within the limits of the true? What else do we do every day in the innumerable translation exercises [thèmes] we venture to make from the works of the old masters?"[12]

In *Richard Wagner,* Baudelaire deftly positions himself between those who object to all programs and those who object only to privileged status for composers' programs. He admits the partial futility of using a text in instances in which music alone cannot make itself understood, but he also sees a certain need for both composers' and listeners' programs: "I have often heard it said that music cannot boast of translating anything with certainty, as can words or paintings. That is true to some degree, but is not wholly true. It [music] translates in its own way, and by the means proper to it. In music, as in painting and even in the written word, which is nonetheless the most positive of the arts, there is always a lacuna [to be] filled in by the listener's imagination" (¶5). Like the journalist who alludes to critics' "innumerable translation exercises," Baudelaire claims that all programs are attempts at translation. Baudelaire also claims, however, that music is itself a translation. The composer's art, he asserts, consists of making a musical translation from an original that precedes and motivates it. Significantly, Baudelaire avoids ever characterizing this original in exact detail, implying instead that no original is completely accessible or comprehensible, even to the composer. As a result, the original can never be translated without gaps and flaws; if printed programs are occasionally useful, it is because "the written word" translates more fully than music and can therefore help listeners over the rough spots in the musical translation. In any event, Baudelaire believes that audiences must always divide their attention between the music and its partially obscured original; the distance between the two must somehow be overcome by "the listener's imagination." For Baudelaire, that is, all concerts inevitably feature program music, whether or not there is a printed text: every composer must translate a piece into music following the program established by its mysterious and inaccessible original, and every listener must then translate the music into an imaginative program leading back toward the original.

As the principal activity of both composers and listeners, translation receives strong emphasis in *Richard Wagner*. What Baudelaire stresses most is its dynamic, permanently unfinished character, as if musical translation were a wandering journey with no definitive ending place. For composers, he indicates, to translate is to move from a hidden or withdrawn source toward audible music, along a path of technical transformations or "combinations" (¶4) that meanders in between the domain of a linguist rendering one language into another and the territory of an artist painting from a model. For listeners, to translate is to move in the opposite direction, to locate or improvise a path through the "lacuna" separating the music they hear from its extramusical origin. This latter path is particularly treacherous: listeners are apt to find not only that the gaps and obstacles to be skirted change with every hearing of the music, but also that they can never manage to travel all the way back to the original. Just as Baudelaire promises to lead his readers back to the "beginning of the question," but not beyond the realm of questioning, Wagner's listeners may journey *toward* his originals, but may not be able to leave the domain of translation. If Baudelaire prefers the verb "translate" to the substantive "translation" in the passage quoted above, it is perhaps in order to emphasize that musical translation involves continual movement: the "lacuna" can always be at least partially crossed and recrossed, but it can never be completely filled in or definitively bridged.

For Baudelaire, then, the main purpose of texts such as Wagner's programs is to serve as maps and maybe also as vehicles for these journeys between musical translations and their originals. Having pushed his aesthetic meditation to this point, he now proposes to support it with some circumstantial evidence drawn from Wagner's concerts. He chooses for this purpose the prelude to *Lohengrin*, one of the more popular works performed on that occasion, and he proceeds to give three separate programs written for this piece. He quotes Wagner's own program from the concert booklet first, then adds a program written by Franz Liszt as part of a larger study on *Lohengrin*, and finally adds a program he claims to have written himself after the concerts. With a comparison of these three texts, Baudelaire wants to show that the two listeners followed roughly the same path away from the music that Wagner followed toward it. By finding similarities among the programs, that is, Baudelaire hopes to demonstrate that Wagner translated an original so faithfully into music that listeners were consequently able to retranslate the music into something close to its original: "[I]t still remains incontestable that the more eloquent the music is, the more rapid and precise is its [power of] suggestion, and the greater are the chances that sensitive people will conceive ideas in rapport with those that inspired the artist" (¶6). If Baudelaire is successful, moreover, his readers will also be able to conclude that movement across the distance that separates listening from writing—or music from literature—is practically effortless: like Wagner himself, Liszt and Baudelaire can best travel between the music of the prelude and its original by writing a text. But since Baudelaire fails to state this conclusion in advance, and since he makes an alarming allusion to "chances" for and against success, he gives readers cause for skepticism from the outset: the three programs are complex, and the resemblances between them are by no means obvious. Before agreeing with Baudelaire that his *Lohengrin* demonstration is "incontestable," therefore, it is important to study the programs both separately and in combination.

ALLEGORIES

Baudelaire begins the demonstration with Wagner's program for the prelude, which he quotes at length. Except to acknowledge his source as the concert booklet and to say that the italics he adds to the quotation will be discussed later, Baudelaire gives no immediate indication of how the program should be interpreted:

> From the first measures onward, the soul of the pious recluse who awaits the sacred vessel *plunges into infinite spaces.* He sees a strange apparition take shape little by little in the form of a body, a face. This apparition becomes clearer still, and *the miraculous host of angels,* carrying the sacred cup in its midst, passes before him. The holy procession approaches; the heart of God's chosen one is exalted little by little; it swells, it dilates; ineffable aspirations awaken in him; *he gives way to growing bliss,* finding himself ever closer to *the luminous apparition,* and when the Holy Grail itself finally appears in the midst of the sacred procession, *he sinks into ecstatic adoration, as if the whole world had suddenly disappeared.*
>
> Meanwhile, the Holy Grail pours out its blessings on the saint in prayer and consecrates him as its knight. Then *the burning flames progressively soften their brightness;* in its holy joy, the host of angels, smiling at the earth it leaves behind, regains the celestial heights. It has left the Holy Grail to the care of the pure, *in whose hearts the divine liquid has been poured out,* and the august host vanishes *into the depths of space,* in the same way that it had come. (¶7–8)

Since he does not explain otherwise, Baudelaire implies that this program simply illustrates his preceding meditation. In other words, he leaves readers to assume that this text lies closer to the original than Wagner's musical translation, that this text renders the original more faithfully than the music of the prelude, which must then be an incomplete, secondary rendering. But such is not the first impression produced by the program. By writing "From the first measures onward" and continuing in the present tense, Wagner suggests that his narrative is neither more coherent than the music nor independent of it, but rather that the story accompanies the prelude in the manner of a flowing commentary or a series of subtitles. While it is obvious that the text is not literally bound up with the prelude as an accompaniment is with a melody or as subtitles are with a film, Wagner at least aims toward the illusion that the program runs parallel to the music and proceeds simultaneously with it. Wagner deepens this illusion, moreover, by using the third person throughout the program. It might be possible to imagine Wagner himself or some fictional narrator assuming responsibility for the story and pretending to recite it roughly in time to the music, as if the opening line of the text should read: "I say that from the first measures onward . . ." But since this "I" is in fact excluded from the program, the story appears instead to emanate directly from the prelude, almost as if there were little to choose between the verbal and the musical representations of the events in question.[13] Far from prescribing or "programming" the course of the music in advance, Wagner's program would seem to help listeners hear the music in the midst of narrating its own story.[14] To put this another way, it would seem that as translations of Wagner's original, his prelude and his program are equally accurate; in the absence of the original, each would appear to translate the other with precision.

Although Baudelaire may not have read the program this way, some of the other listeners at the Théâtre-Italien were happy to look for strict parallels between the text and the music, as if the prelude and its text could narrate each other with the same exactitude. One such listener was Louis Lacombe, himself a partisan and an occasional composer of program music. After the concerts, his review of the *Lohengrin* prelude began with a full quotation of Wagner's text and proceeded to argue that the music told precisely the same story. (For a piano reduction of the prelude, see Appendix 2 below; I have tried to cast my argument in a way that encourages—but does not require—readers to consult the music. It would be helpful for readers to have at least enough listening familiarity with the prelude to follow basic remarks relating to its structure.) According to Lacombe, both the descending angels and the saint's increasing ecstasy appear musically in a melodic phrase that is restated several times with different instrumentation in each instance. It is played at first very softly in a high register by violins divided into four parts (measure 5 through the downbeat of m. 13): "To these four parts others [i.e., strings] are joined [mm. 20–28], then the wind instruments enter one by one [mm. 36–44], and soon all the voices of the orchestra, uniting in a harmonious chorus, undulate and settle for a moment in the low register [mm. 50–58]."[15] This final, climactic restatement of the phrase, the moment of the Grail's appearance, features trumpets and trombones emphatically supported by the rest of the orchestra. The angel host's reascent to heaven is then marked by a slowly rising line in the double basses, while a descending line in the violins and high woodwinds simultaneously indicates the gradual calming of the saint's mystic emotion (mm. 58–67). Like Wagner, who insists that the story ends just as it began, Lacombe concludes that "the suave melody, arriving back at its point of departure, issues forth [s'exhale] in ethereal sounds."[16]

Another reviewer who summarized the music of the prelude in much the same fashion as Lacombe was Hector Berlioz. With Lacombe, Berlioz concentrates on the variety of instrumental timbres that accentuate the harmonic and melodic design, declaring that the piece is "a marvel of instrumentation" from beginning to end.[17] Surprisingly, however, Berlioz avoids drawing any parallels between the music and Wagner's text for it. Given Berlioz's penchant for programs in both his compositions and his music criticism, one might have expected him to linger over their controversial role in Wagner's concerts. Instead, Berlioz contents himself with the following summary of the prelude: "One could give an idea of it by speaking to the eyes with this figure ⟨⟩. It is actually an immense, gradual crescendo, which, having reached the ultimate degree of sonorous power, following an inverse progression, returns to the point from which it had departed and finishes in a harmonious murmur that is almost imperceptible."[18] In other words, Berlioz offers his own program for the prelude. If he pointedly ignores Wagner's program ("I do not know what relations exist between this form of overture and the dramatic idea of the opera"), this is apparently so that he can himself translate the music, first into the visual symbols for a crescendo followed by a diminuendo, then into a verbal sequence that makes the meaning of the symbols explicit. Yet Berlioz's program clearly does not stray very far from Wagner's. What both highlight is above all the symmetry of the prelude, its division into two halves that mirror each other. As Lacombe shows, it is tempting to read Wagner's program and listen to the prelude as if the two are structurally equivalent, as if the music's crescendo and diminuendo correspond exactly to the angels' arrival and departure. And while Berlioz ostensibly resists this temptation, he in fact strengthens it: with his emphasis on musical symmetry, he shows even more insistently than Lacombe how the prelude may be understood as a sort of literal translation of Wagner's program, in which timbres and dynamics are methodically substituted for segments of the narrative.

Just before beginning his *Lohengrin* demonstration, Baudelaire notes in passing that "M. Berlioz has written a magnificent encomium in technical style" for the prelude (¶6). But he never returns to Berlioz's review, and although he thus never challenges either Berlioz or Lacombe, he nonetheless makes it clear that he understands the relation between the prelude and Wagner's program differently. Later in his demonstration, while attempting to summarize each of the three programs, Baudelaire arrives at the following formulation: "Wagner indicates *a host of angels that brings a sacred vessel*" (¶14). Where Lacombe finds in Wagner's program an angel host that ceremoniously descends to earth and then ascends to heaven "in the same way that it had come," Baudelaire discovers a company of angels whose sole mission is to deliver the Grail. That is, Baudelaire summarizes not a symmetrical narrative with corresponding elements centered around a climax, but rather a nonsymmetrical sequence of events directed toward an ultimate goal. In contrast to Berlioz and Lacombe, Baudelaire makes no attempt to interpret the prelude as a literal rendering of its program. Wagner's text, he indicates, is a narrative expansion and elaboration of one dominant image or idea: "*a host of angels who bring a sacred vessel.*" Baudelaire suggests that the music may be rigorously related only to this main image, which it transforms, extends, or elaborates independently of the actual narrative. Although he offers no supporting arguments, Baudelaire raises the possibility that the prelude is a musical figure for the program rather than a literal translation of it.

He might have argued for this possibility, however, simply by quoting at greater length from Wagner's program booklet. In a passage omitted from Baudelaire's demonstration, Wagner writes: "The Holy Grail was the cup from which the Savior had drunk at the Last Supper and in which Joseph of Arimathia had received His blood at the Crucifixion. Tradition tells that the sacred vessel had at one time been withdrawn from unworthy human beings, but that God had decided to place it once more in the hands of a privileged few who, by their purity of soul, by the saintliness of their life, had merited this honor. It is the return of the Holy Grail to the mountain of these holy knights, in the midst of an angel host, that the introduction to *Lohengrin* has tried to express."[19] Like Baudelaire, Wagner stresses the nonsymmetrical, end-oriented logic at work in his narrative, so as to summarize the program with a single, dominant image ("the return of the Holy Grail . . . in the midst of an angel host"). Wagner thus confirms that the music is closely related to this image, but may be less closely associated with the encompassing story. Contrary to the implications of his third-person, present-tense narrative, Wagner denies that the prelude either directly narrates or literally translates the story given in the program. In other terms, Wagner confirms Baudelaire's hint that listeners such as Berlioz and Lacombe cannot travel on any straight path connecting the program with the prelude; even Berlioz's laborious detour through formal description and visual symbols may not enable them to construct a passage between the narrative and the music. Departing from Wagner's angel story in the direction of a literal translation, they enter into an "encomium in technical style" that may never lead all the way to the music.

With their summaries, Wagner and Baudelaire both imply that if the music translates the program, it does so only by elaborating musically on the principal image or the dominant event of the narrative. Under these conditions, the music is neither an imitative equivalent nor a systematically transformed version of Wagner's text; the prelude might perhaps be described instead as an extended musical figure for "the angels' deposition of the Grail on earth." But this removes the prelude to a great distance from its program: it is unclear exactly how the musical figuration relates to the summary image, and it is even more unclear just how—or if— the music relates to the complete narrative. In summarizing the program, neither Baudelaire nor Wagner suggests that the full text is unnecessary; it appears, on the contrary, that they must begin with the complete version of the story in order to make their interpretive reductions. Further, by taking care to separate the two summaries from his quotation of the program, Baudelaire emphasizes that the complete narrative is indispensable and that readers must at first avoid any reductive interpretations of it. Baudelaire's manner of quoting Wagner, therefore, does not encourage readers to describe the prelude as a musical figure for a summarized narrative: it indicates that readers ought perhaps to adopt an inverse perspective, which would prompt them to regard the program as an extended narrative figure for the music.

Baudelaire's readers thus wind up in a predicament. After venturing on several deceptive paths between the narrative and the music, they find only that the distance between the two has become wider and more obscure. Wagner's program seems at first to be a simple story of saints and angels; it unfolds in a measured series of events, enticingly calculated to suggest that no narrator intrudes between readers and the music, that readers listen to the prelude as it narrates its own tale. But Baudelaire's demonstration reveals this apparently intimate connection between the story and the music to be an illusion. By diverging from Lacombe's and Berlioz's descriptions, Baudelaire denies that the music can fully or literally represent the story; and by first withholding, then offering a summary, he upsets any impression that the story tells itself in time to the music. As a result, Baudelaire actually works against one of the goals set for his demonstration, since he implies that no path of translation smoothly connects the program with the prelude. Instead, he makes the distance between them look more like a gap or a chasm than a stretch of ground; the program and the prelude seem to face each other across a gulf that cannot be crossed by ordinary modes of travel.

But it does not follow from this that Baudelaire necessarily strays from the larger goal of his essay. Although he shows readers a gap between the narrative and the music, he does not forbid them even to look out across it. In a well-known passage from his essay on Théodore de Banville, Baudelaire associates "mythologies and allegories" with "vast strides like syntheses" [des enjambées vastes comme des synthèses].[20] When he adds that these immense strides of allegory cover a "landscape that is clothed . . . in hyperbolic magic," he intimates that allegorical travelers must send their gaze leaping over terrain that would be impossible to cross otherwise (2:165). Baudelaire explicitly associates allegory with translation, moreover, in an equally well known passage from his unfinished essay "L'Art philosophique." After describing a series of woodcuts by Alfred Rethel, Baudelaire makes the general claim that "one must, in the translation of philosophical works, apply meticulous precision and great attention to detail; the scenes, the decor, the furniture, the utensils (see Hogarth), everything there is allegory, allusion, hieroglyphs, rebus" (2:600). But if Baudelaire here suggests that it is possible, by dint of careful translation, to move step by step from each allegorical sign to its corresponding referent, he quickly revises this opinion. A paragraph later, he instead declares that no matter how laboriously one undertakes to translate from one to the other, an allegory and its referent always remain separated by distances that can be crossed only by leaps of creative vision: "Besides, even for the mind of an artist-philosopher, accessories do not present themselves with a literal and precise character, but with a poetic, vague and confused character, and it is often the translator who invents *intentions*" (2:601).

In his Wagner essay, Baudelaire maintains that a similar situation awaits any translator who attempts to cross the gap between Wagner's program and his *Lohengrin* prelude. Despite the lacunas revealed by his method of quotation and summary, Baudelaire indicates that the program and the music remain somehow visible to each other: the Grail narrative still offers a view—imprecise but compelling—over the distance that separates it from the prelude. Following Baudelaire's lead, therefore, one might characterize Wagner's program as an allegory of the prelude. Like Banville's or Rethel's allegories, which stand permanently apart from their referents, the program never overcomes the gap between itself and the music. Readers of the program, deprived of practical help from either Berlioz's analysis or Wagner's summary, find that not even a plodding translation will carry them all the way to the prelude; they can only peer across the gap toward a musical "promised land" that they cannot reach.[21] Further, they may have to be content with an overview not only of the prelude itself, but also of the terrain lying between the prelude and its original; their chances of actually approaching this original by means of the Grail narrative, as proposed at the outset of the *Lohengrin* demonstration, seem slight. By inviting them to interpret Wagner's program as an allegory that refers obscurely and remotely to the music, Baudelaire instead climbs with his readers to a textual vantage point overlooking the distant landscape of the prelude.

As if unaware that the Wagner quotation has unsettled his demonstration, Baudelaire turns immediately to Liszt's program for the prelude, first published in 1850 and reprinted in 1851 as part of a book.[22] Baudelaire once again quotes at length, pausing only to acknowledge his source and to claim that at this stage of the demonstration, his goal is to show a listener who moves away from Wagner's musical translation toward its original: "I now take up Liszt's book, and I open it to the page where the imagination of the illustrious pianist (who is an artist and a philosopher) translates the same piece in his own way" (¶9). With this allusion to Liszt as an artist-philosopher and not as a composer, Baudelaire partially prepares readers for differences between this program and Wagner's. Instead of a story, Liszt offers explicit commentary on the music, and as a sophisticated listener self-consciously guiding other listeners, he often uses the first person plural to convey his comments. His program is divided into two parts, the first of which gives a general explanation of the prelude as a whole:

> This introduction encompasses and reveals *the mystic element,* always present and always hidden in the piece . . . [*sic*] In order to teach us the indescribable power of this secret, Wagner first shows us *the ineffable beauty of the sanctuary,* inhabited by a God who avenges the oppressed and asks nothing but *love and faith* from His followers. He initiates us to the Holy Grail; he causes to shimmer before our eyes the temple of incorruptible wood, with fragrant walls, doors of *gold,* beams of *asbestos,* columns of *opal,* partitions of *cymophane,* whose splendid porticos are approached only by those with an uplifted heart and pure hands. He does not allow us to perceive it in its real and imposing structure, but, as if sparing our feeble senses, he shows it to us at first reflected in *some azure wave* or reproduced *by some iridescent cloud.* (¶10)

Liszt first describes the music of the prelude as a transparent container that gathers and displays in concentrated form the "mystic element" hidden and dispersed throughout the rest of *Lohengrin.* Although Baudelaire's quotation does not make it clear, this "element" refers specifically to the contents of the Holy Grail, whose mystic power indirectly motivates the plot of the whole opera: in a passage outside the quotation, Liszt highlights the Grail as the receptacle for both the wine from the Last Supper and the blood from Jesus' wounds; and in a clause replaced by Baudelaire with an ellipsis, Liszt stresses that the Grail is the "divine secret, the supernatural force [ressort], the supreme law of the characters' destiny and of the succession of incidents that we are about to contemplate."[23] But Liszt next asserts that the music is not the immediate receptacle of the Grail and its contents. Instead, the music reveals only the temple in which the Grail is housed; and Liszt's elaborate description of this temple, listing its exotic substances and emphasizing its "splendid porticos" that remain closed to all but the few elect, suggests that the music gives no direct view of the relic hidden within its imposing walls. For Liszt, therefore, the music of the prelude acts as an indirect container for the "mystic element," which is concealed from listeners within both the holy chalice and the particularly opaque walls of the temple. The prelude is a sort of musical metonym that refers to the mystery of the Eucharist only through two intermediate layers of metonymy.

Liszt does not stop, however, with this metonymic proliferation of barriers. He now claims that even if the music is a container for the temple, it must initially display no more than a wavering reflection or a cloudy reproduction of the sanctuary. In order not to overwhelm its frail listeners, the music gives a dim likeness of the temple; but it does so only "at first," as a preliminary step. Liszt thus hints that the music will eventually offer more substantial representations, that it will gradually harden the outlines and deepen the colors in its portrayal of the temple. As if to guarantee that listeners will come to understand the mystic secret sheltered within the music, the prelude undertakes to furnish a progressive series of visions or pictures: leading from a misty blur to clear vision, the likenesses of the temple invite listeners to consider and admire what might lie inside its walls. But it follows that the music undertakes an extremely complex task, although Liszt does not signal this explicitly. In addition to containing the temple by metonymy, the prelude must display the temple by analogy; the music must act as a type of metaphor that relates to the temple as a painting to its model. What is more, the music must provide a carefully measured sequence of metaphors: at the same time that it refers metonymically to the temple as a place of eternal transcendence, the music must also defer to human frailty by figuring the temple metaphorically as a temporal structure. With the first part of his program, Liszt shows the prelude to be a complicated figure engaged in the difficult enterprise of transcending time while making it visible.

With the second part of his program, Liszt explains more precisely how the music goes about this task:

At the beginning, it is a *wide, still sheet* of melody, *a vaporous ether that spreads out,* so that the sacred picture may be drawn on it for our profane eyes; [this is] an effect confided exclusively to the violins, divided into eight different parts, which, after several measures of harmonics, continue on the highest notes of their registers. The motif is next taken up by the softest wind instruments; the horns and bassoons, in joining them, prepare the entrance of the trumpets and trombones, which repeat the melody for the fourth time, *with a dazzling burst of color,* as if in this unique instant the holy edifice *had blazed* before *our blinded gaze, in all its luminous and radiant magnificence.* But *the vivid sparkle,* brought by degrees to *this intensity of solar radiance,* is rapidly extinguished, like a *celestial glimmer.* The *transparent vapor* of the clouds closes in, the vision disappears little by little into the same *variegated* incense from the midst of which it appeared, and the piece ends with the first six measures, [which have] become *still more ethereal.* Its character of *ideal mysticity* is above all made perceptible by the *pianissimo* [that is] always maintained in the orchestra, and that is barely interrupted during the brief moment when the *brass instruments* make the marvelous lines of this introduction's sole motif *glisten.* Such is the image that, upon our hearing this sublime *adagio,* first presents itself to our excited senses. (¶11)

At first sight, this description resembles Louis Lacombe's story of the prelude, structured primarily by a long crescendo and diminuendo. But Liszt differs considerably from Lacombe in his interpretation of this structure and in his choice of descriptive terms. Instead of a "phrase musicale" that is restated several times, Liszt writes about a "motif" that appears in four guises so as to play a striking variety of roles. It acts first as a "*still sheet* of melody," a uniform surface devoid of marks or contours. On this blank, melodious background, the motif proceeds during its second appearance to make something like a light sketch of the temple; and it continues during its third appearance to add detail and color to the representation. Not until its fourth appearance, however, does the motif exercise its full artistic power: rather than simply displaying the completed "sacred picture,"[24] the motif nearly blinds listeners by taking on the vividness and the radiance of the real temple, as if at that "unique instant" the painting were changed by transubstantiation into its model. Following this sudden glimpse of the Grail's sanctuary, listeners find they can hardly see at all; the motif seems either to have disappeared entirely or to have assumed once more the guise of an empty canvas.

In order to review this spectacular progression from blank background to colored picture to intense reality, listeners might look to several passages from Baudelaire's art criticism. Baudelaire clearly has much in common with Liszt when he writes, in his *Salon de 1859*, that "a harmonically [harmoniquement] conducted painting consists in a series of superimposed paintings, each new layer giving the dream more reality and raising it another degree toward perfection" (2:626). Like the prelude, which proceeds by stages from a hazy outline to a radiant temple, Baudelaire's painting advances gradually through a sequence of elaborations and improvements. But Baudelaire particularly insists that this sequence is not a laborious itinerary: although the "harmonically conducted" painting may always continue its progress toward perfection, it is never reluctant to linger at stops along the way. Any other kind of painting, claims Baudelaire, travels tediously and erratically over "a long road divided into a great many stages. When one stage is finished, it is no longer of any concern, and when the whole road has been traveled, the artist is relieved of his painting" (2:626). Unwilling to put up with such a journey, Baudelaire prefers paintings that move without apparent effort from one stage to another or that paradoxically still move toward completion when they have already arrived there. Baudelaire discovers this strange mobility throughout Constantin Guys's work, where "at any point in its progress, every drawing looks sufficiently complete" (2:700). And by quoting Liszt, he seems to find it in Wagner's prelude as well.

When Liszt evokes the prelude as if it were a picture in progress, he does not imply that it seems complete at each of its four stages; he writes, on the contrary, that every appearance of the motif "prepares" the next. The word "motif," however, draws attention to itself in this context. It suggestively bridges gaps between the temple and the painting and the music, linking temporal recurrence with visual emphasis so that the musical phrase may appear to be sculpted into every arch and column of the temple. But even if understood only as a musical term, "motif" stays in constant motion among a number of meanings. Liszt clearly uses it for the eight-measure melody that occurs four times in the prelude, easily recognizable in each instance despite changes of key, register, timbre, and so on. This use of the word, however, was not entirely standard in the mid-nineteenth century: while theorists such as Reicha and Czerny agreed that a motif was a full, eight-bar melody, others such as A. B. Marx held that motifs were minimal melodic fragments from which full melodies might be constructed.[25] Outside of composition treatises, the word appeared frequently in writings on dramatic music; opera composers well before Wagner relied on instrumental motifs, or *Reminiszenzmotiven,* that were intended to bind the orchestra to the stage drama.[26] From this operatic context, the word led musicians toward discussions of program music, where it served to indicate both composers' techniques, involving the transformation or circulation of melodic motifs, and composers' intentions, requiring that melodies be anchored to a dramatic program.[27]

In relation to program music, therefore, *motif* poises significantly between movement of melodies and fixity of intentions; it strains not so much to immobilize contrary meanings within a single structure as to motivate free communication between them. The consequence of such a strain is that *motif* becomes unreliable as an analytical term, since it may easily fail to maintain movement between its various connotations of mobility and immobility. With respect to the *Lohengrin* prelude, this failure is particularly evident in Alfred Lorenz's formal-motivic analysis of the music.[28] Lorenz describes the prelude as an instance of "strophic form," one of four fundamental "form types" by means of which he tries to account for both the large- and the small-scale organization of *Lohengrin.*[29] Defining it as "repetition of the similar" [die Wiederholung von Gleichartigem], Lorenz claims that strophic form allows Wagner to construct music from one melodic unit that is repeated and minimally elaborated. Lorenz discovers in the prelude four strophes of nearly equal length and similar content, framed by a closely related introduction and coda. The first strophe (mm. 5–19) sets forth the "Grail theme," which consists in a "principal motif" [Hauptmotiv] (mm. 5–12) and two "subsidiary motifs" [Nebenmotiven] (mm. 13–16 and 17–19): even within a single strophe, that is, Lorenz finds rigid segments made of homogeneous materials.[30] The second and third strophes each present an embellished restatement of the *Hauptmotiv* (mm. 20–27 and 36–45), followed by an extended and developed version of the first *Nebenmotiv* (mm. 28–35 and 44–49). The fourth strophe, in addition to an altered presentation of the *Hauptmotiv* (mm. 50–57), gives a considerably expanded revision of the second *Nebenmotiv* (mm. 58–66). According to Lorenz, therefore, the entire prelude is composed of a single motif that seems more insistently reiterative in proportion as it is altered, elaborated, or extended; although Lorenz notes changes of key and differences of instrumentation from strophe to strophe, he clearly interprets these only as incidental alterations in the motif's context, unable to affect the uniform integrity of the motif itself. Lorenz also emphasizes the particularly immobile character of this motif by assigning exactly the same programmatic meaning to every recurrence of it: refusing it the right to engage in storytelling or any other movement of figuration, Lorenz forcibly ties the melody to its identity as the "Grail motif."

When set beside this analysis of the prelude, Liszt's program appears to critique and correct Lorenz's understanding of the motif. Like Baudelaire, Liszt evokes the strange mobility of a musically drawn picture that gradually leads listeners from an unmarked canvas toward brilliant reality. But while Baudelaire explicitly states the paradox of a painting that is always and never finished, Liszt uses his description of the prelude's motif to imply that the music changes constantly so as to act as an unchanging figure for the Grail temple. With the first part of his program, Liszt shows that this temple is like the topmost layer of color on an elaborate canvas, since its ornate walls surround and conceal the Grail, which in turn holds and conceals the Eucharistic element. The second part of the program then relies on the mobility of the signifier "motif" to imply that the temple is not as completely opaque as it first seems: the mystic element, suggests Liszt, is continually visible within the sanctuary musically built to hide it, because the motif moves from layer to layer (or from violins, pianissimo, to trumpets, fortissimo) without ever rendering the temple and its contents unrecognizable. As a metonymic structure, the temple permanently withholds the transcendent power of the Grail; but once it is understood metaphorically as a painting in progress, the temple becomes a temporal means of beholding the Grail's transcendence of human time. For Liszt, it is the prelude's motif that makes the temple visible as both a monumental model and an ephemeral image of eternity.

It is far from certain, however, that the prelude's motif could accomplish this alone, without help from Liszt's program. In his second paragraph, Liszt tells not only how the motif moves between metonymy and metaphor, but also how listeners come to make sense of this musical figuration: by gradually following the motif's progress, listeners arrive at an understanding of its relation to the Grail and its temple. The second paragraph of Liszt's program must therefore double as both a figural evocation of the music and as a story of listeners' progressive efforts to interpret the music in the light of the program's first paragraph. Alternatively, one might say that the second paragraph doubles as both a figural evocation and the story of listeners trying by stages to write this same evocation upon hearing the music. In either case, Liszt's program functions simultaneously at two levels: it is at once a program and an allegory of how programs work; it aims both to lead listeners toward the prelude and to show how roads between music and texts are constructed. But as an allegory of how successfully programs function, Liszt's second paragraph contradicts itself. After describing the picture's transfiguration into the real temple, Liszt stresses that this vision "is rapidly extinguished"; listeners end up staring at a dense haze in which they vaguely sense *"ideal mysticity"* without seeing it at all. Because they are not allowed to linger in a place where they might concretely experience and minutely explore the music as a complex housing for the Grail, listeners come out at an impasse where they can only guess at the temple walls from an obscure distance. While giving listeners a program, Liszt also allegorizes his program's failure to provide more than a brief glimpse of the music. It follows that while quoting Liszt, Baudelaire undermines for the second time his attempt to reveal a passage between the prelude and a program; his demonstration shows no unbroken route from one to the other. Once again, readers arrive at the edge of a cliff, peering over the gap between Wagner's music and Baudelaire's text.

Even a cursory glance shows that Baudelaire's program for the prelude is very unlike either Liszt's or Wagner's. As if partly to anticipate this observation and partly to allay any other doubts that readers might have conceived about his *Lohengrin* demonstration, Baudelaire pauses between Liszt's program and his own. He tries first to assure readers that his program harmonizes with the two others, that it constitutes a necessary step in his demonstration: "I certainly would not dare to indulge in talking about my *reveries,* if it weren't useful to attach them here to the preceding *reveries*" (¶12). In addition to introducing his program as an intimate narrative, a record of his dreamlike response to the prelude, Baudelaire's emphasis on *reveries* suggestively echoes the title of Rousseau's *Rêveries du promeneur solitaire.* Baudelaire hints that his program will be thematically linked to Wagner's ecstatic saint and Liszt's mystic temple by way of a subjective listener who, like Rousseau, experiences "the death of all terrestrial and temporal concerns," but Baudelaire at the same time joins both Liszt and Rousseau in admitting that he cannot dispense with a temporal account "of the modifications of [his] soul and their successions."[31] More indirectly, the allusion to Rousseau suggests a close relation between figurative paths for the mind and literal paths for the feet, thus recalling Baudelaire's search for literal distances that might figure the distance between music and texts.

Baudelaire also prefaces his program with an elaborate reminder of his reasons for meditating so long on the prelude: "The reader knows what goal we are pursuing: to demonstrate that true music suggests analogous ideas to different minds" (¶12). Baudelaire continues to keep the problem of musical translation clearly in view; he calls his own program an "inevitable translation" in an earlier sentence. But he now states more specifically than before that his demonstration involves following a trail of analogies from program to program in search of the original that authorizes "true music," so that "translate" serves as a general metaphor for the movement of both composers and listeners between a piece of music and its original.[32] Baudelaire next claims, however, that this translating movement leads far beyond the domain of music. He writes that his quotation of programs is somewhat unnecessary: "[I]t would not be ridiculous here to reason *a priori,* without analysis and without comparisons; for what would be really surprising is that sound *could not* suggest color, that colors *could not* give the idea of a melody, and that sound and color were unsuited to translate ideas; things having always expressed themselves by a reciprocal analogy, since the day when God proffered the world as a complex and indivisible totality" (¶12). After this hyperbolic declaration, Baudelaire plunges directly into the quatrains from his sonnet "Correspondances," leaving readers aghast at the dimensions so suddenly attributed to his demonstration. Readers are confused, moreover, by the wealth of synonyms for "translate"—"suggest," "suggest analogous ideas," "give the idea of," "express by a reciprocal analogy." During this proliferation of apparently synonymous terms, it seems less and less certain that the trail of programs will lead all the way to an original that lies outside the far-flung realm of interconnected translations. Readers might briefly consider that "Dieu" is a true original, situated safely beyond the domain of translation, but Baudelaire's quotation from "Correspondances" throws doubt on this possibility as well. Because it comes so soon after Liszt's program, the poem's famous first line ("Nature is a temple . . .") resonates differently than it might in other contexts. For Liszt, the temple is both a building that hides and a painting that reveals God's presence in the element of the Grail; it is a uniquely musical structure, founded and built by the prelude's motif in order to guarantee listeners' passage between ephemeral artworks and eternal transcendence. With Baudelaire's quotation of his quatrains, however, the temple itself becomes a motif, passing from musical painting to poetry: mobile enough to wander from concert programs to programmatic sonnets and back, the temple can assure passage only from one art to another rather than to higher spirituality; its "splendid porticos" may well lead from translation to translation without revealing an ultimate original.[33]

Perhaps as a result of this uncertainty, Baudelaire declines to quote the tercets of his poem, which would declare that "the transports of the mind and the senses" [les transports de l'esprit et des sens (1:11)] follow a smooth path between translations and originals. Baudelaire instead embarks immediately on his program, as if to replace the tercets with a text that might lead toward the prelude's original by other routes:

> I will continue, then. I remember that, from the first measures onward, I was subject to one of those happy impressions that almost all imaginative people have experienced in a dream while sleeping. I felt myself freed *from the bonds of gravity,* and I rediscovered through memory [par le souvenir] the extraordinary *voluptuousness* that circulates in *high places* (let us note in passing that I was not familiar with the program quoted just now). Next I involuntarily pictured to myself the delicious state of someone [un homme] who is prey to a prolonged reverie in absolute solitude,

but solitude with *an immense horizon* and a *vast, diffuse light: immensity* with no decor but itself. Soon I felt the sensation of a more vivid *brightness, of an intensity of light* growing with such rapidity that the nuances furnished by the dictionary would not suffice to express *this continually increasing overabundance of burning passion and whiteness.* Then I fully conceived the idea of a soul moving in a luminous setting, of an ecstasy *consisting in voluptuousness and knowledge,* and soaring above and very far away from the natural world. (¶13)

From the outset, Baudelaire categorizes his program as a memory, an account of past experience. This in itself is not surprising, either when considered as a practical necessity, since Baudelaire stresses his unwillingness to cope with the technicalities of a musical score, or when considered as an example of Baudelaire's customary emphasis on the interdependence of art and memory. Moreover, the juxtaposition of the first two sentences— "I will continue . . ."/"I remember . . ."—suggests that the tension invoked in the first line of Baudelaire's essay stretches all the way through this program, so that forward, outward movement into Wagner's music requires a backward, inward climb into memory. But it quickly becomes clear that for Baudelaire, the program not only describes one level of memory, but also leads toward other, more distant levels: "I remember that . . . I rediscovered *through memory* the extraordinary voluptuousness that circulates in high places" (emphasis mine). For Baudelaire, to listen to the prelude is to engage in remembering, and to write about the prelude is to remember remembering. By itself, however, such remembering is not enough to produce a program, since Baudelaire notes in the preceding paragraph that he must try to "translate with words the inevitable translation that [his] imagination made of [the prelude]" (¶12).[34] Parallel to his act of memory within memory, Baudelaire needs an act of translation within translation; he accounts for two layers of memory with two stages of translation, the first spontaneous, sensual, nonverbal, the second analytical, narrative, literary. Like an artist who insists on the strangely inadequate perfection of each layer of his painting, Baudelaire calls attention to the necessity for each poetic level of his program.

At the same time, Baudelaire takes care not to isolate the various layers superimposed on one another throughout the program. This complicates his task considerably, because he nonetheless tries to exaggerate some of the distances between layers just enough to make them visible without overtly obstructing his readers' progress. He claims, for example, to describe impressions imposed on him by the music at the intimate level where physical sensation is not clearly distinguishable from mental activity; since he did not read Wagner's program before the concert, his impressions of the prelude were immediate and involuntary. But Baudelaire then makes it plain that the "I" in his text is not the unique, spontaneous subject of all the impressions dictated by the music: the euphoria of weightlessness is recalled from a past experience common to "all imaginative people"; the pleasures of absolute solitude are attributed imprecisely to "someone"; and the final, floating ecstasy of mind and senses belongs to an indefinite "soul" invented by "I" for the occasion. Another discrepancy appears in the sequential ordering of these impressions. As abstractions associated neither with specific musical events nor with episodes in a story, the sensations of weightlessness, solitude, brightness, and ecstasy are difficult to define and delimit in strict relation to one another. Yet Baudelaire refers to them as if to a well-ordered series of distinct segments, and he punctuates the program with adverbs such as "next," "soon," and "then" that imply clear temporal demarcation and succession. A third disjunction in the program separates vivid, subjective experience from remote memory by means of verb forms: while "I" recalls intensely personal impressions from recent experience, the simple past tense of verbs in locutions such as "I felt" [j'éprouvai] and "I conceived" [je conçus] pulls the description toward a more distant, more impersonal past.[35] Baudelaire thus perplexes readers by marking gaps between layers of memory and stages of translation with both conceptual and grammatical incongruities in his program.

Baudelaire hints, however, that this perplexity is unavoidable and that he shares in it himself. When he asks, "Am I myself permitted to recount, to translate with words the inevitable translation that my imagination made of the same piece?" (¶12), the question may be more than a polite formula: Baudelaire implies that the music of the prelude is such that it nearly prevents him from translating it into a coherent program. He prolongs this implication in a later paragraph, where he finds himself unable to summarize his own program; he can say only that in relation to the two others, it is "more vague and more abstract" (¶14). Before trying to decide whether the confusion of the program is in fact "inevitable," readers should note that at least one other commentator strongly agrees with Baudelaire: Theodor Adorno also discovers vagueness to be a fundamental interpretive concept for the *Lohengrin* prelude. Adorno accuses Wagner of overlooking, in his eagerness to give listeners the impression of ethereal floating or wavering, the fact that "the aesthetic idea of vagueness technically calls for representation by the most definite means."[36] Using the prelude as an example for a broader argument, in which he claims that Wagner abandoned clarity of form in his search for striking effects, Adorno cites Baudelaire as the first listener to hear this in Wagner's music: "But [Wagner] is the first to elevate ambiguity to a stylistic principle, to make the category of the interesting prevail over the consistent logic of musical language. This is what so excited Baudelaire, the most advanced consciousness of his own era."[37]

To defend his assertion that the prelude is too vague to represent vagueness, Adorno draws almost all his evidence from the first occurrence of its principal "theme," the same eight-measure phrase that Liszt called the motif.[38] For Adorno, this theme is divided into two halves that aim to illustrate the gradual emergence of angelic shapes from surrounding mist; but the dramatic import of the music is blurred because the formal relation of the two halves cannot be decisively determined. Adorno notes that the first four bars of this theme (mm. 5–8) seem unarticulated, almost formless, owing to a sort of disproportion between the melody and its supporting harmony. Although the melody hovers constantly around E and F♯, the repetition of these two pitches does not seem intentional or significant because the harmony underneath is too sparse: the lower voices form only chords built on the first, fifth, and sixth scale degrees, a minimal arrangement in which the sixth degree has no independent status and acts as a shadowy substitute for the first. Above this, the melodic E appears to alternate with the F♯ in an aimless, ill-defined pattern, directed by no clear harmonic progression.[39] Adorno next claims that in the second half of the theme (mm. 9–12), harmony and melody are better suited to each other. The melody continues to linger near the two main pitches, but the lower voices are much more active, so that E and F♯ now appear as components of a recurrent melodic figure that undergoes continual harmonic reshaping or reemphasis. Despite the formal clarification effected by these second four measures, Adorno concludes that the theme as a whole shows an ill-balanced economy. By saving harmonic complexity for the second half without similarly elaborating the melodic structure, Wagner does not succeed in drawing clear contours from a formless, two-note obsession; Wagner only makes it impossible, declares Adorno, to decide whether the second half relates to the first as its logical, proportionally developed conclusion (*Nachsatz*) or rather as its protracted, increasingly elaborate extension (*Fortspinnung*). Instead of deliberate vagueness resolved into clarity, Adorno hears the disconcerting vagueness of "technical inconsistency."[40]

It is tempting, although unproductive, to search for analogies between Adorno's critique and Baudelaire's program, in order to conclude that Baudelaire understood the prelude so accurately as to include even its compositional flaws in his translation. Such analogies might be discovered, provided they were general enough: the tension between temporal boundaries and indefinite duration in Baudelaire's text might correspond to the opposition in Adorno's analysis between thematic elaboration and aimless repetition in the melody; and Baudelaire's reluctance to decide between intimate memory and impersonal experience might bear a formal resemblance to Adorno's hesitation to choose between calling the theme's second half a consequent or a continuation. But apart from the question of whether Adorno's technical discussion translates the music any more faithfully than Baudelaire's imaginative program, the analogies between Baudelaire and Adorno point to something other than successful translation. Implicitly or explicitly, both writers refer to the prelude in terms of the listener's incomprehension and indecision; and both show that this uncertainty does not come to the listener at a specific instant, but vaguely pervades the entire course of listening. Both suggest, in fact, that this uncertainty is what gives duration to the experience of listening, or more precisely, that it is what permits listeners to recount their experience of the music as a sequential narrative. With his step-by-step description of the prelude's theme, Adorno pedagogically enacts the predicament that he criticizes Wagner for imposing on every listener: he misleadingly describes two halves of the theme in successive order, one after another, for the contradictory purpose of showing that they constitute a violation of musical logic and therefore cannot be heard as an orderly succession. Similarly, with his fantastical series of remembered impressions, Baudelaire makes a sequential program out of a fundamentally nonlinear and atemporal experience of the prelude, which forces him among other things to set pronouns, verbs, and adverbs in conflict with other elements of his text. In this manner, both Baudelaire and Adorno adhere to what Paul de Man has called the "fundamental structure of allegory," since they submit in their accounts of the prelude to "the tendency of the language toward narrative, the spreading out along the axis of an imaginary time in order to give duration to what is, in fact, simultaneous within the subject."[41] In addition to suggesting that even the poet of "Correspondances" is unable to translate the music into figurative language, Baudelaire's program indicates how far his listening must remain from his writing: as an allegory of listening, his program is a narrative that figures the essentially nonnarratable act required of a listener confronting the prelude. Baudelaire's text therefore remains at an unmeasurable distance from the music: rather than leading readers across the gap between music and literature, it allegorizes both the isolated indecision of the listener and the unavoidable inaccuracy of the listener's writing.

ITALICS

Up to this point in his demonstration of the *Lohengrin* prelude, Baudelaire's chances for success appear to be small. Wagner's program, quoted in order to serve as a "positive" link with the original that he translated into music, offers instead an allegory of the prelude, a narrative that figures the music from a distance rather than approaching it literally. The programs by Liszt and by Baudelaire, cited as evidence that sensitive listeners "conceive ideas in rapport with those that inspired the artist" (¶6), are also allegories; whereas Liszt allegorizes his own program's failure to translate the musical motif for listeners, Baudelaire allegorizes the listeners' inability to translate the prelude for themselves. Each of the three programs, therefore, figuratively narrates an unsuccessful attempt to identify the music as a translation susceptible of being retranslated into an original. In addition, the programs suggest the inadequacy of writing that aims to be more literal, more "technical" than allegory: included in each allegory's incapacity to translate the prelude directly is its refusal to translate through the mediation of a description or an analysis of the music. Although the programs all relate to analyses in a manner that focuses attention on the prelude's recurrent motif, they also insist in various ways on the impossibility of leading this motif beyond the music into the texts.

But Baudelaire carries out his *Lohengrin* demonstration more thoroughly than is at first evident. Following his lengthy quotation of the programs, he tries in a brief paragraph to summarize his argument and to draw conclusions:

> Among these three translations, you could easily note the differences. Wagner indicates *a host of angels that brings a sacred vessel;* Liszt sees *a miraculously beautiful monument* reflected in a vaporous mirage. My reverie is much less illustrated with material objects: it is more vague and more abstract. But the important thing here is to grasp the resemblances. Even if they were not numerous, they would still constitute sufficient proof; but, happily, they are numerous and striking to the point of superfluity. In the three translations we find the sensation of *spiritual and physical bliss;* of *isolation;* of the contemplation of *something infinitely great and infinitely beautiful;* of *an intense light* that delights *the eyes and the soul to the point of rapture* [*pamoison*]; and finally the sensation of *space extended to the ultimate conceivable limits.* (¶14)

Baudelaire here leaves readers to infer that all such similarities are manifestations of Wagner's original, still perceptible despite "lacunas" (¶5) in the musical and textual translations. That Baudelaire does not explicitly draw the inference is consistent with the rest of his demonstration; just as he has already declared that "it would not be ridiculous here to reason *a priori,* without analysis and without comparisons" (¶12), he now shows less interest in arguing logically than in proposing an article of faith. With this end in view, he italicizes both his conclusions and the possible objections to them, as if to offer visible proof that apparent differences ("*a host of angels*" as opposed to "*a monument*") actually participate in more basic resemblances ("*bliss,*" "*isolation,*" and so on). These italicized similarities, moreover, are apparently linked to the numerous italics scattered throughout the three programs. Just after quoting Wagner's program, Baudelaire laconically promises that "the reader will understand in a moment why [he] underline[s] these passages" (¶9), and his concluding paragraph now indicates that all italics are intended to reveal resemblances between the programs. Once again, Baudelaire does not make his intention explicit; he seems instead to presume that visual emphasis added to an emphatic tone will command unquestioning acceptance of his demonstration.

At the same time, however, Baudelaire places his italics in such a way as to invite closer scrutiny. It is not clear, first, that all the items on Baudelaire's list of resemblances may be discovered—properly italicized— in every program. For example, "*isolation*" appears without emphasis as "absolute solitude" in Baudelaire's program; it is ambiguously italicized in Wagner's program only after the "pious recluse" has been surrounded by angels and "*sinks into ecstatic adoration, as if the whole world had suddenly disappeared*"; and it is not mentioned at all in Liszt's program, unless isolation is understood as a necessary condition for perceiving the "*mystic element*" contained in the music. One might overlook these inconsistencies, on the assumption that the list is meant as a suggestive collection rather than a rigorous enumeration of similarities, but in that case Baudelaire's mysterious choice of segments to italicize within each program still demands explanation. The italics in Wagner's narrative call the least attention to themselves, because they follow to some extent the sense and the syntax of the text: they generally intensify important nouns and their complements ("*the miraculous host of angels*"), prepositional phrases ("*into the depths of space*"), or complete propositions ("*he gives way to growing bliss*"). In Liszt's text, Baudelaire applies italics in a manner that is less conventional and less respectful of the narrative. He continues at intervals to emphasize key phrases, but he now chooses segments less precisely according to meaning and syntax; this is clear in such fragments as "*still more ethereal,*" in which the missing antecedent weakens the emphasis, and "reflected in *some azure wave* or reproduced *by some iridescent cloud,*" in which the uneven treatment of prepositions is puzzling. In addition, Baudelaire dots Liszt's program with isolated words that inexplicably appear in italics. Such words as "*opal*" and "*cymophane*" might perhaps fall under the rubric of infinite beauty on Baudelaire's list of italicized resemblances; but "*pianissimo,*" "*brass instruments,*" and "*adagio*" do not fit into the list and seem all the more unmotivated in that they might, as musical terms, have been italicized by Liszt himself.[42] It is in his own program, however, that Baudelaire's erratic use (or abuse) of italics reaches its height. He not only emphasizes isolated terms and nonsyntactic word groups, but also in one instance he applies emphasis in such a way as to conflict with both sense and syntax: the italics in "I felt myself freed *from the bonds of gravity*" [Je me sentis délivré *des liens de la pesanteur*] work against the general meaning by stressing the weight of gravity but not the subject's freedom from it (particularly since the French "*des liens*" can mean either "*from the bonds*" or "*some bonds*").

Confronted first with these enigmatic italics and then with Baudelaire's unwillingness to explain them, readers may legitimately wonder exactly what he means to emphasize. When Baudelaire declares that analytical argument is not really necessary to his demonstration, and when he insists as well that every item on his list of resemblances is a "sensation" (¶14), he suggests that the italics are not a riddle to be studied and resolved, but rather a novelty to be experienced with the senses. He intimates that if readers submit to the repeated sensation of seeing italics throughout the texts, they may eventually *feel* the fundamental similarity of all three programs and understand their common relation to the prelude "*a priori,* without analysis and without comparisons*" (¶12). Even further, Baudelaire implies that his italics may succeed at the task shown to be impossible for the allegorical narratives alone: as recurrent configurations, never identical but always recognizable, bound so lightly and intricately to their context that their movement matches neither the unfolding of meaning nor the patterning of syntax, the italics are perhaps intended to translate the musical motif of the prelude into the text of the programs. In order to accomplish this, the italics must mobilize the programs to function as constellations of visual images that are neither perpetually constrained nor permanently forbidden to bear meaning; the italics must motivate a relation between the music and the texts that is not limited to the level of signification, but that involves a continual movement of exchange or substitution between sound and sense and shape. It therefore appears that the italics carry an enormous share of the persuasive burden in Baudelaire's *Lohengrin* demonstration. They seem specially designed to cross boundaries and to overcome distances: intended first to guarantee communication between the three programs, the italics are also responsible for leading over the separation between the prelude and the allegorical narratives, for overcoming the gaps between music and figurative language and literal inscription.[43]

Such an intention and such a responsibility, however, are greater than the italics' power to fulfill them. Despite their ability to avert attention from the unfolding of the narratives, the italics' freedom to move at textual levels other than signification is for the most part an illusion. Whatever their semantic, syntactic, or visual context, all the italicized portions of the programs are bound to a single, rigid meaning, because they all to some degree signify *emphasis*. As a means of altering and differentiating fragments of a larger inscription, Baudelaire's italics enjoy only partial mobility: they are free to mark exceptions within one or more contexts, but unfree to occur independently, unfree to move beyond their determination as a way of affecting other marks that are understood to precede them on the page. The result, for the italicized segments of the programs, is a sort of *paralysis* that prevents them from translating the musical movement of the prelude into a principle of circulation among the visual, grammatical, and allegorical levels of the texts. Fastened into the programs at irregular intervals and detached from their conventional usage, the italics nevertheless continue to confer emphasis with blank, unvarying regularity. Their immobility is increased, moreover, by Baudelaire's use of italics throughout his essay to set quoted titles apart from the rest of the text; as if riveted to these titles, the italics in the *Lohengrin* demonstration take on the arbitrary rigidity of proper names. Baudelaire also habitually uses italics as a visible analogue for vocal intensity, as a way to mark moments that would require, were the essay to be read aloud, an altered tone of voice.[44] But even this cannot bring the programs any closer to translating the music: because italics are tied to them in such a way as to violate both the sense and the punctuation of phrases, the programs baffle any attempt to apply audible emphasis, and they consequently remain further than ever from musical sonority.

Whether they function as visual exceptions, as proper names, or as signals for voiced intensity, Baudelaire's italics are remarkable for their immobilizing force. Far from transporting the prelude's motif into the printed texts, they paralyze each program with their monotonous repetition of emphasis; they obstruct readers' movement from the level of grammar and syntax to the levels of narrative and of allegory. By virtue of their immobility and their enigmatic prominence, the italics emphasize above all their own status as inscriptions, as marks materially fixed to the page and literally distant from either musical or allegorical figuration. In addition, bound as they are to the context of roman typeface, the italics serve as a reminder that even the nonitalicized parts of the programs, as well as the rest of Baudelaire's essay and the other writings mentioned there, are also inscriptions. During the aesthetic meditation just before his demonstration, Baudelaire distinguishes between music, painting, and "the written word, which is . . . the most positive of the arts" (¶5); and his italics now indicate that as printed pages, as substantial objects, the three programs are even more distant from the musical motif than painted images. This explains more clearly than before why Baudelaire uses the word "translation" more reluctantly than "translate": although the verb may signify a way of moving from the prelude to the programs and back, the substantive marks the irreducible separation between the two poles of this movement, between the mobility of the prelude's motif and the fixity of the programs' italics.

Readers will recall, however, that Baudelaire opened his meditation on musical and textual translation only after evoking the struggle at the Théâtre-Italien of Wagner's music against its own program as well as its listeners. In this account, Baudelaire explicitly uses "program" only to mean Wagner's choice of opera extracts; he does not state until later that titles and descriptive texts were printed into a booklet. But he suggests that the prescriptive force of Wagner's concert strategy is linked to the printed texts, since the public only acclaimed a few "irresistible pieces whose thought was most clearly expressed for it" (¶4): the audience reacted best to the music with the clearest text. As Baudelaire then tries to demonstrate, the "thought" of the prelude may also be understood as its original, partially obscured behind the musical translation and discoverable only with the aid of texts written by listeners as well as by Wagner himself. For Baudelaire, in other words, Wagner's prelude is entirely surrounded by interrelated inscriptions, since texts are bound up with its composition from an original "thought," with its manner of performance, and with its listeners' response.[45] The menace of the program therefore consists not simply in imprudent concert arrangements, but in "the written word" that threatens to invade the prelude from all sides, to govern its composition and reception as well as to translate the musical motif into an immobile inscription. Baudelaire contributes to this threat by writing one program and adding italics to others; but he is nonetheless unable to overcome the prelude, which defends itself by maintaining a literal gap between its motif and the complex figuration of italicized allegories. Baudelaire hints, moreover, that the prelude will always successfully resist any effort to translate it: by writing that "Wagner's music triumphed by its own strength" (¶4), Baudelaire predicts the failure of his *Lohengrin* demonstration.

This musical triumph and the corresponding failure of translation may already be inscribed in the first paragraph of Baudelaire's essay, where a single word appears in italics: *I*. Prefiguring the disaster of the prelude demonstration, these italics intensify *I* and set it apart from the rest of the paragraph; despite *I*'s call for "friends" (¶1) to share in writing the essay, the italics warn even "impartial readers" to stay at a respectful distance from *I*'s emphatic authority to represent Baudelaire. The italics thus immobilize *I*, contradicting its stated intention and hindering its attempt to bridge the gap between writer and readers. As a result, it is unlikely that *I* will be able to lead readers on paths of detailed exploration through Wagner's music: after the unsuccessful *Lohengrin* demonstration, the odds are considerable against other attempts to reach a definitive "beginning of the question" (¶1). But if he loses a gamble on the possibility of traveling between music and texts by means of translation, Baudelaire also wins a triumph for the prelude against its programs. By demonstrating the literal distance between musical motifs and textual figures, part 1 of *Richard Wagner et "Tannhäuser" à Paris* may have improved the essay's chances for a good view of the Wagnerian landscape.

3 } *Music in Person*

It is not until after his meditation on the *Lohengrin* prelude that Baudelaire openly declares his personal admiration for Wagner's
music. In a passage that combines a conclusion for the first section of
Richard Wagner et "Tannhäuser" à Paris with a transition to the body of the
essay, Baudelaire writes: "As of that moment, that is to say, as of the first
concert, I was possessed by the desire to enter more deeply into an understanding of these singular works. I had undergone (at least so it seemed to
me) a spiritual operation, a revelation. My voluptuous pleasure had been so
strong and so terrible that I could not stop myself from wanting to return to
it constantly. . . . For several days, for a long time, I said to myself: 'Where
on earth could I hear some of Wagner's music this evening?' Those of my
friends who possessed a piano were more than once my martyrs."[1] Seized
without warning by Wagner's music, Baudelaire experiences something
like an invasion of mind and body, an intrusion against which he is unable
to defend himself. As a result, he is almost literally not himself after listening to it, although he retains limited freedom to study his own sensations
and to write about them. His admiration takes the form of a voluptuous
obsession, an idée fixe that imposes both mental distortion and physical
craving. As if drunk or "possessed" by a powerful opiate, Baudelaire is
essentially unable to distinguish himself from the music he has incorporated. He makes no effort to resist the addiction and begins immediately to
spread the seductive violence of the music among his acquaintances, the
"martyred" pianists.

Baudelaire gives, however, differing accounts of his exact symptoms while under the influence of Wagner's music. In his essay, near the passage just quoted, he insists on his inability to analyze his reaction to the musical narcotic, observing that "this powerlessness caused in [him] anger and curiosity mixed with a bizarre delight" (¶16). But in a letter written to Wagner in February 1860, just after the three concerts, he claims to know precisely how the music has enslaved him. Part of this letter runs as follows:

> At first it seemed to me that I knew this music, and in reflecting on it later, I understood where this mirage came from; it seemed to me that this music was *mine*, and I recognized it just as everyone [tout homme] recognizes the things he is destined to love. . . . And another thing: I often experienced a feeling of a rather strange nature, [a feeling of] pride and sensuous pleasure in understanding, in letting myself be penetrated, invaded, a truly sensual voluptuousness, which resembles that of rising in the air or rolling on the sea. And at the same time, the music occasionally breathed out [or exuded: respirait] pride in living [l'orgueil de la vie]. Generally, those profound harmonies seem to me to resemble those stimulants that accelerate the pulse of the imagination.[2]

Baudelaire claims at first to have recognized the music instantly upon hearing it, as if it were an old friend or a former mistress unexpectedly encountered at the concerts.[3] Unwilling to trust this impression, he subsequently decides that it must have been an illusion, a "mirage" that impersonated loved ones without actually restoring them. But Baudelaire next declares that the mirage deepened into intimate and "sensual" reality; after flickering at the edge of recognition, the music solidified around him until he could feel it caressing his skin like wind or like seawater. The music in fact penetrated Baudelaire's skin, invaded his body, and saturated his imagination, so that it might borrow his lungs in order to "breathe out pride in living." During the concerts, then, Baudelaire found himself in strikingly intimate contact with the music, which seemed either to approach him like a lover or else to surround and suffuse him, like a substance absorbed into his body.

In his letter to Wagner, Baudelaire refers to both these experiences under one name, citing them as varied manifestations of his "admiration" for the music.[4] The two instances of admiration seem to differ more in their immediacy than in their fundamental character: whether it appears to Baudelaire as the image of another person or as a force inhabiting his own body, the music impresses him as a presence that is strangely and compellingly human. Its humanity is in fact concentrated and magnified to an extraordinary degree, as Baudelaire observes at the end of his *Lohengrin* demonstration: "Wagner possesses the art of translating, by subtle gradations, everything that is excessive, immense, ambitious, in the spiritual and bodily nature of man. It seems sometimes, while listening to this ardent and despotic music, that one rediscovers, painted on a background of shadows torn apart by reverie, the vertiginous conceptions of opium" (¶15). If Wagner has mastered the art of rendering all the subtleties and the gradations of human experience into music, claims Baudelaire, he nonetheless specializes in exceptional cases, human beings who exceed mental or physical boundaries and human bodies animated by something beyond the limits of human vitality.[5] Wagner's music therefore produces extreme effects on listeners: it invades their bloodstream and projects before them a vision of half-familiar, half-exaggerated figures. As one of the "stimulants that accelerate the pulse of the imagination" mentioned in Baudelaire's 1860 letter, the music first demands to assume human form—both literally within listeners' bodies and figuratively before their minds' eye—and then pushes its acquired humanity instantly to excess.

Under these circumstances, it is clear that Wagner's music is not altogether safe, and Baudelaire indirectly acknowledges its dangers. He hints that listeners should beware of their own exhilaration: once subdued from within by "this ardent and despotic music," they are likely to be overwhelmed and disconcerted by their visions.[6] Baudelaire warns more explicitly against the music's power of bodily invasion with a brief allusion to an event preceding the 1861 performances of *Tannhäuser*. Just after a dress rehearsal open to members of the public, one of Wagner's Parisian adversaries, the music critic Paul Scudo, created an extraordinary scene at the Opéra. He placed himself near the entrance, "confronting the crowd to the point of blocking its exit, and trying hard to laugh like a maniac, like one of those unfortunates who, in asylums, are said to be *agitated*. This poor man, believing that his face was known to the whole crowd, seemed to be saying: 'See how I'm laughing, I, the famous S . . . ! So take care that your judgment conforms to mine' " (¶3). Apparently overcome by what he heard at the rehearsal, Scudo lost all self-restraint. That he was moved by dislike rather than admiration made little difference: the music was nonetheless able to fill him with excessive, unnatural animation. At the same time, the music emptied him of all capacity to reason and to speak for himself; despite his eagerness to communicate with the crowd, he could produce only exaggerated gestures of scorn and rebellion. Violently seized by Wagner's music, Scudo was both struck mute and made to flail madly about, as if he were a sort of epileptic statue.

Baudelaire himself furnishes a corresponding example of what happens when the music bodily appropriates a willing subject instead of a recalcitrant one. Rather than depriving him of his faculties, it goads him into desperate action: he not only martyrs the pianists of his acquaintance, but also haunts nightclubs where the musicians occasionally squander excerpts from *Lohengrin* on the "unsavory crowds" (¶16). More important, Baudelaire's admiration drives him to read, and ultimately to write, about Wagner's music: "[P]ossessed by the desire to enter more deeply into an understanding of these singular works," he declares, "I resolved to inform myself about the why and the wherefore, and to transform my voluptuous pleasure into knowledge before a stage performance might come to furnish me with a perfect elucidation" (¶16–17). It is to the music itself, therefore, that Baudelaire attributes the motivating force behind the rest of the essay. Whatever its latent dangers, he is dependent on his exaggerated admiration to carry his writing forward and, in the same movement, to provide new perspective on the problem of distance between his text and Wagner's music. When he declares himself to be wholly possessed by the music, Baudelaire suggests that he has in effect lent it his body and thus enabled it to write for itself. Readers, he consequently implies, ought to understand the essay as a text inscribed by Wagner's music with little or no mediation from Baudelaire; their reading should bring them into close, articulate communication with the music. By extension, admiring readers may discover that they are similarly possessed by the music, so that they share in the essay as if they had written it themselves. In several senses, then, parts 2 and 3 of the essay consist of an attempt to bring Wagner's music literally to life by rhetorical means. Despite the warning in his allusions to opium addiction and to Scudo's madness, Baudelaire writes as if the privilege of giving human existence to the music were worth the risk.

LIVE QUOTATIONS

In part 2, Baudelaire relies heavily on a number of quotations from prose texts by Wagner. Although he mentions several books in passing, Baudelaire quotes largely from two letters that Wagner published in 1860 as part of his Parisian publicity campaign and that were designed to summarize his aesthetic principles.[7] Together with Baudelaire's accompanying comments, the quotations give this section of his essay the appearance of a summary research report on Wagner's artistic goals and on the theories underlying them. Baudelaire also gives this section the air of a mild polemic, since he frames it with complaints about the vulgar and irresponsible treatment Wagner frequently received from the French press.[8] He implies that his own essay, by contrast, presents only accurate, well-documented information from direct sources. Moreover, by grouping his quotations in pairs according to the similarity of their themes and assertions, Baudelaire apparently wants to emphasize the consistency both of Wagner's thinking and of his own argument.

Partially protected by these appearances of scholarly convention, however, Baudelaire also uses part 2 for some less straightforward pursuits. It is surprising, in view of his earlier demand for permission to "speak often in [his] own name" (¶1), that he should devote so much of his energy to quoting others; but his admiration, as it is described at the end of part 1 and in his letter to Wagner, offers a preliminary means of accounting for the quotations. If Baudelaire has incorporated Wagner's music to such a degree that the *I* in his text must represent them both at once, then a series of quotations surrounded and supported by commentary provides one method for reminding readers at steady intervals of *I*'s composite status.[9] In addition, it quickly becomes clear that the sequence of quotations and comments is designed to reopen the question of distance between music and language in more than one manner. The quotations not only deal thematically with Wagner's struggle to unite music and poetry, but they also evoke this struggle rhetorically by personifying the two arts in various ways and to varying degrees: the quotations begin to populate the Wagnerian landscape with human figures. Developing his earlier personification of "this ardent and despotic music," Baudelaire now uses the quotations to present music and writing as animated by or embodied in human beings.[10]

Baudelaire prepares readers for this rhetorical tactic at the opening of part 2, where he argues that the relation between Wagner's music and his poetry has been badly misinterpreted by "vulgar journalism":

> Since Wagner had never stopped repeating that (dramatic) music ought to *speak* sentiment, to adapt itself to sentiment with the same exactness as words, but obviously in a different manner, . . . a crowd of people, persuaded by the jokers in the press, imagined that the master attributed to music the power to express the positive form of things, in other words, that he inverted the roles and functions. (¶17)

> I see from the notes that he [Wagner] himself has furnished on his youth that, even as a child, he lived in the midst of the theater, . . . and soon, as years and studies accumulated, it was impossible for him not to think in a double manner, poetically and musically, [impossible for him] not to glimpse every idea in two simultaneous forms, one of the two arts taking up its function just where the other reached its limits. (¶19)[11]

In both these passages, Baudelaire maintains that Wagner has established a perfectly clear division of privileges and duties in his operas: he treats music and language like actors who are assigned to separate but equally important roles. Although both must "speak" their parts in direct response to each other, they must also go independently about their respective "functions" in the theater. Baudelaire further declares that music and language are manifestly well cast in their complementary roles, since the talents of each make up for the inadequacies of the other. Limited by their individual skills, the two must pool their full-time activity and their separate genres of expertise, as if only their meticulously combined efforts were sufficient to bring Wagner's works to life. Consequently, the French press seems all the more irresponsible when it charges Wagner with confusing or "inverting" the roles of music and language; by twisting his words and reporting them out of context, this misquotation deadens the impact of Wagner's artistry even before it has appeared on stage.

As if to remedy the ills caused by other writers' misquotation, Baudelaire now offers four long quotations in which Wagner explains how he has used music and poetry to vivify modern drama. More accurately, these quotations describe an act of *re*vivification: rather than trust completely in the vitality of his own brain children, Wagner claims to resurrect classical Greek drama and to adapt it to life in the nineteenth century. The first of these quotations is drawn from a letter to Berlioz that Wagner published in late February 1860 as a response to Berlioz's review of his three concerts.[12] Although Berlioz had made reasonably favorable comments about the music performed, he had ended his article with an unfavorable discussion of Wagner's aesthetic theorizing, and Wagner wanted to answer this attack. In his reply, he proclaimed his intense dissatisfaction with most contemporary opera and then explained his esteem for classical Greek drama. Part of the passage quoted by Baudelaire reads as follows:

> "We are rightly astonished today that thirty thousand Greeks were able to follow with sustained interest the performance of Aeschylus's tragedies; but if we look for the means by which such results were obtained, we find that it was by the alliance of all the arts working together toward the same goal, that is, toward the production of the most perfect and the only true work of art. This led me to study the relations among the diverse branches of art and, after having grasped the relation that exists between *plastic art* and *gestural art* [la *plastique* et la *mimique*], I examined the one that is found between music and poetry: from this examination there suddenly sprang an enlightenment that completely dissipated the obscurity that had until then worried me.
>
> "I recognized, in fact, that precisely where one of these arts reached insurmountable limits, there began, with the most rigorous exactness, the other's sphere of action; that, consequently, by the intimate union of these two arts, one could express with the most satisfying clarity what neither of them could express in isolation; that, on the contrary, all efforts to render with the means available to one of them what could only be rendered by both together would inevitably lead first to obscurity, to confusion, and then to the degeneracy and the corruption of each art in particular." (¶20–21)

In one of his many evocations of the *Gesamtkunstwerk*, Wagner here describes the relation between different arts as an "alliance." Given the concern he expresses in the second quoted paragraph with both separation of territories and terms of cooperation, Wagner evokes a sort of political accord among independent, self-interested parties. Once Baudelaire begins to quote, that is, poetry and music no longer appear solely as actors who unite their efforts in the theater for the sake of their art; they now also join forces on a larger scale in order to gain power. Wagner measures this power partly by its effect on the audience, since he insists on its capacity to enthrall thousands upon thousands of Greek spectators. But Wagner's text also suggests another, less obvious measure for this power: at the moment it gave him sudden and complete "enlightenment," the alliance of poetry and music appeared forceful enough to limit or at least determine the participation of other arts. Wagner stresses that he initially studied the connection between *"plastic art* and *gestural art,"*[13] but he indicates that he subsequently laid this study aside so as to devote himself to the relation between music and poetry. The second paragraph of the quotation then concentrates on this latter pair, with no explanation (here or elsewhere in the letter to Berlioz) of its ties to the visual and gestural arts. Wagner hints, moreover, that music and poetry collaborate not out of sheer ambition, but rather for basic survival; sequestered behind "insurmountable limits," the two arts pool their strength so that each can better protect its individual "sphere of action." Therefore, although Wagner's reference to "the union of these two arts" might be interpreted as a kind of politically expedient marriage intended to prevent the internal "degeneracy" or "corruption" of each art "in isolation," it might also be understood as a diplomatic arrangement designed to fortify the external borders of music and poetry. Threats to these frontiers may not come solely or explicitly from the realm of the plastic arts, but Wagner's text leaves them under suspicion.

Beside this passage from the letter to Berlioz, Baudelaire's second quotation seems at first to be somewhat oddly chosen. It comes from the piece of Wagner's writing that was most fully and easily accessible to Baudelaire, the *Lettre sur la musique* addressed to Frédéric Villot, curator of paintings at the Louvre. Published in Paris at the end of 1860, this *Lettre* served as the preface for a volume containing four of Wagner's opera librettos in French translation.[14] Baudelaire observes that in addition to various aesthetic and autobiographical reflections, the *Lettre* includes summaries of

Wagner's major theoretical works, *Die Kunst und die Revolution, Das Kunst-werk der Zukunft,* and *Oper und Drama.* The second quotation, taken from the *Lettre*'s summary of *Die Kunst und die Revolution,* apparently has little to do with the preceding one; it dwells on the social conditions of Greek theater, with no mention of how separate arts were combined:

> "[H]istory in turn offered me the model and the type for ideal relations between the theater and public life as I conceived them. I found this model in the theater of ancient Athens: there, the theater opened its precinct only for certain solemnities during which a religious festival was celebrated and accompanied by the delights of art. The most distinguished men of state took a direct part in these solemnities as poets or directors; they seemed like priests in the eyes of the assembled population of the city and the country, and this population was filled with such high expectations for the sublimity of the works that were going to be performed before it, that the most profound poems, those of an Aeschylus and a Sophocles, could be offered to the people and assured of being perfectly understood." (¶22)

Except for its parting reference to the poems of Aeschylus and Sophocles, this quotation appears to leave the dramas themselves aside, focusing instead on the people involved in their production and reception. Baudelaire chooses Wagner's statements about the grandeur of the festivals, the social distinction of the performers, and the absolute awe of the spectators. The dramas do not entirely disappear from this passage, but they are now visible primarily through the various human beings who set them in motion and experience their effects. It is as if the composite, cooperative art of Greek drama, which appeared in Baudelaire's first quotation as an abstraction to be figured and analyzed, were now absorbed and made concrete in the living bodies of actors, poets, and spectators. To put this another way, one might say that the first quotation rhetorically personifies Greek poetry and music as allies in the protection of certain aesthetic boundaries and the search for certain kinds of expressive power; this second quotation presents Greek citizens who, in a different, more literal sense, person-ify these arts, bringing them fully to life in the persons of performers and spectators.[15] What the two quotations have in common is their aim to invest the arts concerned with unusual force and vitality, since the human figures involved are either powerful leaders engaged in affairs of state or members of an immense, surprisingly gifted populace; music and language no longer appear as the anonymous actors evoked at the beginning of part 2. Further, Baudelaire subtly stresses the vitality of these arts and of the people who embody them by cutting off his second quotation just before Wagner turns, in the *Lettre,* to a discussion of the weakening and decline of Greek drama.[16]

Baudelaire's third quotation gives an outline of Wagner's methods for bringing ancient drama back to life. Specifically, it concentrates on the procedures that enable Wagner to overcome the enormous gaps between ancient and modern audiences, to surmount the differences of viewpoint and situation that separate contemporary European spectators from their Greek ancestors:

> "The only picture of human life that may be called poetic is the one in which motifs [motifs] that make sense only to the abstract intelligence give way to purely human motives [mobiles] that govern the heart. This tendency (the one relative to the invention of the poetic subject) is the sovereign law that presides over poetic form and representation [or performance: représentation] . . . [*sic*] The rhythmic arrangement and the (almost musical) ornament of rhyme are the means by which the poet guarantees that the verse, the phrase, will have a power that captivates as if by a spell and governs feeling as it wishes. Essential to the poet, this tendency leads him to the limit of his art, a limit that immediately touches music, and, consequently, the most complete work of the poet should be the one that, at its final culmination, would be perfect music.
>
> "From there, I saw myself necessarily led to designate *myth* as the poet's ideal material. Myth is the primitive and anonymous poem of the people, and we rediscover it taken up again during all epochs, unceasingly reworked anew by the great poets of cultivated periods. In myth, in fact, human relations almost completely shed their conventional form, intelligible only to abstract reason; they show what life has that is truly human, eternally comprehensible, and they show it in that concrete form, excluding all imitation, which gives to all true myths the individual character that you recognize at first glance." (¶24–25)

The ellipsis in the first part of this passage marks Baudelaire's intervention in the *Lettre;* like Greek drama, resurrected only in altered form, this quotation is adapted to present circumstances. Baudelaire omits not only a sentence from the middle of the passage, but also a related one that immediately precedes its beginning. In both of these, Wagner describes language as an instrument that poets adjust for their own, abnormal purposes: instead of using it to express conventional abstractions, they make language act directly on the senses and, in consequence, on the emotional sensibility of listeners.[17] When he excludes these sentences, Baudelaire simultaneously lessens Wagner's emphasis on the activity of poets and highlights the active, apparently self-sustaining power of their language. The elliptical quotation thus seems to confer on poetry a sort of autonomy, so that it appears less as an inert instrument than as an individual "power," willfully inclined to capture and govern listeners. Such autonomy, however, is short lived and illusory. Whether or not poetry has dissociated itself from poets, it is by nature unable to separate itself from musicians; by virtue of its intrinsic rhymes and rhythms, claims Wagner, it is inevitably drawn into the domain of music.

This absorption of poetry into music is the first in a layered series of similar transformations that take place in Baudelaire's third quotation. Once music has incorporated poetry, the resulting "perfect music" may in turn be assimilated into myth. Because it absorbs an ideally proportioned union of poetry and music, myth is livelier, more animated than either of its components taken separately; Wagner suggests its greater freedom of movement when he tries to differentiate rigid or intellectualized "motifs" from spontaneously affective "mobiles." But in addition to this fundamental dynamism, myth has the power to gather and concentrate the most active, least artificial "human relations" into a "concrete form." Further still, myth effects this concentration again and again, tirelessly; Wagner insists that myth shapes universal relations into specific human dramas as poets recast it "anew" in "all epochs."[18] For Wagner, then, the resurrection of Greek drama must proceed by cumulative stages of incorporation and vivification: poetry is absorbed into music, which subsequently animates myth so that this latter may finally—and endlessly—embody human drama.[19]

Baudelaire moves from this third quotation to his fourth one with almost no break, as if anxious not to interrupt Wagner's progress in reviving ancient arts. Drawn from one of the final sections of the *Lettre sur la musique* and constructed by means of several ellipses, the fourth quotation focuses on Wagner's success in introducing resurrected drama into nineteenth-century society. Baudelaire first chooses several sentences intended to explain why myth, in contrast to history, lends itself to incarnation equally well in Greek theaters or German opera houses:

> "All the detail necessary to describe and represent historical fact and its accidents, all the detail that a special and distant epoch in history requires in order to be perfectly understood and that contemporary authors of dramas and historical novels deduce, for this reason, in such an elaborate way, I could leave it [such detail] aside . . . [*sic*] Legend, to whatever epoch and whatever nation it may belong, has the advantage of exclusively comprising what is purely human in that epoch and that nation . . ."

The quotation then skips from the technical use of myth to its effect on audiences. Regardless of place or circumstance, writes Wagner,

> "The character of the scene [or stage: scène] and the tone of the legend both contribute to plunging the mind into that state of *dream* that soon carries it all the way to full *clairvoyance,* and the mind then discovers a new chain of links among the phenomena of the world, [a chain] that the eyes could not perceive in the ordinary state of waking . . . [*sic*]" (¶26)[20]

The ultimate phase in Wagner's series of incorporations thus depends on his spectators: after myth has been animated by poetry and music and has taken shape within characters on stage, it comes at last to life within members of the audience. This final incarnation involves actual human beings, but it stimulates them to a degree of animation that surpasses normal human faculties; once they have been captivated at a performance, spectators' vigor of perception and understanding far exceeds ordinary human limits. Clearly, the inordinate vitality of such spectators recalls Baudelaire's own condition during and after the 1860 concerts. With his fourth and last quotation in part 2, Baudelaire implicitly attaches himself to the "clairvoyant" spectators who have brought Wagner's works literally and intensely to life.

This conclusion to the four quotations confirms the importance of their ordering, which shows a steady progression that Baudelaire's commentary does not make explicit. Taken in sequence, they confer increasing animation on Wagner's music, rhetorically imbuing it with several kinds and degrees of humanity. In preparation for this crescendo, part 2 begins with Baudelaire's declaration of the harm caused by misquotation: the claims falsely attributed to Wagner in the press make his works appear lifeless and ludicrous by casting music and language in the wrong roles. Introduced by Baudelaire's subsequent sketch of music and language as independent, well-matched performers, the first pair of quotations corrects the false reports from two complementary perspectives. In the extract from Wagner's letter to Berlioz, music and poetry find themselves rhetorically personified as allies whose power sharing is mutually profitable; in the excerpt from Wagner's *Lettre* to Villot, it is actual Athenian citizens who, by fervent participation in their immense public festivals, concretely person-ify the arts. Baudelaire's next pair of quotations further accentuates the power and energy that characterize both the preceding kinds of personification. With its series of vivifying transformations, the third quotation shows how the absorption of poetry into music comes to be embodied in stage characters, and the fourth quotation extends this process of incarnation to spectators such as Baudelaire.

Within this progression, the first and third quotations personify music and poetry in a different manner than the second and fourth. It is the first and third that insist the least on figuring music as a fully identifiable human being, complete with visible contours and a discernible character. While allusions to music's "sphere of action" or its "power that captivates" may suggest human endeavors, they summon no more than a passing image; they draw more attention to the music's forceful animation than to its recognizable human qualities. These evocations of vaguely humanized music conform to traditional definitions of personification, such as the one proposed by Pierre Fontanier in his *Manuel classique pour l'étude des tropes* (1830). "*Personification,*" he writes, "consists in making an *inanimate, non-sentient being, or an abstract and purely ideal being, into a type of real and physical being, endowed with feeling and with life, in short, that which is called a* person."[21] Fontanier particularly stresses the fleeting, noninsistent character of genuine personifications, which occur only *"by a simple manner of speaking, or by an entirely verbal fiction"*;[22] as rhetorical embellishments, they by no means attribute actual human status to the objects personified. Fontanier therefore includes only instances of the figure that are "short, rapid, that are only made in passing, on which no emphasis is laid, and that are visibly nothing but a somewhat more elaborately refined expression [une expression un peu plus recherchée], substituted for the ordinary expression."[23] He further specifies that personification must arise from other, more broadly defined tropes, such as metaphor, metonymy, or synecdoche.[24] In Fontanier's terms, for example, Wagner's personification of different arts "working together toward the same goal" (¶20) metaphorically ascribes human actions and intentions to something nonhuman.

When Wagner personifies the arts in Baudelaire's second and fourth quotations, however, the results correspond less well to Fontanier's definition. Both quotations focus on real people overwhelmed by music, either as performers realizing the potential vitality with which music invests myth or else as listeners absorbing this vitality to an extraordinary degree; in both cases, the music is held to be so pervasively powerful that it takes entire possession of its human associates. By thus appropriating minds and bodies, music makes an irresistible but relatively inconspicuous entrance into ancient Greek or modern European society: outwardly indistinguishable from other people, music in human form blends naturally into the crowds on stage or in the audience. This humanized or person-ified music also slips discreetly into the text of the *Lettre sur la musique,* where it appears as a flesh-and-blood person rather than as a rhetorical ornament. When Wagner describes the rapt concentration of ancient audiences and the "clairvoyance" of recent ones, he does not treat listeners as passing metonyms for the music they hear; nor does he regard the performers, ancient or modern, simply as metaphors for the abstract transformation of music and poetry into myth. In order to characterize these authentically human incarnations of music, one might turn to the distinction Paul de Man has proposed between tropes and anthropomorphism. For de Man, anthropomorphism "is not just a trope but an identification on the level of substance. It takes one entity for another and thus implies the constitution of specific entities prior to their confusion, the *taking* of something for something else that can then be assumed to be *given.*"[25] In the second and fourth quotations, Wagner uses performers and spectators not as rhetorical figures that enliven his argument, but rather as concrete embodiments that lend music a corporeal, human identity. It follows that readers, taking music for someone much like themselves, should find it strangely familiar: once incarnated by such theatergoers as those from Athens or Weimar or Paris, music should have little trouble approaching the readers of Wagner's *Lettre.*[26]

By extension, the same music should be able to mingle with the readers of Baudelaire's essay, but its relations with this second crowd are more complex. As an admiring listener, Baudelaire claims literally to embody Wagner's music at the same time that he writes figuratively about "this ardent and despotic music" (¶15) whose task is to "*speak* sentiment" (¶18). While maintaining that he shares his own person with the music, that is, Baudelaire also personifies it in his essay; nothing in part 2 suggests that the two activities are inconsistent with each other. On the contrary, Baudelaire quotes Wagner in such a way as to highlight their compatibility, arranging his quotations in pairs so that each instance of rhetorical personification leads into an instance of physical embodiment. This gathering vitality is especially evident in the second pair, where it is possible to trace the transition from music personified by mythical personages to music incarnated in actual listeners. Baudelaire's quotations therefore serve a double purpose: they imply that there is a difference only of intensity between texts that figure music as a person and texts that identify music with a human being; and they also intimate that the passage from a text about music to a living incarnation of music is natural and immediate. The quotations, that is, appear to act as catalysts that permit the transformation of textual figures into living persons. Baudelaire charges them in this way with the task of infusing human life into Wagner's music, first by engaging in figurative personification, then by implicating readers in a process of literal embodiment.[27] And as if to force this responsibility on his quotations, Baudelaire largely passes over his own role in selecting and ordering them. Except for limited commentary and occasional ellipses, Baudelaire obliges the excerpted passages to fulfill their task independently, thus lending support to Antoine Compagnon's assertion that every quotation "is a mutilated organ, but it may already be a body in its own right [un corps propre], living and sufficient: . . . it moves by itself, it roves around, and I can no longer stop it."[28] If these active and headstrong quotations are able to bring elements of Wagner's dissected texts back to life, then they may also reasonably be expected to carry on in their new context with his revivification of Greek art. By reenacting their drama of figurative and literal personification in part 2 of Baudelaire's essay, the quotations aim to resurrect ancient music as a citizen of modern Paris.

REBELLIOUS MELODIES

Baudelaire continues in part 3 to depend on long quotations, but he deploys fewer of them than in part 2 and draws them from different sources. Turning to the translated opera librettos for which the *Lettre sur la musique* serves as an introduction, he gives three plot summaries embel-lished with comments based either on his own impressions or on his study of Liszt's *"Lohengrin" et "Tannhäuser" de Richard Wagner*. In the course of this commentary, Baudelaire extends and explores an assertion advanced at the end of part 1, but left temporarily undeveloped. When he first de-scribes the symptoms of his addiction to Wagner's music, Baudelaire notes in passing that it is linked to his fascination with recurrent motifs: he feels driven to read and write about Wagner partly because "frequent repetitions of the same melodic phrases, in pieces taken from the same opera, implied mysterious intentions and a method that were unknown to me" (¶17).[29] In part 3, Baudelaire elaborates on the relation between these melodies and his compulsion both to embody the music in himself and to personify it in his essay. It is in the course of this elaboration that the risks and difficulties involved in either manner of bringing the music to life become implicitly clear: literal embodiment and figurative personification in the end reveal not only their intermittent incompatibility, but also the threat they pose both to Wagner's music and to Baudelaire's writing.

Part 3 opens with a discussion of *Tannhäuser* that concentrates particu-larly on the overture and its ties to the rest of the opera. Baudelaire at first seems to make only hesitant use of personification in his account. He claims that the music of the overture anticipates a human conflict later acted out on stage, but he does not insist that the musical confrontation must be figured by means of human combatants: "*Tannhäuser* represents the fight between the two principles that have chosen the human heart for their main battlefield, that is, between flesh and spirit, hell and heaven, Satan and God. And this duality is represented right away, by the overture, with incomparable skill. . . . The overture, I say, thus summarizes the thought of the drama with two songs [or melodies: chants], the religious song and the voluptuous song, which, to use Liszt's expression, 'are posed here like two terms that, in the finale, find their equation'" (¶28). A "fight" on a "battlefield" initially evokes an image of human activity, conjuring a brief and conventional version of the psychomachia. But rather than lingering over this warlike personification, Baudelaire immediately goes on to characterize the opposing forces with several traditional pairs of concepts and then borrows Liszt's allusion to mathematical abstractions. Consequently, the two principal motifs both come to appear as intangible and impersonal entities that resist attempts to endow them with human contours.[30]

As his discussion proceeds, however, Baudelaire begins to distinguish between the two motifs precisely in terms of their abstraction. He describes the religious "*Pilgrims' Chorus*" as an inspiring but inscrutable manifestation of the Christian God, a musical expression of "the authority of the supreme law" (¶28). As if to hint at its connection with the Christian doctrine of incarnation, Baudelaire later sketches a vague personification of this melody; but he writes only that after a successful fight against its rival motif, the pilgrims' hymn tune "comes little by little to reestablish order" and "rises up anew, with all its solid beauty" (¶29). In contrast, the opposing "voluptuous song" has little difficulty in assuming bodily form. Baudelaire asserts that from the moment the conflicting motif is heard, "the true, the terrible, the universal Venus already rises up in every imagination" (¶28); the motif obliges its listeners to personify it not merely as a sensuous woman, but rather as the superhuman goddess of passion. Inevitably, this "furious song of the flesh" (¶29) pushes listeners even further, assailing their ears with "languor, delights mixed with fever and cut off by anguish" (¶28) until they have no choice but physically to absorb the music: "From the first measures onward, the nerves vibrate in unison with the melody; all flesh endowed with memory begins to tremble" (¶29).[31] For

Baudelaire, then, the two motifs of the *Tannhäuser* overture oppose each other on at least three levels. In addition to representing a conflict between abstract principles, they suggest violent discord between music that barely allows rhetorical personification and music that demands physical incarnation; and they intensify this latter division by associating personification with the reduction of divinities to human form (the Christian motif) while linking incarnation with the elevation of human listeners to superhuman status (the Venus motif).

These layers of opposition recall some elements of a theory of motivic confrontation that Wagner himself outlined in an early essay entitled "De l'ouverture." Published in 1841 in the *Revue et Gazette musicale de Paris,* this essay reviewed the past development and current prospects of the opera overture as a genre, concentrating on the overtures most frequently performed in Paris at that time.[32] Prominent among these is the overture to Gluck's *Iphigénie en Aulide,* a work in which the composer "has traced . . . with grandiose and powerful strokes the principal idea of the drama and has personified it [l'a personnifiée] with the clarity of the obvious" (1:235). More precisely, since the drama consists of a struggle between "the army of Greek heroes" and "a tender young girl," Gluck's achievement lies in having "musically personified [personnifié musicalement] these enemy elements" (1:244). These two instances of the term *personnifié* are unclear but also suggestive: without indicating how it might be possible, they nonetheless imply that musical motifs may serve as well as literary figures to personify the general notion of discord, as if the music could somehow lend recognizably human lineaments to an otherwise abstract concept. Wagner reinforces this implication when he later tries to establish an analogy between the dramatic conflict in the opera and "the essence of instrumental music"; as if they were hostile characters in a play, Gluck manipulates rival melodies so as to figure human violence with "the movement given to these motifs by the working-out of the music [le travail musical] inspired by the idea of a fight" (1:245–46). Despite his lack of clarity, therefore, Wagner intimates that the motifs of Gluck's overture are well adapted to processes of figuration, since they can represent either human opponents or the concept of opposition.

Wagner further suggests that the same is not true of all overture motifs. When he discusses Mozart, Wagner focuses on "that fight personified by his overture" to *Don Giovanni*, a combat that pits a human being against the inhuman powers animating the stone statue of the Commendatore. In this overture, claims Wagner, "the dominant idea . . . of the drama is, so to speak, indicated by two principal strokes, and draws the complement [puise le complément] of a real, incontestable life from the movement of the musical working-out" (1:240). Unlike Gluck, Mozart nearly allows his motifs to exceed the bounds of figuration, to come fully and concretely to life. Mozart prevents this, according to Wagner, only because he declines to compose a conclusion for the motivic struggle, thereby discouraging the listener from wholly embodying the music; because he does not allow the overture music to preempt the outcome of the opera, "the listener is seized by the alternatives of a fierce combat, but he never expects to see it transformed into a drama" (1:240). Beethoven, on the other hand, lacked Mozart's restraint in this regard, so that in Wagner's opinion his third *Leonora* overture imposes on listeners "that violent anxiety that dominates us when we witness the immediate development of a striking action" (1:241). Beethoven's motifs thus invade their audience in order to commandeer human vitality; they abandon figurative processes of personification in their pursuit of literal incarnation. The *Leonora* overture, that is, rebels against its status as instrumental music and acts out "in advance the complete drama, in its ardent and precipitate movement" (1:243).

Wagner's account of these overtures therefore agrees with Baudelaire's discussion of the *Tannhäuser* melodies; both indicate that certain musical motifs are best adapted for personification, whereas others lend themselves instead to incarnation. Baudelaire and Wagner both note as well that one consequence of this division is an ambiguous relation between the motivic drama begun in an overture and the sung drama subsequently acted out on stage. Wagner touches on this problem when he remarks that Gluck's motifs, which encourage personification, introduce and complement the stage play, whereas Beethoven's motifs, which demand incarnation, compete or interfere with it. Baudelaire addresses this issue less systematically, but with equal concern. He initially tackles it in two passages from part 3, the first devoted to *Tannhäuser* and the second to *Lohengrin:*

> This overture contains not only the mother idea, the psychic duality constituting the drama, but also the principal formulas, clearly accentuated,

[that are] destined to paint the general sentiments expressed in the rest of the work, as is demonstrated by the forced returns of the diabolically voluptuous melody and of the religious motif or *Pilgrims' Chorus,* every time the action demands it. (¶32)

We have observed that in *Tannhäuser* the recurrence of the two principal themes, the religious motif and the song of voluptuous pleasure, served to awaken the attention of the public and to put it once again into a state fitted [analogous: analogue] to the current situation [in the opera]. In *Lohengrin,* this mnemonic system is applied much more meticulously. Each character is, so to speak, emblazoned by a melody that represents his moral nature and the role he is called to play in the fable [or story: fable]. (¶38)

While obviously related, these passages contradict each other with respect to the role played by the melodic motifs in the two operas. In the first instance, Baudelaire describes the melodies as subordinate—as useful but inanimate tools. However "voluptuous" or "religious," the melodies are no more than "formulas" that are "forced" to punctuate the stage action whenever the fundamental dualism of the drama needs to be accentuated. In the second passage, however, Baudelaire recognizes in the same melodies considerably more autonomy. Far from appearing as mechanical devices, the motifs now serve as intermediaries between the performers and the audience; they are largely responsible for summoning the spectators to participate, if only by analogy, in the situation evolving on stage. Further, the motifs in the second passage interpret the drama to some extent for the audience: when he observes that each character is "emblazoned" [blasonné] by a melody, Baudelaire suggests not only that the melodies function as stylized figures or as the *blasons* traditional in French poetry, but also that they dynamically mark or "emblazon" characters with critical description.

As if aware of the ambiguity created by these two accounts, Baudelaire abandons his own efforts and instead borrows a detailed consideration of motifs from Liszt's book *"Lohengrin" et "Tannhäuser" de Richard Wagner.* As the longest and most complex quotation in the whole essay, this excerpt nearly brings the movement of Baudelaire's commentary in part 3 to a standstill. But it points more clearly than Baudelaire's own remarks to latent tension between Wagner's melodic motifs and his stage dramas, and it also makes partially explicit the related antagonism between figurative personification and literal incarnation. It is therefore worth studying in some detail:

"The spectator, prepared and resigned not to look for *any of those detached pieces that, strung one after another on the thread of some plot, compose the substance of our habitual operas,* will take a singular interest in following throughout three acts the profoundly considered, astonishingly skillful and poetically intelligent combination with which Wagner, *by means of several principal phrases,* has tightened *a melodic knot* that constitutes his whole drama. The twists these phrases make, in binding and interlacing themselves around the words of the poem, create an effect that is moving to the last degree. But if, after having been struck and impressed by this at the performance, one still wants to understand better what it was that so vividly affected one and to study the score of this work belonging to so new a genre, one remains astonished by all the intentions and nuances that it encompasses and that one could not immediately grasp. What dramas and epics of great poets is it not necessary to study for a long time in order to master their whole meaning?

"Wagner, by a procedure that he applies in a wholly unforeseen manner, succeeds in extending the influence and the ambitions of music. Not content with the power it exercises over hearts by awakening in them the entire range of human feelings, he gives it the possibility of inciting our ideas, of speaking to our thought, of appealing to our reflection, and [he] endows it with a moral and intellectual meaning . . . [*sic*] He melodically draws [*dessine*] the nature of his characters and of their principal passions, and these melodies reveal themselves, *in the vocal line or in the accompaniment,* each time that the passions and sentiments they express are put in play. This systematic persistence is joined to an art of arrangement that would offer, by the refinement of the psychological, poetic and philosophical insights it shows, the most unusual interest even to those for whom eighth notes and sixteenth notes are dead letters and pure hieroglyphs. Wagner, solely by forcing our meditation and our memory into such constant exercise, tears the action of music out of the domain of vaguely tender feelings and adds to its charms some of the pleasures of the mind. By this method that complicates the facile delights procured by *a series of arias* [*chants*] *rarely related to each other,* he demands singular attention from the public; but at the same time he prepares more perfect emotions for those who know how to savor them. His melodies are in a way *personifications of ideas;* their return announces that of feelings which the words pronounced do not indicate at all explicitly; it is to them that Wagner confides the task of revealing to us all the secrets of the heart. There are some phrases—the one, for example, from the first scene of the second act [of *Lohengrin*]—that wend their way through the opera like a venomous serpent, twining around its victims and fleeing before their holy defenders; there are others, like the one from the introduction, that return only rarely, with supreme and divine revelations. The situations or the characters of any importance are all expressed musically by a melody that becomes their constant symbol. Now since these melodies are of rare beauty, we will say to those who, in studying a score, restrict themselves to judging internal relations between eighth notes and sixteenth notes, that even if the music of this opera had to be deprived of its beautiful text, it would still be a production of the first order." (¶39–40)[33]

Baudelaire begins this quotation by adding emphasis to Liszt's assertion that Wagner's motivic technique saves his works from the chaotic fragmentation typical of operas at the time. Instead of *"detached pieces"* mechanically wired together or a string of *"arias rarely related to each other,"* Wagner organizes a melodic ensemble of *"principal phrases"* that engage in lively interchange with one another. Active and energetic, these melodies are constantly in search of new positions: they make room for themselves with equal determination either *"in the vocal line or in the accompaniment,"* obliging both actors and instruments to collaborate with them. But it is not clear from the quotation that this collaboration is entirely beneficial to all parties concerned, because Baudelaire oddly underlines the already strange statement that the motifs form *"a melodic knot"* [*un nœud mélodique*] that Wagner has pulled tight [serré], with "twists" [replis] that are bound and woven around the libretto. Some of the French words involved in this formulation suggest amicable or even amorous relations initiated by the motifs: their way of "binding and interlacing themselves" [se liant et s'entrelaçant] could signal either bonds of friendship or erotic intertwining, and the *"knot"* could refer either to dramatic tension built up in the opera's plot or to melodic curlicues that adorn the music like ribbons. But none of these connotations is strong enough to overpower the hostile implications also raised by the words used here. Especially in light of the serpent pictured later in this quotation, the *"knot"* could equally well insinuate the snakelike coils of the motifs,[34] just as the "twists" mobilize a common French term for reptile twining. In addition, a tightened *"knot"* "binding itself" around the libretto sharply calls to mind a noose, or at least a rope that constricts and lacerates limbs rather than embracing them. Taken together, then, as strands of an ominously resonant *"knot"* that tightens around and between the words sung on stage, the motifs apparently have as much power to stifle as to support or caress. Instead of joining in the stage drama, the motifs might succeed only in immobilizing and eventually choking it; the melodic knot might create a drama of its own that paradoxically tears the opera apart.

The quotation also suggests that the ties between Wagner's motifs and his listeners are possibly more strained than might be expected. Near the end of the first quoted paragraph, one reads that even by devoting complete attention to the music as it is performed, one "could not immediately grasp" "all the intentions and nuances that it encompasses"; as with any masterpiece, one would have to take up the score and "study [it] for a long time" in order to understand the true extent of the motifs' activity. Slightly modified, this admonition returns in the last sentence of the quotation, which declares that even without a libretto or a performance, an examination of the score will still reveal a "production of the first order." Liszt by no means denies the motifs' spontaneous influence over spectators in the opera house; on the contrary, he insists that the audience will be "struck and impressed at the performance" and, further, that the motifs will exercise both an aesthetic and an intellectual fascination over listeners. But the quotation nonetheless indicates that the motifs are not fully able to seize listeners by sheer force, without their consent and studious cooperation. Unless listeners are willing to prolong the strenuous effort of "meditation" and of "memory" begun in the theater, to examine the method by which Wagner "melodically draws the nature of his characters and of their principal passions" on paper as well as on stage, the motifs will have somewhat limited powers of animation. In other words, the audible dynamism of the intertwining motifs depends partly on the listeners' silent, synthesizing gaze.

It is perhaps in view of this dependence that Liszt, with Baudelaire's

emphatic help, calls Wagner's motifs *"personifications of ideas."* This formulation presents some of the same difficulties here as it does in "De
l'ouverture," but it also provides some means of understanding the uncertain status assigned to the motifs. As figures that "speak to our thought"
and communicate "moral and intellectual meaning," the motifs serve a
mainly rhetorical purpose; they give roughly human outlines to the music
by associating it with the stage characters, or else with their "principal
passions." As melodies "of rare beauty," on the other hand, the motifs take
immediate, visceral hold of listeners with a grip that tightens in proportion
to time spent studying the score. According to this quotation, therefore,
Wagner's motivic melodies invite both rhetorical personification and concrete incarnation, but they lend themselves fully to neither: as musical
"personifications of ideas," they make listeners hesitate between imagin-
ing them figuratively as players in the drama and embodying them literally as living members of the audience.[35] In this ambiguous and unstable
situation, it seems likely that Wagner's motifs may betray—or at any rate
surprise—both the performers and the spectators. From some points of
view, in fact, the motifs engage in a sort of espionage directed against
the drama by announcing "feelings that the words pronounced do not indicate at all explicitly" and by uncovering "all the secrets of the heart."
Whereas Baudelaire's own commentary earlier described the melodies as
consistently useful formulas and helpful mediators, the motifs here seem
to participate in occasional acts of subversion; like Ortrud, the conniving
sorceress of *Lohengrin,* certain motifs "wend their way through the opera
like a venomous serpent." By the end of the Liszt quotation, Wagner's
melodies have begun to appear as something of a threat to the coherence
of his operas and a distraction to his audiences.

   The snakelike melodies evoked near the close of the quotation recall
the *"melodic knot"* mentioned near its opening; both suggest, among other
things, that the motifs often operate by stealth and with taut discipline. If
they ever foment rebellion against human participants in *Tannhäuser* and
Lohengrin, it is a decidedly covert revolt. The motifs work not by wreak-
ing conspicuous violence, but rather by spreading a kind of slow paralysis
that eventually immobilizes those involved in the stage drama as actors or
as spectators. The quotation hints at this static insurrection when it says

that every major character and situation is bound up with "a melody that becomes its constant symbol." Thus permanently attached, the melodies have as much opportunity to restrict as to encourage dramatic movement; they may easily begin to deaden the characters' spontaneity, to harden their passing gestures into stiff or repetitive attitudes. Further, after declaring that listeners would do well to study the score, Liszt soon admits that the motifs may well appear to them there as nothing but "lettres mortes," frozen and meaningless patterns rather than dynamic agents of the drama. But Liszt's text points most clearly toward the immobilizing tendency of Wagner's motifs in two sentences that Baudelaire omits from his long quotation. Replaced by an ellipsis early in the second paragraph quoted, they compare Wagner's motifs to those in Meyerbeer's opera *Les Huguenots:* "Already we had seen, in les Huguenots [*sic*], the role of Marcel, inlaid [incrusté] so to speak into Luther's chorale, which personifies not only his faith, but all the inflexible exaltation of his mind, all the meaning of his actions. Wagner has surpassed even this happiest of Meyerbeer's intentions" (68). Like a statue elaborately "inlaid" or "encrusted" with the sparkling elements of a hero's life, Meyerbeer's Lutheran chorale melody hardens Marcel into an "inflexible" image that concentrates all his actions into a single, frozen shape; and Wagner's motifs, according to Liszt, surpass even this example of sculpted immobility.

It is precisely in the course of some reflections on statues, rather than on music, that Liszt first introduces the expression "personification of ideas" in *"Lohengrin" et "Tannhäuser"* (35). He begins his book with a detailed explanation of the circumstances surrounding the premiere of *Lohengrin,* which took place in Weimar during a series of festivities in honor of Herder and Goethe. The main event of the festival was the unveiling of a newly completed statue of Herder; and before describing this ceremony, Liszt indulges in a lengthy excursus on the various means by which peoples from antiquity to the present have expressed their admiration for men of genius. With the spread of modern civilization, claims Liszt, "one can observe that with few exceptions, it is the Statue [*sic*] of men whose memory one wants to perpetuate and popularize that one erects in the place of their birth, their death, or their habitual residence. This mode of glorification has the advantage of prolonging, so to speak, for generations yet to come, the existence of these privileged beings" (34). But as Liszt subsequently remarks, the sculptor of such a statue must do much more than "prolong" life: he is forced to "rob death of what it has already swallowed up," to resurrect someone already dead (37). In order to restore a genius to temporal history, so that he can once more live naturally in his "habitual residence," the sculptor must outdo himself in "the personification of more nuanced ideas" than are necessary for any other occasion (35). Whereas Wagner's motifs may prove partially unable either to personify ideas after the manner of rhetorical figures or to incorporate themselves into actual human beings, the commemorative statues seem to remedy these failings; they serenely undertake both to represent genius figuratively by means of a human likeness and more literally to reanimate the existence of genius within "generations yet to come." But as if to anticipate the freezing force of the melodies he will discuss later in his book, Liszt intimates that the statues' permanent immobility stifles their power of animation. No amount of admiring artistry will completely suffice to bring dead geniuses back to life: reconstructed with a chisel "from a death mask or a mute portrait" (36), statues such as Herder's are born paralyzed "in an immortal bronze" (50).[36]

Although Baudelaire does not mention this opening section of *"Lohengrin" et "Tannhäuser,"* he intimates with the italics added to his Liszt quotation that he senses the motifs' surreptitious rebellion and the sculptural rigidity with which they contaminate Wagner's operas. In addition to highlighting the motifs as *"personifications of ideas,"* he accentuates the tightening of the *"melodic knot"* and the melodies' power to infiltrate every part of an opera, from the *"vocal line"* to the *"accompaniment"*; and he subtly reminds readers of the suspicion expressed toward *"plastic art* and *gestural art"* in the first Wagner quotation of part 2. Further, the dubious relation that Liszt's book suggests between melodies and statues recalls Baudelaire's own uncertainty with respect to sculpture. In his *Salon de 1846,* he roundly condemns sculpture for many of the same reasons that, in Liszt's text, make it a threat to Wagner's music. Comparing it adversely to the art of painting, Baudelaire complains that sculpture is "brutal and positive like nature," a condition that involves paradoxical disadvantages (2:487). As the representation of a human being, a statue is at once insultingly obvious and disturbingly inscrutable: the most primitive observer can recognize its shape; but the most sensitive connoisseur, examining it from every angle and in every light, is disappointed to find it "vague and elusive, because it shows too many sides at once" (2:487). In the *Salon de 1859,* where he revises many of his earlier judgments, Baudelaire still claims that the lifelike textures and dimensions of sculpture render it "more barbaric and more childish" than painting, but he no longer views this as an unqualified drawback (2:670). A sculpted figure, he claims, can slip into a garden (or a library, or a church, or a public square) almost as easily and naturally as a living passerby. Once poised in any of these settings, the statue balances itself delicately, not quite able either to move or to freeze; apparently alive in every detail, it also serves as a motionless emblem of mortality. Like Liszt's melodic and statuesque "personifications of ideas," Baudelaire's sculptures make observers hesitate: "[T]he phantom of stone takes hold of you for several minutes, and commands you, in the name of the past, to think about things that are not of the earth" (2:670).[37]

For Baudelaire, therefore, statues are problematic because they are alternately too human and too inhuman; they either frustrate observers with the swarming minutiae "of the wrinkle, the hair and the wart" or else baffle them with frozen grandeur (2:488). The same alternative, in Baudelaire's opinion, also menaces both the art of painting and the art of acting. In *Le Peintre de la vie moderne,* he notes that the same risks are involved for the actor Frédéric Lemaître to bring a role to life as for the painter Guys to "resurrect" a subject on canvas. Lemaître must take care that his acting neither dissolve entirely into a shower of "luminous details" nor freeze completely into a "sculptural" representation; similarly, should Guys fail to control "a riot of details, all of which demand justice with the fury of a crowd in love with absolute equality," he would find his artistic faculty "paralyzed" and his work reduced to a lifeless "phantom" (2:698–99). The parallel dangers of hyperanimation and paralysis—arising here from excessive detail and overly blatant simplicity—thus harass sculpture, painting, and drama in Baudelaire's art criticism, so that it is not surprising to find them haunting music in his Wagner essay.[38] Introduced into part 3 by way of the Liszt quotation, they take the form of melodies whose subversive complication works at times against Wagner's operas, simultaneously undermining the drama and petrifying the audience. Like statues, these rebellious melodies are paradoxically human as well as inhuman, "brutal and positive" as well as "vague and elusive." They seem both to invite figurative personification and to demand literal incarnation, while also setting the two at odds: the more Wagner's music appears to take on a multisided, fully human identity, the more it freezes into a simplistic, inanimate figure.

As if dimly aware of this complex danger, Baudelaire presents his long quotation of Liszt more warily than the Wagner quotations in part 2. Although he recommends Liszt's book and assures readers that Liszt "knows how . . . to translate with infinite charm all the rhetoric of the master," Baudelaire cautions them about "this slightly bizarre language that he affects, a sort of idiom composed of extracts from several languages" (¶38).[39] But without further warning or explanation, Baudelaire then proceeds to add touches of his own to the quoted text, just as he had earlier altered his Wagner quotations with italics and ellipses. By thus heightening the composite character of the quotations, Baudelaire draws attention to the amalgamated quality of his essay in general; shaped by a mixture of quotation, emendation, italicization, and argument, the essay might itself be called an "a sort of idiom composed of extracts from several languages." Such composite writing, indicates Baudelaire just after the Liszt quotation, may in fact be the only adequate means of studying the "rhetoric of the master"—or of Wagner's melodic motifs—at close range: "In fact, without poetry, Wagner's music would still be a poetic work, endowed as it is with all the qualities that constitute well-made poetry; explanatory on its own, since everything in it is so closely united, conjoined, reciprocally adapted, and, if it is permitted to use a barbarism in order to express the superlative of a quality, prudently *concatenated*" (¶41). With this ensemble of carefully enchained elements, Baudelaire evokes not only well-crafted poetry and well-composed music, but also well-formulated criticism; he raises the possibility that the relation of intertwined parts to an animated whole is nearly the same in his essay and in Wagner's music. Simultaneously, however, Baudelaire recalls the tangled "*melodic knot*" that covertly works to paralyze the operas. Just as motivic melodies threaten quietly to revolt against fellow components of Wagner's works, Baudelaire's quotations menace the body of his essay with their subversive implications and their treacherous rhetoric. Whereas the quotations in part 2 seem to put Baudelaire's admiration into action, vivifying Wagner's prose and revivifying Greek music, the Liszt quotation in part 3 threatens to invalidate admiration and to deaden musical movement: the quotations join in a subtle rebellion against other elements of the essay. Behaving as much like statues as Wagner's motifs, Baudelaire's quotations sometimes hinder his attempt to bring music to life.

POISONED STATUES

From several points of view, Baudelaire's sudden discovery and his single, journalistic essay on Wagner have little in common with Friedrich Nietzsche's long acquaintance and diverse philosophical meditations on the composer. There are, however, some striking resemblances in their manner of writing about music in general and about Wagner's music in particular. Nietzsche himself was perhaps mainly struck by what he felt were disturbing similarities between Baudelaire and Wagner; both before and after learning of his essay, Nietzsche regarded Baudelaire as "a sort of Richard Wagner without the music"[40] and as the writer who seemed to him "the most naturally and most intimately Wagnerian, despite and without Wagner."[41] But as Henri Thomas notes, Nietzsche's later writings occasionally reveal marked sympathy toward Baudelaire, "a sort of grateful recognition between two minds (or rather two sensibilities) so close to each other that their languages come to merge together [se confondre]."[42] One indication of this closeness may already be glimpsed in some of Nietzsche's early works, where he shows an explicit preoccupation with personification and embodiment in relation to music. This concern persists and intensifies through Nietzsche's final books on Wagner, although it changes somewhat in character. Following an itinerary reminiscent of the one in Baudelaire's essay, but with a different pace and purpose, Nietzsche considers first the uneasy compatibility and then the subversive hostility between rhetorically personified and physically embodied music.

Throughout *The Birth of Tragedy*, Nietzsche studies and manipulates various personifications of music. Already in the first paragraph, he personifies the "Apollinian art of sculpture" and the "Dionysian art of music" as mutually antagonistic partners whose eventual "coupling" leads to the birth of Attic tragedy.[43] Nietzsche accentuates the rhetorical nature of this personification by introducing his metaphors of "birth" and "coupling" with an explicit comparison: "[T]he continuous development of art," he writes, "is bound up with the *Apollinian* and *Dionysian* duality—just as procreation depends on the duality of the sexes."[44] Nietzsche then indicates that such personifications, effected with metaphors and similes, furnished the ancient Greeks with their primary means of reflecting upon art, since they formulated their aesthetics "not . . . in concepts, but in the intensely clear figures of their gods."[45] As a protective reaction against the frenzy induced by Dionysian music, claims Nietzsche, Apollinian poets elaborated the figurative world of Olympus and peopled it with gods who differed from their human worshipers only in grandeur and intensity. Like Apollo and Dionysus themselves, these divine personifications reassured the Greeks by figuring humanity as something "exuberant, triumphant," "desirable in itself"; the gods both represented every detail of human existence and idealized it with their own "fantastic excess of life."[46]

While admiring and exploiting the ancient Greeks' gift for extravagant personification, however, Nietzsche also engages in another literary maneuver. He declares that all modern readers participate to some degree in the Apollinian and Dionysian conflict, because they are all subject to the "physiological phenomena" of dreaming and intoxication.[47] Nietzsche's readers are therefore unable to avoid embodying the two fundamental principles of art; whenever they engage in dreaming or reveling, his readers incarnate within themselves the basic "artistic energies which burst forth from nature herself."[48] Every dreamer, Nietzsche asserts, is a natural artist who molds and polishes images with the same detachment that the Greeks attributed to the sculptor Apollo. Similarly, every reveler, whether actually drugged or simply overwhelmed by the emotion of the surrounding crowd, incarnates the same ambiguous mixture of joy and pain that characterized the Greek Dionysus. Such a reveler "is no longer an artist, he has become a work of art: in these paroxysms of intoxication the artistic power of all nature reveals itself to the highest gratification of the primordial unity. The noblest clay, the most costly marble, man, is here kneaded and cut."[49] As if to emphasize the solid reality of these incarnations, Nietzsche relates both of them to the visual, tactile art of sculpture, thus creating a confusion of Apollinian and Dionysian attributes: the dreamer, no matter how serene, must actively struggle with the sculptor's tools, while the reveler, even in the midst of his frenzied dance, appears to freeze in the shape of a half-formed statue. Whereas Nietzsche's personifications accentuate the separation and the often divisive relation between music and sculpture, his allusions to literal embodiment emphasize their interdependence.

It follows that in *The Birth of Tragedy*, rhetorical personification and physical incarnation are implicitly at odds with each other, despite their potential for joining together; their latent antagonism reflects the relation between music and sculpture or between the Dionysian and the Apollinian. In his fragment *On Truth and Lie in an Extra-Moral Sense*, Nietzsche touches on this relation more explicitly when he defines truth as "a moving army of metaphors, metonymies and anthropomorphisms, in short a summa of human relationships that are being poetically and rhetorically sublimated, transposed, and beautified until, after long and repeated use, a people considers them as solid, canonical, and unavoidable."[50] As Paul de Man interprets it, this definition partially hides the incompatibility of anthropomorphism on the one hand and tropes such as metaphor and metonymy on the other. Derived from these tropes, personification shares their mobility, their sometimes aggressive capacity to replace one image with another until the beginning of the process has been completely obscured. But anthropomorphism carries out a different and perhaps more lethal kind of aggression. Because it imposes on something nonhuman a specific, human identity, anthropomorphism paralyzes metaphor and metonymy; it "freezes the infinite chain of tropological transformations and propositions into one single assertion or essence which, as such, excludes all others."[51] In the terms of *The Birth of Tragedy*, the musical vivacity or flexibility of tropes (such as personification) would seem to oppose the sculptural fixity of anthropomorphism (literal incarnation).

As a result, it becomes important to ask whether tragedy is born, in Nietzsche's text, of the union of personification and incarnation. When discussing the preliminary union of Apollinian verse and Dionysian melody in ancient folk song, which he understands as the precursor of tragedy, Nietzsche pauses to express his suspicion of rhetorical figures as they were applied to the music of his own day:

> Again and again we have occasion to observe that a Beethoven symphony compels its individual auditors to use figurative speech in describing it, no matter how fantastically variegated and even contradictory may be the composition and make-up of the different worlds of images produced by a piece of music. . . . Indeed, even when the tone-poet expresses his composition in images, when for instance he designates a certain symphony as the "pastoral" symphony, or a passage in it as the "scene by the brook," or another as the "merry gathering of rustics," these two are only symbolical representations born of music—and not the imitated objects of music—representations which can teach us nothing whatsoever concerning the *Dionysian* content of music, and which indeed have no distinctive value of their own beside other images.[52]

Despite his mistrust, Nietzsche's objections to the rhetorical devices of programs and programmatic titles are not as strong as they might be; he admits that modern music "compels" its listeners to speak figuratively and in some sense "produces" the resulting images, so that numerous "symbolical representations" are inevitably bound to accompany music such as Beethoven's. But the danger of these figures, for Nietzsche, is that none of them has any necessary or permanent relation to the music: far from suffusing the music with any profound and lasting vitality, they simply slide past it in an endless succession of "fantastically variegated and even contradictory" tropes. Nietzsche suggests, however, that figurative language maintained entirely different relations with the music of Attic tragedy. For the audiences of ancient Greece, he claims, music literally enlivened figures of rhetoric and set them dancing, first in the guise of the tragic chorus and then in the form of individual actors. This was possible because every spectator simultaneously embodied both the visual or figural art of Apollo and the visceral, musical energy of Dionysus:

> For a genuine poet, metaphor is not a rhetorical figure but a vicarious image that he actually beholds in place of a concept. A character is for him not a whole he has composed out of particular traits, picked up here

and there, but an obtrusively alive person before his very eyes, distinguished from the otherwise identical vision of a painter only by the fact that it continually goes on living and acting. . . . At bottom, the aesthetic phenomenon is simple: let anyone have the ability to behold continually a vivid play and to live constantly surrounded by hosts of spirits, and he will be a poet; let anyone feel the urge to transform himself and to speak out of other bodies and souls, and he will be a dramatist.

The Dionysian excitement is capable of communicating this artistic gift to a multitude, so they can see themselves surrounded by such a host of spirits while knowing themselves to be essentially one with them.[53]

Nietzsche thus indicates that Greek tragedy depended on a complex association of personification and incarnation. While spectators might attempt to understand the dramas figuratively, as personifications of metaphysical concepts, this understanding by itself was not enough. Spectators also needed to recognize, first, that they were themselves literally doubled, reincarnated in members of the chorus and, second, that the solo actors gave physical substance to the chorus's changing personifications of Dionysus.[54] According to Nietzsche, tragedy was born during the dynamic, multilayered intensification of rhetorical personification into concrete embodiment.

As in Baudelaire's essay, however, this smooth process of intensification appears no longer to characterize the nineteenth-century resurrection of ancient drama: Nietzsche's text suggests that the latent incompatibility of personification and incarnation obstructs the rebirth of tragedy in Wagner's music dramas. Near the end of *The Birth of Tragedy,* in his discussion of Wagner, Nietzsche chooses an example from *Tristan und Isolde* to demonstrate the modern reunion of the Apollinian with the Dionysian. He claims at first that the music from the third act would fatally overwhelm listeners if its energy were not condensed and embodied in the actors on stage; because listeners are themselves too weak to incarnate the musical vitality directly, they must rely on the protective mediation of characters such as Tristan, Isolde, and Kurwenal. But Nietzsche does not thereafter present these characters as living embodiments in which Wagner's music takes on a human identity. He describes Tristan and Kurwenal instead as figures that stand for universal longing or jubilation, as visual representatives of metaphysical conditions that are also figured verbally in the dialogue and musically in the orchestra.[55] Although he does not entirely deny Tristan's status as a human being, Nietzsche immobilizes and simplifies his humanity until it is nearly drained of living substance. Consequently, Nietzsche is obliged to conclude that "the glorious Apollinian illusion makes it appear as if even the tone world confronted us as a sculpted world, as if the fate of Tristan and Isolde had been formed and molded in it, too, as in an exceedingly tender and expressive material."[56] Uncertain whether tragedy may truly be revived by joining personification with incarnation, Nietzsche treats it as music embodied in an "expressive" but inanimate statue.

Statues reappear at intervals throughout Nietzsche's later critiques of Wagner, in which they often continue to mark moments of hesitation over the kinds of language it is possible to use in writing on music. Whatever the changes in Nietzsche's evaluation of Wagner, his successive attempts to write about him are haunted by the same tension between physical incarnation and rhetorical personification already evident in *The Birth of Tragedy*. In *Twilight of the Idols*, for example, when reviewing "the conceptual opposites which [he has] introduced into aesthetics, *Apollinian* and *Dionysian*," Nietzsche states that the Apollinian principle is above all a "power of vision," so that "the painter, the sculptor, the epic poet are visionaries" engaged in fashioning and substituting images one for another.[57] By contrast, the Dionysian principle forces an artist to undergo constant "metamorphosis," so that "he enters into any skin, into any affect," and thus makes his whole body inseparable from his art.[58] But Nietzsche next claims that this Dionysian impulse is barely alive in nineteenth-century music, which is therefore unable to animate the entire human body: "To make music possible as a separate art, a number of senses, especially the muscle sense, have been immobilized . . . so that man no longer bodily imitates and represents everything he feels";[59] once prevented from dancing within a living body, music stiffens and eventually freezes into a sculpted image. From this perspective, Nietzsche's dilemma as a critic of Wagner is suggested by his allusion to idols in the wordplay of his title, as well as by his declaration that these hollow gods "are here touched with a hammer as with a tuning fork."[60] Since it resists full incarnation, but requires more than rhetorical personification, Wagner's music tempts Nietzsche to give it a vibrating semblance of life even at the risk of smashing it to pieces.

Nietzsche's most decisive confrontation between personification and incarnation, however, is staged in *The Case of Wagner*. Nietzsche alludes to both in the opening sections of this essay, almost as if experimenting with a variety of possible relations between them; but he then uses these variations as one means of suggesting the dangers that set Wagner's works apart from all other music. Nietzsche claims, for instance, that the perfection of Georges Bizet's music is evident from the manner in which it allows listeners to embody it. Rather than violently seizing and inhabiting its listeners, the music of *Carmen* permits them to incorporate it gently, to their benefit: by incarnating such music, states Nietzsche, "one becomes a 'masterpiece' oneself."[61] This is at least partly because, as Nietzsche's quotation marks around "masterpiece" indicate, listeners are not completely consumed by their effort of incarnation: not only are they continuously aware of their own real transformation into musical masterworks, but they also remain free to personify the music as an imaginary figure who "approaches lightly, supplely, politely" and who "treats the listener as intelligent."[62] In the case of Bizet's music, then, Nietzsche finds no conflict between concrete incarnation and rhetorical personification, since listeners may easily and beneficially engage in both at the same time.

With respect to Wagner, however, Nietzsche intimates that this is impossible. In order to convey the threat he finds inherent in Wagner's music, Nietzsche demands near the beginning of *The Case:* "Is Wagner a human being at all? Isn't he rather a sickness? He makes sick whatever he touches—*he has made music sick.*"[63] If Nietzsche here personifies music, or at least figures it as something animate, he does so only to emphasize its frailty and ultimately its mortality. Further, Nietzsche personifies music at the expense of its composer, dematerializing Wagner until he is nothing but a poisonous infection; Wagner appears in a related passage as a "clever rattlesnake,"[64] a cause of death more tangible but no less inhuman than an undefined "sickness." But at the close of the book, Nietzsche contradictorily insists that in Wagner, "falsehood itself has become flesh and even genius";[65] made corporeal, falsehood so completely infiltrates Wagner as to become identical with him. Nietzsche thus sets personification (music figured as "sick") in conflict with incarnation (falsehood identified with Wagner's very "flesh"). At the same time, Nietzsche uses both to signal the threat faced by Wagner's listeners. Whether deceived by Wagner/false-hood or contaminated by the sickness of his music, listeners are continually menaced with a nearly fatal invasion that both weakens and overstimulates them: "Wagner represents a great corruption of music. He has guessed that it is a means to excite weary nerves—and with that he has made music sick. His inventiveness is not inconsiderable in the art of goading again those who are weariest, calling back into life those who are half dead."[66] Rather than genuinely enlivening listeners, Wagner's music perversely undermines their health; it is able to produce a semblance of resurrection only because it also nearly causes death.

As Nietzsche presents it, therefore, the sickness that spreads from Wag-ner to his music to his listeners is best suggested by a kind of rhetorical infection that successively figures the music as a human sufferer and identi-fies it with actual invalids. To describe the exact symptoms manifested both in the music and in listeners, Nietzsche evokes almost the same paradox that arises in part 3 of Baudelaire's essay with regard to motivic melodies. On the one hand, Nietzsche emphasizes the excessive, overanimated de-tails that engage in covert rebellion against Wagner's music as a whole; he declares that "Wagner was unable to create from a totality; he had no choice, he had to make patchwork, 'motifs,' gestures, formulas."[67] But as the progression from (circulating) "motifs" to (fixed) "formulas" implies, Nietzsche on the other hand stresses the immobility induced by the music; both the stage actors and the audience are frozen by "the way Wagner's pathos holds its breath, refuses to let go an extreme feeling, achieves a terrifying *duration* of states when even a moment threatens to strangle us."[68] Just as Baudelaire and Liszt together explore the relation between rebellious parts and a lifeless whole, Nietzsche observes that the sepa-rate components of Wagner's music aim constantly to injure or to poison one another, thus provoking "anarchy of atoms, disgregation of the will, 'freedom of the individual,' to use moral terms—expanded into a political theory, '*equal* rights for all.' Life, *equal* vitality, the vibration and exuberance of life pushed back into the smallest forms; the rest, *poor* in life. Everywhere paralysis, arduousness, torpidity *or* hostility and chaos."[69]

Like Baudelaire, Nietzsche also observes that these complementary symptoms of decline may afflict not only music, but other arts as well.

He specifically notes that such symptoms characterize "every *literary deca-dence*,"[70] confirming that for Wagner musical and literary sickness are not far apart. With this allusion to the twin maladies of music and literature, Nietzsche echoes the beginning of part 2 in Baudelaire's essay, where music and language appear as fellow actors accused of corruption for having ex-changed roles. But whereas Baudelaire declares this to be a false accusation or a misquotation, Nietzsche finds a certain truth in it: he indicates that Wagner's music tends to usurp declamatory roles, so that "the musician now becomes an actor, his art develops more and more as a talent to *lie*."[71] By way of illustrating this claim, Nietzsche proposes an experiment that occupies the whole sixth section of *The Case of Wagner* and that begins with the following scenario: "Suppose it were the case that Wagner's *suc-cess* became incarnate, took human form and, dressed up as a philanthropic music scholar, mixed with young artists. How do you suppose he would talk?"[72] Nietzsche then answers this question with an extended exercise in the rhetorical art of prosopopoeia, pretending to report a long speech that Wagner's success delivers to the surrounding artists. The speech deals en-tirely with methods for corrupting music and poisoning listeners until both are too severely weakened to recover; it proclaims, for example, that "it is easier to write bad music than good. . . . Why, then, have beauty? Why not rather that which is great, sublime, gigantic—that which moves *masses?*"[73] In other words, Nietzsche elaborates a fictive quotation on the subject of deceit and uses it to show both the danger that confronts listeners when Wagner's music invades their bodies and the distance that is apt to separate the literally toxic reality of his music from any rhetorical discourse about it. What is more, Nietzsche arranges this maneuver in such a way that it is not easy to decide whether he starts out from an instance of personification or a reference to literal embodiment: while the falsely "philanthropic music scholar" may serve as a passing metaphor for deceitfulness, Nietzsche also deliberately stresses this scholar's essential identity as falsehood made cor-poreal. By deceptively blending personification with incarnation and then revealing their combined untrustworthiness with an imaginary quotation, Nietzsche doubly and triply emphasizes the gap that he is convinced will always separate Wagner's music from the writing devoted to it.

Much of *The Case of Wagner*, consequently, may be read not only as an evaluation of the composer, but also as a critique of Baudelaire's effort to bring music to life within the text of his essay. As already noted, Baudelaire appears himself to be aware of dangers in this enterprise, which he launches in part 1 amid allusions to the overbearing force of "this ardent and despotic music" (¶15) and especially to the mad scene created by Paul Scudo at the Opéra (¶3). Flailing about in mute rebellion against Wagner's music, the Scudo of Baudelaire's description bears a resemblance both to the silent statues implicated in part 3 and to the poisoned, hyperstimulated listeners evoked by Nietzsche. Transformed into a kind of poisoned statue, Scudo illustrates the double risk involved in Baudelaire's admiration for Wagner's music: Scudo's mad gestures signal the peril of trying to give the music human life by means of incarnation, just as Scudo's mute incoherence suggests the danger of trying to incorporate the music into a text by means of quotations. It is therefore almost as if Nietzsche were reformulating this image of Scudo in the opening section of *Nietzsche contra Wagner*, entitled "Where I Admire." After declaring that Wagner is "a master at finding the tones of the realm of suffering, depressed, and tortured souls, at giving language even to mute misery," Nietzsche confides that Wagner is himself "one who has suffered deeply—that is his distinction above other musicians. [Nietzsche] admire[s] Wagner wherever he puts himself into music."[74] Like Baudelaire, Nietzsche finds no way to admire Wagner's music without immediately encountering evidence of its power to poison and to paralyze, whether this evidence is embodied in false "music scholars" like Scudo or in Wagner himself. Despite their enormous differences, then, the texts of Baudelaire and Nietzsche point toward the same conclusion: whatever the diversity and intensity of their rhetorical efforts, two of Wagner's most complex admirers can discover no reliable means of bringing his music to life from the safe distance of their writings.

4 } *Openings*

THROUGHOUT *Richard Wagner et "Tannhäuser" à Paris,*
Baudelaire is preoccupied by questions of order, position, and context. This
fixation generally reveals itself in attempts to establish various kinds of
chronology or, on some occasions, in efforts to align temporal and logical priority. In part 1, for example, after announcing his search for the
"beginning" of the Wagner question, Baudelaire declares that this question had been falsely resolved before it was ever accurately formulated.
Wagner's advance publicity in France, he charges, was hopelessly misleading; before both the 1860 concerts and the *Tannhäuser* performances,
press reports "had the result of leading public opinion astray in advance,"
thereby unnecessarily encouraging "the instinctive, precipitate need of the
French to make up their minds on everything before having deliberated or
examined."[1] In addition to this irrational predisposition, claims Baudelaire,
Parisians allowed a further distortion to warp their judgment: rather than
wait for a genuinely adequate "stage performance" of his works (¶17),
they dismissed Wagner on the basis of a few concert extracts and three
chaotic attempts to perform a single opera. Wagner's music thus arrived
in Paris bereft of its intended operatic context and deprived of the orderly
sequence that should have led from anticipation to performance to critical
reception.[2]

In part 2, Baudelaire addresses the same problem from a wider perspective. Before embarking on his series of quotations, he tries briefly to
situate Wagner within a broad history of aesthetic creation and reception.
But instead of positioning Wagner within a straightforward progression

of artists and events, Baudelaire toys with a few names and then settles on the following pronouncement:

> In leafing through the *Lettre sur la musique,* I felt coming back to life in my mind, as if by a phenomenon of mnemonic echo, different passages from Diderot which assert that true dramatic music can be nothing other than the cry or the sigh of passion, set to notes and rhythm. The same scientific, poetic, and artistic problems recur unceasingly across the ages, and Wagner does not present himself as an inventor, but simply as one who confirms an old idea that will no doubt again be—more than once—alternately vanquished and victorious. (¶19)

In this statement, Baudelaire considers Wagner not only with respect to a continuing artistic tradition, in which artists act and react with their creations, but also with respect to an endless flow of criticism that prescribes or sustains or opposes these creations. Baudelaire does not clearly articulate the connection between these two sequences, but he stresses that Wagner occupies a middle position in each of them. This implies that no lasting tension divides the two; as in part 1, Baudelaire here suggests that works of art and works of criticism ought to follow each other in an orderly succession, undisturbed by distorting circumstances. But Baudelaire also indicates that if Wagner participates in both an artistic and a critical tradition, it is not as an "inventor" who creatively connects a line of achievements from the past with a potential chain of accomplishments still to come. Wagner's works—his operas and his treatises—are not inventions, but rather echoes: they are not innovative descendants of "an old idea," but only "confirmations" or even reproductions of it. And after the fashion of echoes, they are sometimes truncated reproductions—fragments of "different passages" resonating more or less strongly in a chain of strangely similar fragments. Once launched in a rocky landscape, a chain of echoes is at once unpredictable and unstoppable: although rigidly determined by its original sound, the chain also escapes control as it travels haphazardly along a random collection of surfaces, so that the link between one vibration and the next is never certain. Baudelaire thus finds that as a "mnemonic phenomenon," the Wagnerian echo at once recalls its predecessors and generates its successors in a chain of artistic and critical works, but it does so erratically; now fading, now ricocheting from an unexpected direction, the series of echoes confuses relations of order or priority and makes distances difficult to guess. When he resorts to the image of an echo, therefore, Baudelaire severely complicates the problem of either discovering or accounting for Wagner's place in the series of aesthetic debates that "recur unceasingly across the ages."

The reverberations of Baudelaire's echo metaphor do not stop there, moreover. This "phenomenon of mnemonic echo," as Baudelaire remarks, is not so much something that gradually dies away as it is something that comes alive or, better, that restores life: "I felt coming back to life in my mind different passages from Diderot." An echo, for Baudelaire, not only repeats, but also reanimates: it resuscitates dead or dying utterances. This power of animation is of course interrogated by the body of classical myths in which Echo, personified as a nymph and variously associated with Pan, Syrinx, or Narcissus, eventually turns into a disembodied voice.[3] Her transformation nearly always involves some form of violence: in one myth, for example, a jealous Pan orders shepherds to dismember her; in another, an indifferent Narcissus allows her to waste away from despair. By giving up her life as a nymph, Echo brings new life to the sound of music or of speech, but the sounds renewed at such a brutal price are often fragmented or distorted. According to mythological tradition, then, the life-giving or life-prolonging function of an echo is inseparable from the risk of disfigurement or misshaping. To the extent that Baudelaire allows this tradition to resonate in his essay, his echo imagery binds the problems of historical and aesthetic ordering to the those of hazardous regeneration and deformity.

Baudelaire confronts this cluster of problems most explicitly by means of two passages from parts 2 and 3, in which he tries to articulate the successive phases of aesthetic growth and critical regeneration that are appropriate for artists of Wagner's stature, particularly where their reappropriation of myth is concerned.[4] This theoretical concern finds a practical echo in Baudelaire's critique of *Tannhäuser* and *Lohengrin,* since his argument there raises questions about both the artistic position and the critical function of the overtures with respect to the operas. On the theoretical as well as the practical level, Baudelaire's chief goal is to show that the successive stages

or positions, if aligned in their proper or natural order, may ultimately result in a well-formed, well-integrated whole. That is, he hopes once again
to demonstrate that art and criticism—and, by extension, Wagner's music
and his own writing about it—may join together "Like long echoes that
distantly merge / In a shadowy and profound unity" [Comme de longs
échos qui de loin se confondent / Dans une ténébreuse et profonde unité].[5]
But as with Baudelaire's other attempts to pursue this goal, the distance
separating his essay from the operas proves deceptive: like echoes fading and swelling around an indistinguishable point of origin, Wagner's art
and Baudelaire's text remain at shifting distances that defy efforts to unite
them completely. And in this refusal to take up stable positions or to compose a settled whole, Baudelaire and Wagner find themselves echoed with
particular persistence by Mallarmé.

DIGRESSIONS

Within parts 2 and 3, Baudelaire permits himself two earnest and
elaborate digressions about artistic sequences or processes, each in the
form of a lengthy paragraph that is only tangentially related to the surrounding arguments. Despite their assertive tone, both digressions experiment in an elliptical way with relatively abstract and speculative meditations. Both, however, are sufficiently rigorous and suggestive to sustain
analysis, and they turn out to be closely connected with each other. The
first of these digressions forms a surprise conclusion to part 2. After his
series of quotations, one might expect Baudelaire to summarize Wagner's
theoretical positions and to prepare the discussion of specific operas in
part 3. Instead, as if suddenly exasperated past endurance by Wagner's
detractors and determined to silence them once and for all, he launches
into an emphatic defense of the composer. This unexpected final outburst
of part 2 runs as follows:

> How could Wagner not admirably understand the sacred, divine charac-
> ter of myth, he who is at once a poet and a critic? I've heard many people
> derive from the very range of his faculties and from his lofty critical
> intelligence a reason to mistrust his musical genius, and I think this is a
> propitious occasion to refute a very common error whose principal root

is perhaps the ugliest of human feelings, envy. "A man who reasons so much about his art cannot naturally produce beautiful works," say some who thus strip genius of its rationality, and assign it a purely instinctive and so to speak vegetable function. Others want to consider Wagner as a theorist who has only produced operas in order to verify *a posteriori* the value of his own theories. Not only is this perfectly false, since the master began very young, as we know, by producing poetic and musical essays of a varied nature, and since he succeeded only progressively in creating his own ideal of lyric drama, but it is even something [that is] absolutely impossible. A critic making himself into a poet would be a completely novel event in the history of the arts, a reversal of all psychic laws, a monstrosity; on the contrary, all the great poets naturally, unavoidably become critics. I pity poets who are guided solely by instinct; I believe they are incomplete. In the spiritual life of the former, a crisis infallibly arises, during which they want to reason about their art, to discover the obscure laws by virtue of which they have produced, and to derive from this study a series of precepts, whose divine goal is infallibility in poetic production. It would be incredible for a critic to become a poet, and it is impossible for a poet not to contain a critic. The reader will therefore not be astonished that I consider the poet to be the best of all critics. People who reproach Wagner the musician for having written books on the philosophy of his art, and who derive from this the suspicion that his music is not a natural, spontaneous product, ought equally to deny that [da] Vinci, Hogarth, Reynolds, were able to make good paintings, simply because they deduced and analyzed the principles of their art. Who speaks better about painting than our great Delacroix? Diderot, Goethe, Shakespeare, so many producers, so many admirable critics. Poetry was the first to exist, to assert itself, and it engendered the study of rules. Such is the uncontested history of human endeavor. Now, since each person is the diminutive of all people, since the history of an individual mind represents on a small scale the history of the universal mind, it would be right and natural to suppose (for lack of the proofs that exist) that the elaboration of Wagner's thoughts has been analogous to the work of humanity. (¶27)

At the center of this passage is Baudelaire's vehement declaration that the growth and maturation of every genuine artist follow an unchangeable, three-part progression. There must always be a preliminary, creative stage during which artists work by instinct, unencumbered by consciously specified methods or ideals. This initial period invariably leads to a crisis, a crucial moment at which aesthetic energy begins to stifle for want of intellectual perspective. Although he characterizes it as a crisis, Baudelaire insists that this new phase is in many ways conservative: far from renouncing or rethinking their earlier work, truly great artists need only step back far enough "to discover the obscure laws by virtue of which they have produced"; like travelers who pause to draw maps of territory already covered, such artists only document the aesthetic principles already in force throughout their creations. Similarly, Baudelaire intimates that such artists become "the best of all critics" not because they attack the genius of others, but rather because they have "deduced and analyzed the principles of their art"; the self-confirming crisis of each individual artist also produces a supportive community of critics. Despite its importance, however, this second phase is temporary and transitional. It passes into a third and final stage, the purpose of which is to integrate and harmonize its two predecessors. The artist's dialectical development thus ends not so much with a culminating achievement as with a continuing and miraculous return to its beginning: by allowing critical judgment to sustain and inform a return to instinctive creativity, the third phase aims to ensure "infallibility in poetic production."

Within this tripartite development, the status of the middle phase is doubly critical. On the one hand, according to Baudelaire, the practice of criticism is a normal and foreseeable event; on the other, it is an interruption or a digression that disturbs the artist's original impetus and places his future productivity in question.[6] In an effort to explain more convincingly how criticism can be both a natural necessity and a dangerous crisis, Baudelaire exploits the distance between great artists and mediocre ones. He emphasizes that in artists of authentic genius, the succession of aesthetic phases is genetically predetermined, programmed at birth in much the same way as physical growth: "[I]t is impossible for a poet not to contain a critic," he writes, so that when it is time for their latent critical acumen to develop, "all the great poets naturally, unavoidably become critics." In the case of lesser poets, however, abnormalities often appear. The most common aberration manifests itself in "incomplete" poets, artists who never reach the point of intellectual crisis and whose production therefore remains "purely instinctive and so to speak vegetable." This type of arrested development, complains Baudelaire, is what many skeptics would prefer to find in Wagner, on the mistaken assumption that only a vegetable mentality is by nature capable of artistic inspiration ("'a man who reasons so much about his art cannot naturally produce beautiful works,' say some"). Wagner is also frequently accused of another abnormality, however, and this second aberration strikes Baudelaire as much rarer and more unnatural, so rare as to be almost inconceivable: "A critic making himself into a poet would be a completely novel event in the history of the arts." The moment of crisis in an artist's career can only occur as an effort of reasoning and can only come after a period of instinctive creativity, thus taking second position in an unchangeable sequence. Were criticism ever to precede creation, the resulting disorder would be "a reversal of all psychic laws, a monstrosity," a freakish exception unlikely to produce anything viable. Baudelaire categorically denies that Wagner, whose earliest compositions predate his critical writing, constitutes such a monstrous "theorist who has only produced operas in order to verify *a posteriori* the value of his own theories." Among the imaginable varieties of artists, asserts Baudelaire, Wagner follows the normal course of genius; he is neither a mindless vegetable whose works proliferate like weeds, nor a sterile monstrosity who laboriously fabricates inert creations.

Significantly, Baudelaire expends the greater part of his vehemence on this preliminary progression, depicting criticism as the natural posterity of artworks and theoretical reason as the progeny of instinct. He insists less forcefully on the third generative stage, even though it is vital to his genetic argument. While he dramatizes the initial turn from art to criticism with his forbidding vegetable/monstrosity alternatives, he merely hints at the subsequent return from criticism back to art. He barely mentions the synthetic character that makes the third stage unique, leaving readers to deduce for themselves that the critic contained in every artist must perpetually reinforce his innate genius with "a series of precepts" if he is to attain "infallibility in poetic production."[7] Baudelaire's hesitation becomes more obvious when he calls such infallibility the "divine goal" of artistic development, somewhat as if it were an admirable but improbable aim whose reality in any particular case should be doubted. After arguing so energetically for an inviolable progression in which art precedes criticism, Baudelaire loses momentum when he tries to evoke their eventual confluence; he is almost too preoccupied with establishing the priority of art and the subordinate position of criticism to consider the possibilities of their partnership.[8]

This preoccupation increases toward the end of the passage, where Baudelaire broadens the scope of his argument. He does so first by means of examples: naming a number of celebrated artists from different eras and branches of art, he indicates that all of them matured according to the three-phase pattern he has postulated and therefore finished up as "so many producers, so many admirable critics." This might suggest that Baudelaire has at last overcome his hesitation over the third phase, except that he next proceeds in nearly the opposite direction. In order, perhaps, to close his long digression (and, at the same time, part 2) with greater aplomb, he suddenly extends his argument well beyond the domain of the fine arts. With the grandiose assertion that the development of artists such as Wagner exemplifies that of the human race in general, Baudelaire concludes that on all levels of universal history, "poetry was the first to exist, to assert itself, and it engendered the study of rules." If Baudelaire thus appears to legitimate the course of Wagner's career by making it represent the whole course of human endeavor, he also appears to lose sight of the goal in both histories: he stresses the primacy of art and the ulterior development of criticism, but not the final period of their intermingling.

One aspect of Baudelaire's parting impulse to stress the priority of art calls for further attention. The last sentence of part 2 contains an odd qualification: in view of the proposed analogy linking great artists with all humanity, writes Baudelaire, "it would be right and natural to suppose (for lack of the proofs that exist) that the elaboration of Wagner's thoughts has been analogous to the work of humanity." This insistence on the value of supposition prior to any proof seems to parallel Baudelaire's claim for the necessity of art before any criticism, as if the open-endedness of supposition corresponded to the creative potential of art. At the same time, however, Baudelaire presents his readers with a logical dilemma: since he has just finished a diatribe against the "monstrous" notion that critical reason might sometimes give birth to artistic creation, it is startling to find him now defending the naturalness of reasoning that precedes (or possibly even ignores) actual instances of artistic production. Beyond this immediate inconsistency, moreover, the assertion that "it would be right and natural to suppose . . ." recalls Baudelaire's *Lohengrin* demonstration, in which he similarly insists that "it would not be ridiculous to reason *a priori*," without requiring proof that sounds, colors, and ideas have all been linked by "a reciprocal analogy, since the day when God proffered the world as a complex and indivisible totality" (¶12). When read together, these two statements leave Baudelaire's ordering of priorities thoroughly scrambled. If he is concerned to establish criticism in a secondary position, as an operation dependent on prior artistic achievements, why does he repeatedly emphasize the legitimacy of reasoning a priori about aesthetic matters? Or if he believes, as an article of faith, that criticism has always interacted with art in a "complex and indivisible totality," why does he shy away from analysis of their interaction? And why, if he instead believes in the inviolable priority of art, does he append only the quatrains from "Correspondances" to the passage just quoted (¶12), thus mutilating or deforming one of his artworks to support a critical argument? In other words, how does Baudelaire really understand the relative positions of art and criticism?

The confusion thus fostered by the last sentence of Baudelaire's digression, while not immediately resolvable, directs his readers toward at least three avenues of clarification, one at the beginning of the digression and two others outside it. The first sentence of the digression opens out of Baudelaire's fourth quotation, in which Wagner praises myth as the ideal source material for his operas: "How," Baudelaire then demands, "could Wagner not admirably understand the sacred, divine character of myth, he who is at once a poet and a critic?" (¶27). Coming as it does before Baudelaire has enumerated the successive phases of artistic development, this question gives an initial impression that art and criticism are perfectly compatible, that it is entirely possible to engage in both at once. The question also links their marvelous compatibility to myth: anyone who is an artist and a critic at the same time, it suggests, will necessarily comprehend the nature of myth. This in turn suggests that myth itself is at once a work of art and a work of criticism, or at least that myth somehow by nature requires both creative and critical faculties for its comprehension. But the question specifies that the nature of myth is, precisely, unnatural; its "sacred, divine character" removes it from the ordinary domain of either art or criticism and makes it incomprehensible to anyone who has not miraculously attained the "divine goal" of integrating the two. Therefore, Baudelaire would seem to understand myth not as the primitive, unfinished material with which modern artists begin, but as the final achievement of their maturity. And because of the doubt he casts over this last stage of aesthetic maturation, Baudelaire raises the possibility that the complete coincidence of art and criticism in myth may itself be a myth in another sense, a fiction designed to represent something too remote or too unreal to be conceived otherwise. In this digression, then, much as Baudelaire would apparently like to demonstrate that art may in the end abandon its position of priority so as to merge with criticism, he cannot avoid questioning whether this mythical ideal is in fact possible to realize.[9]

The second place to look for some understanding of the uncertainty in Baudelaire's ordering of art and criticism is Wagner's *Lettre sur la musique*. The digression in part 2 not only arises in response to a quotation from this work, but also forms a veiled gloss on several passages from the *Lettre* not previously mentioned or quoted in the essay. In some instances, Baudelaire actually gives not so much a personal commentary as a thinly disguised paraphrase of pronouncements from the *Lettre*.[10] Thus the unreasonable detractors whom he attacks near the beginning of his digression turn out to be the same ones scorned by Wagner himself: "I recall now and again the antipathy, the hostility of critics who saw nothing but an abomination in my previously published writings on art, who stubbornly insisted that operas written at a much earlier time had been composed as a belated and deliberate confirmation of my theories, and who had, especially in the beginning, unleashed their rage against those operas."[11] Even more noticeably, Baudelaire takes from Wagner some of his thinking about the order of phases in the career of an artist. Wagner insists that the natural progression always starts out from purely creative, nontheoretical activity and leads eventually to a period of critical reasoning: "[C]reative energy is by nature spontaneous, instinctive. . . . Sustained reflection starts to become a necessity for it only at the moment when it runs into some serious obstacle" (iii). Further, Wagner particularly stresses the crisislike character of his own passage through this second phase: "From the pronounced repugnance I now feel upon rereading my theoretical writings, it is easy for me to recognize that at the time when I composed them I was in a completely abnormal state of mind, one of those states in which the artist can find himself once during his life, but into which he cannot enter a second time" (ii).[12]

Wagner also believes in a third phase of aesthetic development, but his approach to it is much less direct and requires a greater interpretive effort from his readers. In the course of summarizing *Oper und Drama,* Wagner briefly recounts his version of music history from the dance forms of ancient Greece to the symphonies of nineteenth-century Germany. The symphonies of Beethoven are particularly crucial to this history, because despite the organizational rigor of these works, "rational thought that proceeds according to principles and consequences finds no hold here," so that Beethoven's artistry "completely confuses and disarms logical reason" (xxxiii–xxxiv). In this way, Beethoven's music focuses on a problem that Wagner believes to be endemic in modern concert halls: nineteenth-century composers and listeners, he maintains, have arrived at "that inevitable phase in the march of human intelligence, where it [i.e., intelligence] feels pressed to discover the law that presides over the linking of causes [enchaînement des causes] and asks itself, in the presence of all phenomena from which it receives a strong impression, this involuntary question: 'Why?'" (xxxvi). Not even a Beethoven symphony is always able to force listeners outside this critical frame of mind; Wagner worries, on the contrary, that precisely because a symphony offers so little of the familiar logic found in rational argument, it disorients listeners and thus aggravates their inclination to respond with critical questions rather than with a more spontaneous, instinctive appreciation. The solution Wagner envisions, of course, is to combine music as powerful as Beethoven's with an equally powerful rational discourse, preferably in the form of a dramatic poem that, by virtue of both its verbal logic and its scenic realization, "penetrates all the way into the most delicate fibers of the musical fabric" (xxxvii).[13]

In this manner, the *Lettre* proposes the model for Baudelaire's three-stage progression leading from primitive artistic instinct to critical reason and finally to their integration; and the *Lettre* also traces this progression on several corresponding levels, since it involves individual composers within the general history of musical forms as well as in the universal "march of human intelligence." With considerably more conviction than Baudelaire, however, Wagner declares not only the strong probability of making art coincide with criticism at an ultimate phase, but also the actual success of this phase in his own operas.

Even so, Wagner's confidence on this point is not completely unshakable. His hesitation appears when he tries to explore the full extent of his success by measuring the effects of his operas on typical audiences. He first declares that each listener, succumbing to the combined force of poetic reason and musical unreason, falls into "a sort of ecstasy, where man forgets that fateful [or deadly: fatal] question of why"; but in the next clause of the same sentence he claims that this ecstatic listener "gives himself up without resistance to the control of the new laws through which the music makes itself so marvelously understood, and, in a very profound sense, gives the only exact response to that question: 'Why?'" (xxxvii). Wagner thus leaves the final status of the "why" in doubt; it is unclear whether this critical question is immediately forgotten, whether it is so quickly and thoroughly answered as to provoke no anxiety, or whether forgetfulness is itself the answer given. Just as Baudelaire avoids a full explication of the third stage in artistic development, Wagner here equivocates about the mutual interaction of art and criticism in his own works. As the *Lettre* continues, moreover, Wagner carefully sustains this uncertainty, arriving several pages later at the concise but ambiguous pronouncement that the intention of his operas is "to forestall and to resolve the question of why" (xlix).

The context of this last statement is significant. Having sketched the history of music up to the mid-nineteenth century, Wagner now undertakes to define more clearly his own position as Beethoven's successor. He asserts that one of his crucial discoveries, made after the composition of *Rienzi*, his first major opera, was the vital importance of founding his work on legend (a term he uses interchangeably with "myth" in the *Lettre*) rather than history. The reasons that Wagner gives for this assertion made a strong impression on Baudelaire, who quotes a number of them just before the opening of his digression in part 2. Baudelaire does not, however, quote the one sentence in which Wagner elucidates the relation between critical questioning and the nonrational, primitively artistic quality that legend gives, in his view, to an opera:[14] "This legendary coloring that clothes a purely human event possesses in addition the most essential of advantages, which is to make extremely easy for the poet the role I imposed on him a moment ago, to forestall and to resolve the question of why" (xlix). For Wagner, in other words, myth does not exactly combine art with criticism, but rather concentrates and focuses the tension between his desire to prevent the latter from ever arising ("forestall") and his conflicting desire to achieve a perfect integration of the two ("resolve"). Wagner further claims in this context that for one of his operas, he consciously allowed myth to make this tension as explicit as possible by thematizing it: the legend adapted in *Lohengrin* turns on the critical (and from most points of view highly reasonable) question, "Where do you come from?" that the heroine Elsa is forbidden to ask her husband Lohengrin. After explaining this in the *Lettre,* Wagner provocatively concludes, "You guess the particular connection between this tragic question and the theoretical 'why' of which I spoke above," thus evading once more an explicit decision as to whether the question should be forgotten or answered (li). Implicitly, it might appear, Wagner's position here becomes clearer, since *Lohengrin* ends in catastrophe as soon as Elsa has uttered the forbidden question and received her husband's answer; and Wagner also implies that he used the lesson of *Lohengrin* to suppress his own tendency to ask, "From where, and why?" at the expense of his compositional creativity (li). But these implications are not decisive, because Wagner claims at the same time that the success of *Lohengrin* derives from the mixture of rational understanding and aesthetic emotion made possible by the "legendary character of the subject" (l). Like Baudelaire, Wagner is unable to say definitively whether this mixture is a blessing actually bestowed by myth or only a tantalizing, but mythical, possibility.

To this point, Baudelaire is content to follow Wagner; the digression in part 2 echoes, with varying degrees of distortion, the ambiguous relations between art, criticism, and myth set forth in the *Lettre*. With a second digression that occurs in part 3, however, Baudelaire takes up these reflections at just the point where he and Wagner had left off and carries them a good deal further. This new digression opens into the middle of a discussion of *Lohengrin*. Following his summary of the plot, Baudelaire transposes Wagner's remarks about the cautionary lesson conveyed by Elsa's tragedy: "Elsa who doubted, Elsa who wanted to know, to examine, to control, Elsa has lost her happiness. The ideal has vanished" (¶35). But then, instead of rehearsing Wagner's indefinite conclusions about the role of myth in this exemplary plot, Baudelaire embarks on a different meditation:

> The reader has no doubt noticed in this legend a striking analogy with the myth of the ancient Psyche, who was herself a victim of demonic curiosity and, unwilling to respect the incognito of her divine spouse, lost all her happiness in penetrating the mystery. Elsa lends an ear to Ortrud, as Eve to the serpent. The eternal Eve falls into the eternal trap. Do nations and races transmit fables to one another, just as people bequeath to one another heritages, patrimonies or scientific secrets? One might be tempted to believe it, so striking is the moral analogy that marks the myths and legends blossoming in different lands. But this explanation is too simple to seduce a philosophical mind for long. The allegory created by a people cannot be compared to those seeds that one farmer gives in a brotherly spirit to another who wants to acclimatize them in his own country. Nothing that is eternal and universal needs to be acclimatized. This moral analogy of which I spoke is like the divine stamp of all popular fables. It is, if you will, the sign of a single origin, the proof of an indisputable kinship, but on condition that one looks for this origin only in the absolute principle and the common origin of all beings. Such and such a myth can be considered as the brother of another, in the same way that the black man is called the brother of the white. I do not deny, in certain cases, either the fraternity or the filiation; I only believe that in many other cases the mind could be led into error by surface resemblances or even by the moral analogy, and that, to take up again our vegetable metaphor, myth is a tree that grows everywhere, in every climate, beneath every sun, spontaneously and without cuttings. Religions and poetry from the four corners of the world furnish us with superabundant proof on this subject. Just as sin is everywhere, redemption is everywhere, myth everywhere. Nothing is more cosmopolitan than

the Eternal. Be good enough to pardon me this digression that opened
out before me with an irresistible attraction. I return to the author of
Lohengrin. (¶36)

Although he explores it from a new angle, Baudelaire returns here to
his earlier preoccupation with order and chronology. In light of the thematic resemblances between the myths of the medieval Elsa, the classical
Psyche, and the biblical Eve, he wonders rhetorically whether Wagner's
heroine is a late descendant or derivative, adapted by stages for survival
in modern Europe. The answer, he asserts, must be negative; Elsa must
be viewed as an original, no matter how strikingly she resembles the protagonists of older myths. Given the vehemence with which Baudelaire
goes on to argue for this view, he seems to be aware that he is not only
indulging his own interest in Wagner's myths, but also responding to a
widespread nineteenth-century theory about the origin and development
of mythology. Defended notably by Jacob Grimm, this theory held that
all the myths recounted in Indo-European languages share an "original
kinship" that has gradually been confirmed and accentuated by "external,
accidental and manifest interchanges of influence between them."[15] For
Grimm and his romantic followers, therefore, different myths were "blos-
soms" descended from one "legendary seed," so that the study of these
myths should show "with what fidelity they propagate themselves, how
exactly they seize and transmit to posterity [their] essential features."[16]
For Baudelaire, however, authentic myths are self-producing, dependent
neither on genetic transmission, like human families, nor on artificial cultivation, like exotic plants in a greenhouse. While he admits that some myths
or versions of myths may be related by "fraternity" or by "filiation," he
insists that such cases are purely contingent and of marginal importance,
that myth is always able to flourish "spontaneously and without cuttings"
and that it therefore need never engender offspring. Myth, in other words,
does not participate in ordered phases or in generative cycles, and it must
therefore lie outside the kind of developmental process described in Baudelaire's first digression. As it is evoked in the present passage, myth in fact
recalls the aberrations that formerly threatened the three normal stages of
an artist's development. On the one hand, myth is now said to grow in
every climate as abundantly and irrepressibly as the local flora, requiring

no special thought or judgment for its cultivation. On the other hand, this mythic undergrowth does not reproduce by any ordinary genetic means, but instead appears by a sort of spontaneous generation; while it does not share the deformation or the sterility traditionally attributed to mythical monsters, it is nonetheless born and reborn through a strange process that obeys no sequence in the natural world. Myth in Baudelaire's second digression thus unites the abnormalities previously attributed to failed artists: its growth, in the manner of both an unreflective vegetable and a reproductive monstrosity, would seem to constitute a "completely novel event in the history of the arts" (¶27).

Myth in this second digression recalls the monstrosity discussed at the end of part 2 for another reason as well. Unlike Wagner, who in the *Lettre* confines himself to the terms "myth" and "legend," Baudelaire uses a richer vocabulary: "myth," "legend," "fable," "popular fable," and "allegory created by a people." Although he apparently regards all these expressions as roughly synonymous, the simple fact of their diversity accentuates their differences of nuance and resonance. Both "legend" and "fable," for example, begin in this context to evoke their traditional connotations of moral commentary or social critique embodied in fictional narrative, thereby subtly reintroducing Baudelaire's concern with the mixture of art and criticism inherent in myth.[17] But the most suggestive term in this respect is "allegory created by a people." Taken by itself, mythical "allegory" points toward Baudelaire's 1861 essay on Théodore de Banville, in which he associates "allegories" with "mythologies" because of their mutual power to evoke concepts and "syntheses" that would otherwise remain inexpressible (2:165). When Baudelaire specifies, however, that the allegory now in question has been "created by a people," he comes closer in tone and in wording to his unfinished essay "L'Art philosophique." In this essay, as in *Richard Wagner*, he attacks artists whose main point of departure is "reasoning, deduction," and in whose works "everything is allegory, allusion, hieroglyphs, rebus" (2:598,600). Such artworks, however refined, always constitute a kind of pedantic "return toward the imagery necessary to a people in its childhood"; since they spring primarily from a spirit of critical argument, and only secondarily from aesthetic feeling, Baudelaire is compelled to regard this "philosophical art" as "a monstrosity in which some fine talents have revealed themselves" (2:598–99). If this opinion is allowed to reverberate in the Wagner essay, then myth and its synonyms appear there as monstrosities that embody not so much the artistic instinct of ancient peoples as the critical lessons that aim to instruct—and thereby possibly to deform—them.[18]

The potential monstrosity of myth in Baudelaire's second digression therefore arises from its failure to follow orderly processes of generation and maturation: it is not born "naturally" from the union of criticism with a preexisting art, nor can it be neatly categorized as either the latest achievement of civilization or the earliest inspiration of primitive peoples. Yet Baudelaire also claims that it is precisely this failure to participate in cycles and phases that accounts for the perpetual flourishing of myth. He lends rhetorical grandeur to this permanent blossoming with the word "eternal," which occurs four times in the passage. If Elsa's myth resembles Eve's, it is not because Elsa is an artistic descendant or a critical revision of Eve but because she actually is, in a certain sense, Eve: "the eternal Eve falls into the eternal trap." That is, myth need never engage in a slow process of aesthetic rebirth or intellectual adaptation; it enjoys a constant, unmediated connection with "the absolute principle and the common origin of all beings," and this privileged connection does not estrange myth from its various surroundings, but instead naturalizes it in every conceivable setting. Myth is thus completely and radically original; but this originality is forever impossible to locate or to identify, since its first effect is to ensure that myth is inconspicuously acclimatized.[19] According to Baudelaire, then, myth is a kind of universally endemic freak, always and never native to its environment, like an indigenous tree with no roots or an aboriginal inhabitant with no local ancestors. Neither the "imagery" of primitive art (2:598) nor the "philosophical spirit" (¶36) of advanced criticism is quite natural to myth; and yet myth somehow allows them both to grow together "spontaneously and without cuttings," in the absence of any planting, genetic processing, or artificial grafting. Or as Baudelaire summarizes the hybrid, slightly monstrous composition of myth, in which the natural and the primary intertwine with the foreign and the secondary: "Nothing is more cosmopolitan than the Eternal" (¶36).

As if he were a little unnerved by his own pronouncements about myth,

Baudelaire suddenly apologizes for them. "Be good enough," he requests, "to pardon me this digression that opened out before me with an irresistible attraction. I return to the author of *Lohengrin*" (¶36). Unlike his first digression, which is to a certain degree camouflaged as a conclusion for part 2, the present one makes no attempt to disguise itself; it freely announces not only its status as a digression, but also the ambiguity of its position among the other passages in part 3. In one way, this digression calls for an apology, as if it were a freakish accident that leaves the main body of part 3 somewhat malformed. In another way, the digression opens outward in a way that irresistibly invites Baudelaire to explore it; the opening is an integral and unavoidable part of his primary argument. In other words, Baudelaire's digression reflects the paradoxical character he finds in myth: it is both a natural outgrowth of its surroundings and a surprising mutation or transplant. Alternatively, one might say that Baudelaire understands myth as a complex principle of digression. When viewed as a whole, myth appears to Baudelaire as a cultural digression, as something that simultaneously belongs to and departs from the context of any given society. At the same time, when viewed as the joining of two elements, as the intertwining of art and criticism, myth appears as both a fertile union and a critical monstrosity, a strange event in which each component opens both naturally and disruptively into the other. Baudelaire's second digression thus reinterprets the artistic and critical stages proposed in his first one, making the succession appear infinitely circular and reversible: as interlacing digressions, art and criticism will never quite coalesce and will never quite diverge; they will continually lead away from and back into each other, so that myth is at once their origin and their point of return. The "divine goal" of merging art and criticism does not turn out to be entirely mythical, but neither does it entirely overcome the distance between them.

OVERTURES

If art and criticism digress from each other within Baudelaire's two digressions, it remains to be seen whether the same is true outside the digressions, especially in the passages between them. For it is here, with the beginning of part 3, that Baudelaire first attempts a really broad overview of Wagner's operas; it is here that he makes his most determined endeavor to show the value of "general views" (¶31) for practical criticism. It is also here, therefore, that he runs his greatest risk: since his acquaintance with the works in question is in fact limited and fragmentary, he must work hard to make it seem panoramic. More than ever, Baudelaire's main enterprise in part 3 is to turn his distance from Wagner into an advantage rather than a handicap, to present his criticism as a natural and productive digression from Wagner's art. His most interesting effort in this direction involves the relation between the operas and their overtures. Since he had seen only one (somewhat incoherent) performance of *Tannhäuser*, but had heard concert extracts and read librettos, Baudelaire not surprisingly tends to divide Wagner's oeuvre into a set of overtures and choruses on the one hand and a series of dramatic poems on the other. Although misleading in some ways, this unconventional perspective on Wagner allows Baudelaire to make a practical study of the questions raised in his digressions. By calling attention to the kinds of articulation that join *Tannhäuser* to its overture and *Lohengrin* to its prelude, Baudelaire helps readers discover in each case how the overture's combination of artistic and critical elements opens unevenly or tangentially into the mythical drama of the opera. More important, however, Baudelaire allows his discussion to digress from each of the operas at a particularly suggestive juncture, and these digressions serve a double purpose. First, they indicate that from Baudelaire's perspective—and despite his claims to the contrary—art and criticism do not in fact achieve a fully adequate balance or collaboration in Wagnerian myth. Second, they also show that even if Baudelaire's knowledge of the operas is too limited for him to consider this flaw directly, he can still approach it precisely by digressing from it.

In part 3, Baudelaire gives his attention first to *Tannhäuser* and describes right away the collaboration he finds between the overture and the rest of the opera: "*Tannhäuser* represents the fight between the two principles that have chosen the human heart for their main battlefield, that is, between flesh and spirit, hell and heaven, Satan and God. And this duality is represented right away, by the overture, with incomparable skill" (¶28).

The overture thus accomplishes much the same thing as the opera, but it does so more briskly and with skill of a different kind. Although Baudelaire later observes that "the overture to *Tannhäuser,* like the one to *Lohengrin,* is perfectly intelligible, even to someone who is not familiar with the libretto" (¶32), he does not particularly stress the independence of either the overture or the opera; he seems rather to think that for a drama as fundamental as the one offered in *Tannhäuser,* two collaborating modes of representation are better than one alone. In this attitude, Baudelaire unexpectedly differs from Liszt, whose opinions on Wagner he otherwise follows so carefully. Liszt argues with energy that the *Tannhäuser* overture forms "so complete a symphonic whole that one can consider it as a piece independent of the opera it precedes."[20] Like Baudelaire, Liszt recognizes that the overture and the opera ultimately achieve something very similar, but he claims that this similarity only increases their independence: "With the same thoughts," he writes, "Wagner has created two different works, and . . . they neither want nor need each other in order to explain themselves mutually" [elles ne s'appellent, ni ne se réclament pour s'expliquer mutuellement].[21]

This discrepancy between Liszt and Baudelaire occurs in the context of a century-long debate about the best way to open tragic operas. The perennial difficulty under discussion among composers and critics was that the overture must introduce its opera effectively, but without giving too much of it away. As Rousseau protested in his *Dictionnaire de la musique,* composers might be misguided "in gathering beforehand in the *overture* all the musical characters [tous les caractères] expressed in the piece, as if they wanted to express the same action twice, and as if what is to come had already happened."[22] A better solution, claimed Rousseau, would be an overture designed more to tantalize than to instruct, an overture "that inclines the spectators' hearts in such a way that they open up without effort to the interest one wants to offer them from the beginning of the piece onward."[23] Rousseau's opinion was frequently challenged in the late eighteenth and early nineteenth centuries,[24] but at least two of its premises survived the debate intact: first, that the instrumental overture had enormous potential power to summarize and preview; and second, that if it were used too freely, this power would interfere with the overture's main task, which was to draw attention not to itself, but rather to what followed it. It was a later opera theorist, the Comte de La Cépède, who best evoked this delicate task when he compared the overture of a lyric tragedy to the peristyle of a palace.[25] Although La Cépède wanted mainly to figure the pomp and magnificence appropriate to serious opera, his image of an open colonnade suggests more than that: just as a visitor stepping into the peristyle would be neither completely outside nor yet quite inside the adjacent palace, an audience listening to the overture would entertain ambiguous relations with the accompanying opera. As entrances leading to greater things, both the overture and the peristyle must exercise exactly the right kind and amount of fascination; their position between implicit promise and explicit advertisement is precarious.

Above all, however, their position is an intermediate one. The overture, like the colonnade around a building, never simply precedes or opens. Instead, it always *stands between:* between the nonmusical everyday world of the audience and the exotic, exceedingly musical one of the stage, for example, or between the listener's ignorance of the opera and the composer's full knowledge of it. The overture's task requires that it simultaneously precede some things and follow others, that it occupy at once a primary and a secondary position; in this respect, it shares the difficulties inherent in any critical preface that an author generally writes last or retrospectively, but that readers usually encounter first or prospectively.[26] By Wagner's time, however, the overture's role had acquired an additional complication, because it became increasingly common in the nineteenth century not only to perform opera overtures separately, but also to compose independent "overtures" intended solely for concert performance.[27] These variations in context actually enhanced rather than diminished the overture's mediating function: when heard alone, most overtures still served as thresholds that enticed listeners to enter into some dramatic intention standing close by, whether this intention appeared as the reminder of an absent opera (for example, Weber's overture to *Oberon*), as the reminiscence of another dramatic work (Berlioz's overture *Le Roi Lear*), or as the indication of some other ceremonial occasion (Beethoven's *Die Weihe des Hauses*). In this way, nearly all overtures acted as gateways; as Berlioz observed, if there was no actual opera waiting beyond them, they nonetheless beckoned to listeners like the "the superb peristyles of ruined temples."[28]

Such gateways were also prone to invite differing interpretations of their status: listeners such as Baudelaire could concentrate on their connection with the more or less shadowy drama behind them, while listeners such as Liszt could just as easily emphasize their detachment. For Wagner, neither of these outlooks was by itself sufficient. In "De l'ouverture," written shortly before he began work on *Tannhäuser,* Wagner argues that as a means of passage from the familiar world of the audience to the unfamiliar one of a drama, the overture must be simultaneously compelling and indirect. He takes the Rousseauian view that "by transporting you into a higher sphere, [the overture] should prepare you, and not exhaust the subject in advance"; and he specifies that in this preparation, "it is not a question, in truth, of the sort of action that one can only find in the drama itself, but of the sort that resides in the essence of instrumental music."[29] With this proviso, Wagner refers partly to a technical question of composition, the much debated problem of how closely to associate overtures with the established repertory of instrumental music by organizing them, for example, according to principles of sonata form.[30] But Wagner also refers more generally to any separation that prevents the musical logic of an overture from mechanically reduplicating the dramatic logic of its opera, any disjunction that lets the overture open dynamically into the opera without exhausting the drama in advance. Such separation, Wagner indicates in a later essay, is equally crucial to the success of concert overtures that open not into an opera, but into some other dramatic intention of the composer; there must always be a gap that permits dynamic passage between the two.[31] Like an open colonnade, the Wagnerian overture should not belong entirely either to the dramatic structure adjoining it or to the musical countryside surrounding it.

In his discussion of *Tannhäuser,* therefore, Baudelaire comes close to Wagner's own point of view when he lays approximately equal stress on the overture's separability and on its ties to the opera. Baudelaire himself summarizes this delicately balanced relation not with an architectural metaphor, but with a genetic one: "This overture," he writes, "contains not only the mother idea, the psychic duality constituting the drama, but also the principal formulas, clearly accentuated, [that are] destined to paint the general sentiments expressed in the rest of the work, as is demonstrated by the forced returns of the diabolically voluptuous melody and of the religious motif or *Pilgrims' Chorus,* every time the action demands it" (¶32). By figuring the opera as a sort of child or descendant, an entity whose growth toward independence is partially determined by "formulas" inherited from the overture, Baudelaire makes their relation seem natural, inevitable, predictable. A suggestion of tension appears, however, in the "forced returns" of these formulas, as if the parental or ancestral authority of the overture threatened to provoke a crisis of rebellion in the opera. This same tension soon reappears, disguised and elaborated, in another part of Baudelaire's discussion. The overture develops, as Baudelaire points out, in a three-part progression: a pious chorale melody representing a pilgrims' hymn is replaced by the voluptuous motifs of Venus and Tannhäuser, which are in turn suppressed by the final triumph of the pilgrim song. Apparently anxious to emphasize this tripartite logic, Baudelaire borrows Liszt's description of the overture as two conflicting "terms" that ultimately "find their equation" (¶28), even though it is not clear that the overture's third part in any way equates or combines the first two. With respect to the opera itself, however, Baudelaire essentially abandons this three-phase description in order to stress the simple "duality" that characterizes its development. Although he gives no systematic summary of the libretto, much less of the music, he explains that the drama begins on a virtuous note when Tannhäuser escapes from Venus just in time to encounter a band of pilgrims singing hymns on their way to Rome. But then, instead of following Tannhäuser through his voluptuous relapse into sin all the way to his salvation in the final scene, Baudelaire stops in the middle: his *Tannhäuser* discussion concludes with the hero's initial failure to receive the pope's forgiveness, upon which "one certainly understands, then, that such a misfortune can only be repaired by a miracle, and one excuses the hapless knight for seeking once more the mysterious path that leads to the cave, in order to regain at least the favors [or charms: grâces] of hell with his diabolical spouse" (¶33). Declining to mention the nature and outcome of the miracle in question, Baudelaire gives the unexpected impression that the opera may not end with the same "bliss of redemption" (¶29) as the overture. Despite the genetic links he finds between the two, his commentary lends unforeseen importance to their rebellious divergence as well.

Something strikingly related happens in the Wagner writings on *Tann-häuser* to which Baudelaire had access. For the 1860 concerts, Wagner naturally included a text about the *Tannhäuser* overture among his other programs; and in this text, Wagner not only accentuates the three-phase organization of the overture, but also relates it to the opera in such a way that Tannhäuser's personal redemption at the end remains merely implicit, and perhaps even a little uncertain. As distributed at the three Paris concerts, the program sketches the following scenario for the overture: at dusk, the singing of pilgrims first swells and then fades into the distance; when night falls, Venus appears with her orgiastic followers and, at Tannhäuser's approach, draws him down into her realm, so that the air around her haunted mountain is now "troubled only by a voluptuous murmur. . . ."[32] With this portentous ellipsis, the program breaks off its long first paragraph. The second and last paragraph follows with a much briefer description of how the pilgrims approach once more at dawn and how their hymn gradually replaces the sensual murmur until one sees "the Venusberg freed from its pagan malediction" and "material life uniting with the life of the soul." Although this program thus makes clear that the overture's third section integrates the first two, it also passes silently over Tannhäuser's individual fate. It thereby leaves open the slight possibility—at least for a skeptical and sensuous reader like Baudelaire—that Tannhäuser may remain in the depths with Venus, too far removed from the pilgrims to share in their redemption.

It would seem, by extension, that this possibility should also be programmed into the rest of the opera, as Baudelaire hints with his summary. The opera's libretto, however, contradicts both the overture program's implication and Baudelaire's text on this point, although it does leave Tannhäuser's fate in doubt up to the last page. At the beginning of act 3, he apparently stands condemned forever, since the pope refuses him absolution in the following terms: "Just as this staff in my hand will no longer adorn itself with fresh greenery, so you will never see deliverance flower again for you in the infernal blaze" (*Quatre poèmes d'opéras*, 166). But this miracle is thereafter realized exactly as specified; just as Venus is leading Tannhäuser definitively back under the mountain, pilgrims arrive to announce that "the dried-up stick, in the hand of the priest, has

adorned itself with fresh greenery. Just so, in the blazing of hell, will de-
livrance flower again for the sinner" (171). Tannhäuser's unquestionable
salvation—and the libretto's final divergence from the overture's program
as well as Baudelaire's summary—are thus signaled by the transformation of a priest's crosier from a dry rod into a live branch surrounded by
flowering greenery. In the Tannhäuser legend, this prophetic blossoming
of the papal staff most immediately figures the Christian hope of redemption springing from Christ's death on the barren wood of the cross. In the
context of *Richard Wagner*, however, the flowering staff also vividly calls
to mind Baudelaire's famous description of a thyrsus in the prose poem
"Le Thyrse" (1:335–36). Like the pope's "dried-up stick" [bâton desséché]
bedecked with foliage, Baudelaire's thyrsus is also made up of a priest's
staff [bâton hiératique] around which "stems and flowers play and frolic
with each other." The priest in "Le Thyrse" is of course Dionysus rather
than the pope, but the prose poem and the opera text both explore the
relations between spiritual discipline and sensual abandon. As Baudelaire
might have said, therefore, Tannhäuser avoids the Christian possibility of
damnation that closes the overture's program by virtue of the surprisingly
pagan symbol of salvation that ends the opera's libretto.

But Baudelaire did not say this: the thyrsus is conspicuous by its absence
from his commentary on *Tannhäuser*.[33] With his refusal to consider the concluding miracle of the opera, Baudelaire apparently forfeits an admirable
occasion to rejoin several other strands of meditation in his essay. As a
spatial metaphor for the relation between the overture and its opera, the
thyrsus—with the small, vital gap between its central rod and its peripheral vines—would suggest both their interrelatedness and the slight but
indispensable distance between them. Further, by entering so effectively
and unobtrusively into Wagner's modern amalgamation of two medieval
Christian legends,[34] the Dionysian thyrsus would illustrate Baudelaire's
theory that myth is always at once native and foreign to its context. Finally,
just as the thyrsus in Baudelaire's prose poem figures both Franz Liszt's
"songs of delight" as a musician and his "abstruse meditations" as a writer
and critic, it might here stand for the digressive relation of art and criticism
in which neither can be permanently defined as the "pretext" for the other
(1:336). In the very act of letting all these opportunities slip by, however,

Baudelaire also seizes one with a broader perspective. Whether he ignores the thyrsus image deliberately or inadvertently, he at any rate prevents it from serving in his essay as the emblem for ideal or redemptive relations between art, criticism, and myth in *Tannhäuser*. He thereby raises, however distantly and negatively, the possibility that these relations are less than ideal, that they are somewhat out of balance, and he further hints that the tension or the divergence between overture and opera is perhaps out of proportion. When Baudelaire lets the end of his discussion stray away from the thyrsus, therefore, he raises a hesitant and implicit question about Wagner's right to the title of perfectly integrated "poet and critic" (¶27), a question that will become more pressing and easier to formulate in the case of *Lohengrin*. Beyond this, one might also say that Baudelaire manages to twine the suggestion of a critique around the straight fact of his overlooking the *Tannhäuser* thyrsus: like De Quincey, in whose writing he discovers and admires the image of a thyrsus, Baudelaire converts the "essentially digressive" character of his discussion into an advantage.[35]

Baudelaire was probably unaware that for the 1861 performance of *Tannhäuser* in Paris, Wagner had hoped to revise his original overture by suppressing its third section and attaching the other two without a break to the first scene of act 1.[36] Such a change would have departed from operatic tradition and would have given *Tannhäuser* a much different kind of opening; it would have engaged the questions of dependence and separability usually involved in overtures. This was exactly what happened from the beginning with Wagner's prelude to *Lohengrin*. With regard to this prelude, Baudelaire's treatment again differs noticeably and suggestively from Liszt's. Despite his fascination with the prelude itself, Baudelaire gives relatively little attention to its connections with the opera. His discussion of *Lohengrin* in part 3 makes no explicit allusion to the prelude; and while he hints briefly that the prelude participates in the "mnemonic system" of motifs pervading the opera as a whole (¶38), he also indicates just as briefly that the prelude is "perfectly intelligible" in the opera's absence. In contrast, Liszt declares that the prelude is by no means dissociable from the rest of the opera. The prelude is too short, he writes, to serve as anything but a "magic formula" leading directly into the main drama; its powers of introduction take immediate effect, so that it accomplishes "a mysterious initiation, [which] prepares our souls for the sight of unaccustomed things with loftier meaning than those of our earthly life."[37] Where Baudelaire finds a largely independent composition, Liszt discovers a work whose sole purpose is to open the opera.

As in the case of overtures, this discrepancy between Baudelaire and Liszt reflects a division within the history of the prelude as a genre. Like the overture, the prelude was fundamentally an instrumental composition intended to introduce some other, more substantial work;[38] but it was in general shorter, less standardized in form, and much less commonly associated with opera than the overture. In the sixteenth and seventeenth centuries, the prelude was a kind of improvisatory "flourish," related metaphorically by this term to the preliminary gestures of a fencer:[39] it gave performers a means of tuning and warming their instruments in public immediately before attacking the main pieces. Such "preluding" sometimes signaled the beginning of operas or stage plays during this period; but by the eighteenth and nineteenth centuries, preludes were associated most often with instrumental performances. In the early nineteenth century, moreover, "preludes" came also to serve as the generic title for sets of brief but comparatively independent compositions for solo piano (exemplified notably by Chopin's Preludes Op. 28).[40] The prelude in Wagner's era thus shared very little of the overture's intermediary character: it was either relatively autonomous or else aggressively attached to the first bars of another piece. Wagner's prelude, or *Vorspiel*, to *Lohengrin*, although it turned out to be detachable for concert performance, was in fact supposed to cling more closely than an overture to the beginning of the opera. Bound there by means of its principal motif, which recurs in the opera at particularly solemn moments, the prelude was not intended to give a dramatic preview or overview; its aim was rather to fill listeners with a sense of anticipation that the later recurrence of motifs would gradually transmute into memory.[41] Consequently, Liszt echoes Wagner when he describes the prelude to *Lohengrin* as a brief but irresistible formula of initiation.

Liszt adds, however, an important reservation about the prelude's initiatory powers. When left to open the opera with nothing but its own devices, the prelude is not sufficiently compelling and will not give adequate access to the drama: "In order fully to understand the unfolding [marche] of the work [pièce] in the theater, and to grasp the intention and the scope of the music from the first measures of the introduction onward, one must be familiar beforehand with the mystery on which all the action of the drama turns, but which is unveiled only in the last scene. This mystery rests on the tradition of the Holy Grail."[42] The prelude, Liszt suggests, cannot fulfill its introductory function unless listeners know or read something in advance about what it will introduce. For most listeners, in other words, the opening power of the prelude depends on prior acquaintance with a program, and this program in turn depends on the ending of the opera (which "is unveiled only in the last scene"). That is, the prelude and its program must work together, first to transport the opera's conclusion to its beginning and then to disguise this conclusion as a genuine opening. In Liszt's opinion, this task of reshuffling positions, so that the ending might appear, veiled, as a beginning and vice versa, is one of the primary operations of all program music. He writes in his essay on Berlioz that this is true from both the listener's and the composer's perspective: if the program provides the listener with a "foreword" that prospectively betrays "the poetic idea of the whole," it also serves the composer as a preliminary, predetermining guide for the completed work.[43] Liszt similarly states in an open letter to George Sand that just as readers often need a preface to a complex book, listeners also need a prefatory program that "summarily indicates" the musical drama they will subsequently discover little by little.[44] Even further, Liszt claims that this program should function as "a sort of philosophical critique" of the music; it should allow the composer to assess the coherence joining the end of his work with its beginning and to forearm listeners with the results of his evaluation.[45] From Liszt's point of view, then, the *Lohengrin* prelude furnishes a magnified instance of such a critique, since its program must anticipate not simply the ending of the prelude itself, but also the coherent completion of the entire opera. Liszt looks to the prelude to exemplify a larger notion of critical and artistic coherence, a notion that Derrida has formulated (complete with italics that immobilize the opening movement and turn it into a conclusion) by writing: "[E]very *pro*gram . . . is already a pro*gram*."[46]

At least two lines of thought from Baudelaire's essay suggest that Liszt's view of the *Lohengrin* prelude is inadequate, that even with help from its program, the prelude does not disguise a retrospective critique as an indispensable formula of initiation into the opera. First, Baudelaire persistently allows all connections between the prelude and the opera to remain vague or implicit, as if unobtrusively signaling that each is accessible without the other. While it is perhaps not surprising that he limits his discussion of musical links between the prelude and an opera he never heard in full, it is noteworthy that he finds so little relation between the program and the libretto. When summarizing the drama in part 3, he does not associate it explicitly with any of the three programs quoted during his *Lohengrin* demonstration in part 1, although he mentions in passing the temple ("the marvelous refuge," ¶34) evoked by Liszt's program. Baudelaire already refuses in part 1 to give logical priority to any one program, which would establish it as a vital preliminary to the opera; and when he lists thematic resemblances between the three programs, he eliminates all narrative elements that would permit the prelude to open or to foretell the sequence of events in the myth to be portrayed on stage. He further denies the prelude any specific powers of either initiation or critique when he writes, early in part 3, that it expresses only "the ardors of mysticity, the longings [appétitions] of the mind for the incommunicable God" (¶29); like his list of similarities, such a description acknowledges no urgent bonds between the prelude and any particular moment of the drama. By holding the prelude a little apart from its opera, Baudelaire suggests that it may act neither as an initiating force necessary to set the myth in motion and give spectators magical access to it, nor as a masked conclusion that surreptitiously ensures coherence by prefiguring the end of the drama.

Baudelaire also intimates in a second, subtler way that relations between the prelude and the opera are not what Liszt takes them to be. With his plot summary in part 3, Baudelaire makes it clear that the opera is precisely about the masking of beginnings or of origins, in order that critical conclusions may not be drawn from them. This masking occurs on several levels, but it is particularly obvious in the case of the hero, Lohengrin; his origins as a knight of the Grail must remain hidden, since his mystical power will evaporate as soon as he is recognized. While Baudelaire summarizes most other elements of the story very briefly, he quotes at disproportionate length from the libretto both Elsa's repeated promise not to ask her husband's identity and Lohengrin's disconsolate reply once she has blurted out the forbidden question (¶¶34–35). In addition, Baudelaire stresses that "Elsa who wanted to know, to examine, to control, Elsa has lost her happiness" (¶35), thus echoing the connection made in Wagner's *Lettre* between Elsa's tragedy and the nefarious "Why?" asked by nineteenth-century audiences. What Baudelaire makes less clear, however, is that the *Lohengrin* prelude places unwary listeners in Elsa's position and, in a certain manner, encourages the kind of questioning forbidden in the drama. Although Baudelaire observes that each character is "emblazoned" (¶38) by a musical motif, his readers must learn or deduce for themselves that the prelude's motif represents Lohengrin and that it recurs notably in act 1 at his arrival and in act 3 during the revelation of his identity.[47] It follows from this that in the absence of any program, listeners are led gradually to question the Lohengrin motif until they have discovered its full relation to the prelude. But at the same time, they learn that the essential condition of Lohengrin's identity is to remain unknown and unquestioned. Listeners must conclude, therefore, that their understanding of the music becomes less and less "innocent" as the opera proceeds: like Elsa, they betray Lohengrin when they go beyond an uncomprehending appreciation of the prelude to an explicit awareness of its role in the drama. The listeners' position is further complicated by programs such as Wagner's or Liszt's, which give extensive but indirect hints about Lohengrin's origins. Once they have come retrospectively to interpret the prelude as a revelation of Lohengrin's most vital secrets, listeners find that their "guilt" as unsuspecting bearers of forbidden knowledge has been ensured by the program from the very beginning. In at least two ways, then, Wagner allows the prelude to betray listeners: without its program, it excites the same questioning about origins for which Elsa will eventually be condemned; with its program, it implants guilty knowledge at the origin of the opera.

One might at the same time suppose, however, that the prelude also offers a way to save listeners from this advance condemnation. Especially in conjunction with Wagner's or Liszt's program, the prelude might seem to impart a kind of privileged omniscience—rather than guilt—at the origin of the opera: by revealing at the outset that Lohengrin comes from the miraculous temple and has received a divine mandate from the Grail, the program gives listeners a similarly "divine" understanding of the hero's identity, so that they need not participate in Elsa's anguished and guilt-ridden questioning. Even without Wagner's or Liszt's program, the prelude might "inoculate" listeners by instilling what they will later understand as a protective and privileged familiarity with the Grail's music. But while these possibilities can perhaps lessen or limit guilt, they cannot wholly save listeners from collaboration in the opera's final catastrophe. Like Lohengrin himself, they are powerless to forestall, reverse, or even mitigate the consequences of Elsa's growing curiosity; if they can avoid sharing or echoing her queries, listeners are nonetheless unable to prevent or escape the tragic repercussions of her betrayal. Nor can listeners know for certain whether the prelude places them among the holy elite rather than among the guilty questioners; with or without its programs, the motif wields no unambiguous power to absolve listeners beforehand by associating them more closely with the Grail knights than with Elsa. So rather than simply initiating or fully forearming listeners, as Liszt would have it, the prelude obliges them to become at least partial or potential collaborators in the disastrous conclusion of the drama.

Even though he does not explicitly describe or denounce this forced collaboration, Baudelaire makes its various conditions visible enough for readers to glimpse the full process. In other words, he indirectly reveals the particular kinds of complicity—actual or potential—between the prelude and the opera, a cooperation that entangles listeners in the progress of a musical motif and consequently takes away their critical distance from the myth being enacted. Listeners are thus obliged to experience at first hand the "solemn excommunication of inquiry" at the heart of this myth;[48] far from allowing artistic sensitivity and critical questioning to intermingle with respect to the myth, the music of *Lohengrin* may well aim to suppress the latter as much as possible. Fostered in particular by the prelude, this exclusion of critical interrogation threatens to unbalance the opera in much the same way that the absence of critical reasoning threatens to warp the half-developed artists evoked in Baudelaire's first digression. Baudelaire thus allows his readers to glimpse in *Lohengrin* a threat that Adorno discovers more generally in Wagner's music dramas. Operas before Wagner, claims Adorno, traditionally maintained some degree of tension between their music and their mythical plots, and this tension permitted listeners who followed the music to question the myths, to retain some critical distance from them. But just as Wagner's listeners may find themselves forced by the *Lohengrin* prelude to share in Elsa's guilty questioning, so in other Wagner operas "music, in collusion with a fate imposed on the powerless, gives up its profoundest critique, a critique that was inherent in it from the invention of opera as a form throughout the whole epoch of bourgeois ascendancy: its critique of myth. . . . The music simply follows after the action, without transcending it."[49] In *Lohengrin*, one might say, the music trails submissively along beside the plot, leading Elsa and her helpless listeners first to irresistible questioning, then to forbidden knowledge. Conspiring with its counterparts in the body of the opera, the prelude's motif not only conforms to the myth, but also deforms the listeners. And their punishment, should they give way—the penalty for uncritically following the motif's lead—is like Elsa's: endless separation, not from Lohengrin, nor from his music, but rather from the possibility of subjecting them to criticism.[50]

Baudelaire is less insistent than Adorno: since he also suggests several ways in which the *Lohengrin* prelude is partially separable from the opera, he hints that the music may retain some power to critique the myth and that listeners may to some extent resist the ban on critical questioning. But he points nevertheless to the imbalance or the disorder that results when art and criticism do not participate equally in myth. With the absence of the thyrsus from his *Tannhäuser* discussion, Baudelaire throws an oblique and unformulated doubt on Wagner's success in achieving a properly digressive equilibrium between art and criticism; and his study of *Lohengrin* hints more clearly that any serious disequilibrium between them will render myth threatening and coercive. However explicitly Baudelaire tries to praise Wagner's understanding of "the sacred, divine character of myth," his essay implicitly reveals in Wagner's operas an art deformed by its imperfect collaboration with criticism.

MYTHICAL POSITIONS

Among all the nineteenth- and twentieth-century echoes of Baudelaire's concern with the relative positions of art and criticism or of music and writing, none is more resonant than Mallarmé. If Baudelaire was himself conscious of how startlingly this concern related him to other writers "as if by a phenomenon of mnemonic echo" (¶19), then Mallarmé was even more so: while meditating on the crisis he believed to have overtaken music and letters in his time, Mallarmé also chooses the figure of an echo to evoke the deformation that his writing on the subject was certain to turn against him. Any critical effort to trace "the act of writing . . . all the way to its origin"[51] or to situate it with respect to music, he claims, will involve rhetoric that is indispensable but unreliable:

> Admire the shepherd, whose voice, once it has struck against cunning rocks never comes back to him according to the disorder/blurring of a snicker. All the better: there is moreover contentment, and maturity, in asking for sun, even a setting sun, on the causes of a vocation. (646)

> [Admirez le berger, dont la voix, heurtée à des rochers malins jamais ne lui revient selon le trouble d'un ricanement. Tant mieux: il y a d'autre part aise, et maturité, à demander un soleil, même couchant, sur les causes d'une vocation.]

The unpredictable character of an echo, which irrepressibly renews all or part of its original sound, but only according to the irregular configuration of the surrounding rocks, is well chosen as an emblem for Mallarmé's reflections on music and literature in general and on Wagner in particular. The echo imagery suggests that there are obvious connections linking Mallarmé to Baudelaire's essay and to the issues raised there; and it also suggests the inevitable distortions of emphasis and context that occur among these connections. Echoes may serve as well to figure the relations Mallarmé hopes to find between art, criticism, and myth; but like Baudelaire, Mallarmé sometimes finds these relations unexpectedly deadened by the hollows and protuberances of the Wagnerian landscape.

For Mallarmé, as for Baudelaire, music refuses to hold a stable position as either an artistic origin or a retrospective critique of mythical drama.

In order to explore the variety of ways in which Mallarmé formulates this instability, it is helpful to begin by glancing over "L'Après-Midi d'un Faune" (50–53). More starkly than his Wagner writings, this poem shows how far Mallarmé pushes Baudelaire's preoccupation with questions of (chrono)logical ordering and aesthetic regeneration. In the poem, the narrating faun tries to articulate not only his uncertainty as to whether a recent encounter with two nymphs was real, but also his inability to decide whether his music was a necessary prelude to the encounter or merely an incident unrelated to it. The nymphs (or their illusion) may have sprung up and flourished in consequence of the "arid rain" falling in line 19 from the faun's flute; but it may also be that his music is a falsely preparatory elixir (or arcanum: "arcane," line 42) unconnected with the nymphs, that the faun and his flute have merely entertained "the beauty of the surroundings with false / Confusions between itself and our gullible song" [La beauté d'alentour par des confusions / Fausses entre elle-même et notre chant crédule (lines 45–47)]. The faun's perplexity on this point deepens when he tries to turn the scene into an orderly narrative:

> O bords siciliens d'un calme marécage
> Qu'à l'envi de soleils ma vanité saccage,
> Tacite sous les fleurs d'étincelles, CONTEZ
> « *Que je coupais ici les creux roseaux domptés*
> » *Par le talent; quand, sur l'or glauque de lointaines*
> » *Verdures dédiant leur vigne à des fontaines,*
> » *Ondoie une blancheur animale au repos:*
> » *Et qu'au prélude lent où naissent les pipeaux*
> » *Ce vol de cygnes, non! de naïades se sauve*
> » *Ou plonge . . .* »
>
> (lines 23–32)

> [O Sicilian banks of a calm marsh
> That in rivalry with suns my vanity ransacks,
> Tacit beneath the flowers of sparks, RECOUNT
> « *That I was here cutting the hollow reeds tamed*
> » *By talent; when, on the blue-green gold of distant*
> » *Greeneries dedicating their vine to fountains,*
> » *Undulates an animal whiteness at rest:*

>> *And that to/in the slow prelude where are born the pipes/lures/traps*
>> *That flight/theft of swans, no! of naiads saves itself*
>> *Or plunges . . .* >>]

As if to emphasize the uncertainty of the nymphs' origin, the narrative makes its own source as difficult as possible to ascertain. It is dramatically separated from the rest of the text by its typography, as though the fertile landscape, urgently summoned by the faun's capitals, were literally producing its own tale in its native Italic accent.[52] This does not relieve the faun of all responsibility for the story, however, because it still takes the form of indirect discourse in which "*I*" implicates the faun as the subjective originator of the tale and thus leaves the countryside at least partially "tacit." Moreover, the narrative is also set apart by quotation marks, as if it has been cut out and removed, like the flute reeds, from some distant site that is perhaps unknown to both the faun and the Sicilian scenery. Conceived in this threefold confusion, the fleeting vision of the nymphs is further entangled in the first sounds of the faun's newborn music, since it is within or in time to "*the slow prelude where are born the pipes/ lures/traps*" that they appear. The suggestive ambiguity of "*les pipeaux*"— which according to *Le Petit Robert* can be synonymous with *appeaux* (lures or decoys), *gluaux* (traps of sticky birdlime), or *flûtes champêtres* (country pipes or pastoral flutes)—here makes the status of the music even more enigmatic than that of the nymphs. It is possible that the faun has lured and trapped the swanlike naiads with his flute prelude, which would thus precede their appearance and might even cause their existence. But it is equally and simultaneously possible that the prelude has given birth to the pipes themselves, trapping the material substance of the instruments as the music lured them into being. This latter possibility would then confer on the music a much more radical kind of anteriority: as the progenitor of its own means of production, the prelude would appear as an absolute and unconditional origin.[53]

If the poem thus assigns to the faun's music varying degrees of priority, from that of an illusory beginning to that of an imperative precondition, it also relegates the music at times to the position of a consequence or an aftereffect:

Tâche donc, instrument des fuites, ô maligne
Syrinx, de refleurir aux lacs où tu m'attends!
. . . .
Ainsi, quand des raisins j'ai sucé la clarté,
Pour bannir un regret par ma feinte écarté,
Rieur, j'élève au ciel d'été la grappe vide
Et, soufflant dans ses peaux lumineuses, avide
D'ivresse, jusqu'au soir je regarde au travers.
                              (lines 52–53; 57–61)

[Try therefore, instrument of flights/leaks, O cunning
Syrinx, to flower again by the lakes where you are waiting for me!
. . . .
Thus, when from grapes I have sucked the brightness,
In order to banish a regret by my feint dismissed,
Laughing, I lift up to the summer sky the empty bunch
And, blowing in its luminous skins, eager
For intoxication, until evening I gaze through them.]

The *"pipeaux"* born of music in the earlier narrative have here become
"Syrinx," or perhaps merely "a syrinx," a pipe named after the nymph who
was not only changed into a reed, but was "herself the wind in the reeds":[54]
the faun's instrument has reclaimed its precedence, its power to generate
music from its own breath. But with this resurgence of its clever and rather
guileful originality ("O cunning / Syrinx"), the flute also becomes an "instrument of flights/leaks," so that its malignantly continuing music helps
the two (illusory?) naiads trickle away or else reflects belatedly on their
escape rather than causing or announcing their appearance. When the faun
tauntingly orders the flute to "flower again," therefore, the challenge rings
somewhat—but not entirely—hollow. Music can still blossom out of the
dead reeds, but it will now be the preludial flourish only to the *memory*
of the two nymphs, which is itself perhaps an illusion; this music is less
an origin than "an anticipation of a future 'afterness,'"[55] the digressive
opening of an afterthought. Like Baudelaire, who sidesteps the miraculous reflowering of the priest's staff in *Tannhäuser,* Mallarmé circumvents
the rejuvenating magic of the flute music, so that the effects of beginning
and ending or of initiative and resignation become hard to disentangle:

the faun's "thyrsus" is composed from the hollow stick of a potentially fertile, yet temporarily abandoned, flute and the equally hollow curves of a permanently ruined, yet temporarily luminous, bunch of grapes. The music of "L'Après-Midi d'un Faune" does not eliminate the difference between origins and aftereffects (or, one might suggest, between songs and echoes), but neither does it allow them to occupy fixed positions relative to each other.[56]

Under these circumstances, it is significant that Debussy composed, specifically, a musical prelude to "L'Après-Midi d'un Faune." Since Debussy twice announced his original intention of composing a "Prélude, interludes et paraphrase finale" for the poem, his ultimate choice of a title situating the music as an introduction to the poetry was almost certainly deliberate.[57] Consequently, it may also be significant that without challenging the title, Mallarmé subtly but persistently characterized Debussy's composition as a follow-up, prolongation, or belated extension: "[T]his music prolongs the emotion of my poem"; "your illustration of *l'Après-Midi d'un Faune,* which would present no dissonance with my text, if not by going further . . ."; "Sylvan *of first breath* / If your flute was a success / Hear all the light / That Debussy will blow into it."[58]

This determination to prevent the music and the poetry from staying in preassigned places reflects Mallarmé's suspicion of the very word "composition," a mistrust eloquently justified in the essay "Crise de vers" when he claims that because of recent poetic reforms, "anyone with his individual playing and hearing can compose himself [or can himself compose: se peut composer] an instrument, as soon as he blows, brushes it or strikes with skill/knowledge" (363).[59] The ambiguity of this formulation, accentuated by the displaced pronoun "se," makes it difficult to say whether everyone may make an instrument *for* herself or *of* herself, or both; the exact source of music (who or what is the instrument?), as well as the exact admixture of language involved (how are poetry and music aligned or positioned together?), cannot be decided. In view of the wary attention directed here to the verb "compose" and generally to the concept of composition, it is not surprising that Mallarmé turns later in "Crise de vers" to one of its more flexible and dynamic variants: the word "transposition" occurs whenever the unsettled relations between music and writing are in question. Its first appearance in "Crise de vers" signals more vehemently than ever the impossibility of ordering the two according to rank or priority. Following his declaration that the unique "magic spell" of "literary art" lies in its allusiveness, in its power to "liberate, out of a handful of dust or reality without enclosing it, in the book, even as text, the volatile dispersion that is the mind, which has nothing to do with anything besides the musicality of everything," Mallarmé pursues: "This aim, I say it [is] Transposition—Structure, another" (366).[60] Perpetually dispersing a musical whole that never disintegrates, "Transposition" holds music together with writing in a (dis)order that cannot remain fixed.

The first part of the preceding quotation appeared originally not in "Crise de vers," but in "La Musique et les Lettres." In this latter essay, which Mallarmé first presented as a lecture in the same year that Debussy completed and premiered his *Prélude à "L'Après-Midi d'un Faune"* (1894), the quoted lines belong to the same passage in which Mallarmé formulates the critical question, "—That is, whether there is reason for writing to take place" (645). It is thus only when "the act of writing scrutinized itself all the way to its origin" (645) that literature could discover "the musicality of everything," completely and pervasively mingled with itself in a "volatile dispersion." Even though "Literature exists and, if you will, alone, with the exception of everything" (646), it can never situate its own origin securely enough to escape invasion by the volatile "musicality of everything": music and literature continuously open into each other in a kind of mercurial oscillation.[61] For Mallarmé, then, the instability of the relation between music and literature prevents their ever poising, together or separately, at a point of origin; there can be no fixed position that would either unite the two in a single identity or give definite priority to one of them. In other words, music transposes itself into literature and vice versa as a kind of permanently wandering digression that permeates all territory, forming and reforming a paradoxical "exception to everything." This is the "conclusion" that Mallarmé, with considerable irony, announces as his "position" in "La Musique et les Lettres":

> I set down, at my risk aesthetically, this conclusion (if, by some favor, absent, always, from a presentation, I led you to ratify it, that would be the honor sought for me this evening): that Music and Letters are the

alternative face here widened/released toward the obscure; scintillating there, with certainty, of a phenomenon, the only one, I called it, the Idea.

One of the modes inclines toward the other and disappearing there, springs out again with borrowings: twice, perfects itself, oscillating, a whole genre intact. Theatrically for the crowd that is present, without awareness, at the hearing of its greatness: or, the individual requires lucidity, from the explanatory and familiar book. (649)

[Je pose, à mes risques esthétiquement, cette conclusion (si, par quelque grâce, absente, toujours, d'un exposé, je vous amenai à la ratifier, ce serait l'honneur pour moi cherché ce soir): que la Musique et les Lettres sont la face alternative ici élargie vers l'obscur; scintillante là, avec certitude, d'un phénomène, le seul, je l'appelai, l'Idée.

L'un des modes incline à l'autre et y disparaissant, ressort avec emprunts: deux fois, se parachève, oscillant, un genre entier. Théâtralement pour la foule qui assiste, sans conscience, à l'audition de sa grandeur: ou, l'individu requiert la lucidité, du livre explicatif et familier.]

When Mallarmé evokes the divided manifestation, public and private, of this "whole genre intact," he describes with surprising accuracy Baudelaire's situation with regard to Wagner. Even to some degree in the case of *Tannhäuser,* Baudelaire's experience of works that he accepted as a dynamic "*coincidence* of several arts" (¶6; Baudelaire's emphasis) was static and divided; it was in the gaps between "theatrical" fragments heard at the 1860 concerts and "bookish" hours spent with Wagner's texts that he conceived his essay. In other words, Baudelaire's Wagner criticism relates to its object in much the same way that literature relates to music in the passage given above: although his essay and the art it discusses remain separate, they take volatile shape in and around each other, so that neither holds a genuinely predominant or preexistent position. Mallarmé is himself concerned with the mutual interpermeation that prevents either art or criticism in general from taking permanent precedence: "Criticism, in its integrity, exists, has value or almost equals Poetry to which it should bring a noble and complementary operation, only by aiming, directly and superbly, also at phenomena or the universe" (294).[62] Just after this pronouncement, Mallarmé further intermingles the traditional attributes of art and criticism by declaring the latter's "quality of primordial instinct placed in the secrecy of our innermost reaches (a divine uneasiness)," a declaration that echoes Baudelaire's longing for a mixture of artistic instinct and critical reason "whose divine goal is infallibility in poetic production" (¶27). But just as Baudelaire never quite manages to present Wagner as a perfectly integrated "poet and critic" (¶27), Mallarmé is unable to find in Wagner's works a dynamic interpenetration of music and letters or of art and criticism. In the essay entitled "Richard Wagner: Rêverie d'un poëte français," Mallarmé tries repeatedly to praise Wagner for uniting music and drama in a "fusion," a "harmonious compromise," or a "marriage," thereby critically renewing a whole artistic tradition that would otherwise have shriveled into "impending obsolescence" (543). But in between these efforts, Mallarmé inserts a skeptical observation:

> Although philosophically it still does nothing there [in Wagner's operas] but juxtapose itself, Music (I enjoin someone to insinuate where it dawns/sprouts, its primary meaning and its fate) penetrates and envelops Drama by dazzling willpower and allies itself with it: [there is] no ingenuity or depth that with alert enthusiasm it does not pour out for this purpose, except that its very principle, for Music, escapes. (543)

> [Quoique philosophiquement elle ne fasse là encore que se juxtaposer, la Musique (je somme qu'on insinue d'où elle poind, son sens premier et sa fatalité) pénètre et enveloppe le Drame de par l'éblouissante volonté et s'y allie: pas d'ingénuité ou de profondeur qu'avec un éveil enthousiaste elle ne prodigue dans ce dessein, sauf que son principe même, à la Musique, échappe.]

In Mallarmé's view, there is a great deal of superficial evidence that Wagner is a master of transposition, that he spins music and drama into a continual, oscillating exchange of places. Beneath all the surface dazzle, however, Mallarmé discerns only a simple juxtaposition, an arrangement that is both static and unequal: it is only Music that must come from elsewhere, as a nameless stranger or a foreign implant, to settle into its pose beside Drama. The reason for this, according to Mallarmé, is that this music is in any case already dislocated; uncertain of its own origin and unable to interrogate its own identity (Mallarmé describes it two sentences later as "the floating and the inborn"), Wagner's music lacks the momentum to engage in an entirely equal interchange with drama. The trouble with this juxtaposition, then, is that while it may seem artistically appealing, it restricts or prohibits critical reflection. Since the music involved remains permanently unable to examine its principles "all the way to its origin," it limits the scope of the whole collaboration; it prevents the drama from joining with it in any rigorously critical enterprise.

The consequence of this, for Mallarmé, would seem to be that in Wagner's achievements, art and criticism are positioned all too fixedly with respect to each other. This is among the implications of Mallarmé's "Hommage" to Wagner, a sonnet concerned with questions of ordering and succession. According to one way of reading it, the poem sketches a large-scale progression of the sort outlined in Baudelaire's first digression: the quatrains evoke a primitive or instinctive art that is about to wither for want of critical scrutiny, while the tercets announce its imminent rejuvenation in a Wagnerian spurt of both critical and aesthetic vitality:[63]

> Le silence déjà funèbre d'une moire
> Dispose plus qu'un pli seul sur le mobilier
> Que doit un tassement du principal pilier
> Précipiter avec le manque de mémoire.
>
> Notre si vieil ébat triomphal du grimoire,
> Hiéroglyphes dont s'exalte le millier
> À propager de l'aile un frisson familier!
> Enfouissez-le-moi plutôt dans une armoire.
>
> Du souriant fracas originel haï
> Entre elles de clartés maîtresses a jailli
> Jusque vers un parvis né pour leur simulacre,
>
> Trompettes tout haut d'or pâmé sur les vélins,
> Le dieu Richard Wagner irradiant un sacre
> Mal tu par l'encre même en sanglots sibyllins.
>
> (71)

> [The already funereal silence of a moiré cloth
> Disposes more than merely a single fold on the furnishings
> That a sagging of the principal pillar should
> Hurl down with the lack of memory.

Our so old triumphal frolic of the grimoire,
Hieroglyphs that excite the thousands
To disseminate a familiar shiver of the wing!
Bury it for me instead in an armoire.

From the smiling primeval din hated
Among them of masterful brightnesses gushed forth
All the way toward a parvis born for their simulacrum,

Trumpets aloud of gold swooning on the velums,
The god Richard Wagner irradiating a rite/consecration
Badly silenced by the ink itself (by ink even) in sibylline sobs.]

At the same time that Wagner's work constitutes a critique of the "old triumphal frolic" that formerly entranced readers and audiences, it would also seem to return with new radiance to the "smiling primeval din" from which all artistic energy springs. On a general as well as an individual scale, then, the "god Richard Wagner" would appear to reach the "divine goal" (¶27) of this Baudelairean sequence, joining his creative origins with the "sibylline sobs" that foretell future infallibility of poetic production. But the sonnet does not wholly affirm this orderly progression; or at least, it gives no assurance that the final joining of art and criticism has yet taken (or can ever take) place. The rhymes in "-moire" that dominate the quatrains, for example, work to distance the possibility of such a joining: although the "moire" of line 1 suggests both stiflingly shrouded beginnings and their critical/creative reweaving in the hands of Fate, the "mémoire" of line 4 pulls attention back toward the dull, dying past, the "grimoire"— or magician's unreadable book—of line 5 hints at the tangled illegibility of past and future alike, and the "armoire" of line 8 rather embarrassingly drags the whole fabric of suggestions off into a remote closet. Thus lexically and conceptually engulfed, the original "moire" seems unlikely to weave art and criticism into anything more than a thin, shimmery semblance of wholeness.[64] The tercets then deepen this unlikelihood. They do so partly by insinuating that it is only a false—if convincing—"simulacrum" of artistic origins that Wagner's critical energy is able to fabricate. More compellingly, the poem's last line points toward a contest staged between sonorously prophetic "sobs" and censorious "ink" that tries to silence them. This contest is not quite resolved by the sonnet's end, even though the artistic creation of the future, "badly silenced" by the (critical) writing of the present, is perhaps winning. But the very image of their combat suggests that any hope of profound cooperation between them is slight and that if they were somehow to make a concerted attempt to reorder or revivify the "primeval din," their success would be at best incomplete. Or as Mallarmé provocatively puts it when he alludes, in his "Rêverie d'un poëte français," to Wagner's halting, ambiguous journey toward rejuvenating origins: "Everything is drenched once more in the primitive stream: not/footsteps all the way to the source" [Tout se retrempe au ruisseau primitif: pas jusqu'à la source] (544).

This last quotation further suggests that for Mallarmé, as for Baudelaire, the uneven juxtaposition of art and criticism adversely affects the myths portrayed in Wagner's operas. In Mallarmé's view, these myths take on a disjointed, mechanically divided character: on the one hand, they seem to represent a past so strange and distant as to be almost inaccessible; on the other hand, they seem to participate in the immediate present. The effect of this disjunction is neither to intrigue nor to confuse the spectators, but rather to numb them:

> Always the hero, who treads on a fog as much as our soil, will show himself in a distance that is filled with the vapor of moans, of glories, and of joy emitted by the instrumentation, pushed back in this way to some beginnings. He acts only when surrounded, Greek-style, by the stupor mingled with intimacy that an audience feels before myths that have almost never existed, so much does their instinctive past melt! without however ceasing to benefit there from the familiar outward appearances of the human individual. (544)

> [Toujours le héros, qui foule une brume autant que notre sol, se montrera dans un lointain que comble la vapeur des plaintes, des gloires, et de la joie émises par l'instrumentation, reculé ainsi à des commencements. Il n'agit qu'entouré, à la Grecque, de la stupeur mêlée d'intimité qu'éprouve une assistance devant des mythes qui n'ont presque jamais été, tant leur instinctif passé se fond! sans cesser cependant d'y bénéficier des familiers dehors de l'individu humain.]

The fog mentioned here does not come from the volatile kind of oscillation evoked in "La Musique et les Lettres." It is a thicker, more deceptive haze that artfully hides any disjunction between the past and the present, between instinctive memory and critical awareness, or between the music and the drama.[65] Unlike the myths Baudelaire discusses in his second digression, the ones Mallarmé finds in Wagner are almost certainly unable to flourish spontaneously in every time and place. They emerge from a haze of multiple "beginnings" rather than from "the absolute principle and the common origin of all beings" (¶36); just as Wagner's music arrives from foreign regions to juxtapose itself with drama, his myths are never wholly and naturally acclimatized in the world of his audiences. For Mallarmé, therefore, Wagner never achieves more than an inaccurate, incomplete understanding of myth. Mallarmé agrees with Baudelaire that genuine myth is possible to conceive and even to put on a modern stage: when he writes, about "Myths," that "the Theater calls for them [or calls them forth], no: not fixed, nor age-long and well-known, but one, freed of personality, for it composes our multiple aspect" (545),[66] Mallarmé is not far from Baudelaire's conception of myth as something paradoxically "cosmopolitan" (¶36), always simultaneously native or primary and foreign or secondary. Much more decidedly than Baudelaire, however, Mallarmé fails to discover such myths in Wagner. Whereas Baudelaire only shies away from the thyrsus image in *Tannhäuser* and hints at the imbalance in *Lohengrin*, Mallarmé denounces a series of artificial juxtapositions. Echoing Baudelaire, but with changes of accent and resonance, Mallarmé finds in Wagner a dry sequence of music and letters rather than "those rarefactions and those natural pinnacles that Music renders, vibratory afterextension of everything like Life" (545).[67]

5 ⟩ Breach of Genius

—However, you would show bad grace if you didn't
observe that one generally refuses to engage in introspection
just as much out Guermantes' way—where the matrimonial
regime of sounds is regulated according to an unchangeable
social tradition, as out Swann's way—where free love is de
rigueur between [musical] notes. Which denotes, in the end, a
very symptomatic mistrust of intelligence, on both sides. May
I quote Baudelaire?

—He won't prevent you.

—True! . . . [sic] Listen: "I pity poets who are guided solely
by instinct; I believe they are incomplete . . . [sic] It is
impossible for a poet not to contain a critic." Listen again!

—Baudelaire again?

—"I want to illuminate things with my mind and project
their reflection onto other minds." Listen some more!

—Still Baudelaire?

—"The divine goal is infallibility in poetic production." Of
course, one can play for a long time with quotations . . . [sic]

Pierre Boulez, "De moi à moi"

WALTER BENJAMIN has claimed that "there can be
no familiarity with Baudelaire that does not include Proust's experience of
him";[1] and while Benjamin was thinking mainly of *Les Fleurs du Mal,* his
statement applies to *Richard Wagner* as well. Proust is, of course, perpetually

concerned with numerous kinds of distance and with complex attempts to overcome them, with the general mystery of "that moral distance . . . proportionate to material distance."[2] When he writes about music, however, and in particular about Vinteuil's music, Proust raises several questions of distance that specifically recall Baudelaire's essay. To judge from some of his critical writings, Proust was a little dubious of Baudelaire's emphatic admiration for Wagner and was therefore hesitant to consider too closely the relation between Baudelaire's poetic genius and his musical sensitivity. But beginning with the enigmatic distance that Swann always senses between himself and the "little phrase" of Vinteuil's Sonata for Piano and Violin, Proust devotes parts of his *Recherche* to a continuing exploration of the gaps between musical understanding and literary interpretation, or between what he once calls the "unanalyzable states" of listeners (3:883) and the apparently more articulate activity of readers and writers. From certain points of view, the passages on music in "Un Amour de Swann" serve almost as a summary of Baudelaire's reflections on music and writing, a useful manner of reviewing the main rhetorical maneuvers of Baudelaire's arguments from a new angle. Following this review, several other sections of Proust's novel will prove helpful in studying the conclusions that Baudelaire offers in the final pages of his essay.

THE WANDERING PHRASE

In his article "Sainte-Beuve et Baudelaire," Proust objects to Sainte-Beuve's behavior toward Baudelaire with something of the same indignation that Baudelaire himself leveled at French critics of Wagner. Proust may even have been (or become) aware of this, since he alludes to Baudelaire's Wagner essay in a later article entitled "À propos de Baudelaire." After quoting the final stanza of the poem "L'Imprévu," Proust writes that "here it is permitted to think that for the poet, along with the impressions of the Parisian idler [badaud] that he was, there is attached the memory of the passionate admirer of Wagner. Even should young musicians of today be right (which I do not believe) in denying the genius of Wagner, such verses would prove that the objective exactness of the judgments that a writer passes on such and such a work belonging to an art other than his own has no importance, and that his admiration, even if false, inspires him with useful reveries."[3] Proust appears in this passage to discount the value of Baudelaire's Wagner essay as a piece of criticism; in "Sainte-Beuve et Baudelaire," he similarly dismisses Baudelaire's critical writing as an "intermediate heaven" needed mostly to fill the huge gap between Baudelaire's poetic genius and his everyday personality.[4] Whether intentionally or not, however, Proust echoes *Richard Wagner et "Tannhäuser" à Paris* twice in the passage quoted above, and he does so in an oddly suggestive way. His allusion to "useful reveries" echoes Baudelaire's insistence, with respect to his own program for the *Lohengrin* prelude, that he "certainly would not dare to indulge in talking about [his] *reveries,* if it were not useful to attach them here to the preceding *reveries,*"[5] a remark that evokes among other things the pathways of Rousseau's *Rêveries du promeneur solitaire.*[6] In addition, the beginning of the Proust passage recalls Baudelaire's hope that his essay will clarify "the works of this man [Wagner] whose person and whose ideal ambitions have for so long been the main subject of idle Parisian curiosity [badauderie]" (¶46). Together with the explicit assertions of the passage, these echoes suggest that Baudelaire's Wagner criticism functions as a path—the curious, digressive kind of path attractive to Parisian "badauds"—winding not only from his own art toward Wagner's, but also toward some elements of Proust's.[7]

One other *flâneur* (or rather, *flâneuse*) leads by a circuitous route from Proust's criticism of Baudelaire to *À la recherche du temps perdu.* Proust writes in "Sainte-Beuve et Baudelaire" that Baudelaire's works are only isolated stretches of "that country of his genius"; but Proust then claims that each single fragment, "as soon as one reads it, attaches itself to the other fragments with which we are familiar, much like [what happens when] in a salon, in a frame that [you] had not yet seen there, [with] some mountain of antiquity where the evening reddens and where there passes a poet with a woman's face followed by two or three Muses, . . . all that, in a moment, at a certain hour, in the ephemeralness that gives something real to immortal legend, you feel a fragment of the country of Gustave Moreau."[8] Just as Baudelaire proposes to lead his readers high enough above some scattered pieces of Wagner's art to give them "general views" (¶31), Proust indicates that such a climb may prove equally necessary in the mountainous country native to other artists, including Baudelaire himself. Proust suggests, like Baudelaire, that the way to approach such landscapes is not to study them from a minute distance, but rather to stand so far away that the strangeness of lighting and perspective induces an impression of more intimate reality ("something real") than could have resulted from literal proximity. Further, Proust's text hints that this impression comes close to being a musical one, because the "poet with a woman's face" on the mountain path in Moreau's painting is like a companion to the "promeneuse" wandering through Vinteuil's sonata during one of the Verdurins' soirees: "[B]eneath the agitation of the violin tremolos that protected her with their sustained trembling two octaves away—and just as in a mountainous country, behind the apparent and vertiginous immobility of a cascade, one perceives, two hundred feet below, the minuscule form of a woman walking [promeneuse]—the little phrase had just appeared" (1:260).

In effect, much of Swann's fascination with the "little phrase" corresponds to Baudelaire's experience with Wagner. Like Baudelaire, who called himself "someone who . . . *does not know music,*"[9] Swann also "did not know music" (1:206) at the time of his original acquaintance with Vinteuil's sonata; and it is almost as if this parallel ignorance of music prompted the narrator of "Un Amour de Swann" to pursue rhetorical strategies reminiscent of those in Baudelaire's essay. Even before he associates it with Odette, the "little phrase" appears to Swann as a personification, a figure that leads the "fugitive phrases" (1:206) of the sonata closer to him than would otherwise be possible. The relation between quotation and personification is not as evident as it is in Baudelaire's essay; but Swann's first encounter with the "little phrase" is suggestively *like* a quotation, since it might easily serve as a free paraphrase that reanimates the tercets of Baudelaire's sonnet "À une passante": "[Swann] was like a man into whose life a passing woman he perceived for a moment has just introduced the image of a new beauty that gives greater value to his own sensitivity [sensibilité], without his even knowing whether he will ever again be able to see her whom he already loves and about whom he knows nothing, not even her name" (1:207).[10] This first "passante" is not identical with the "promeneuse" Swann later meets in the Verdurin salon, nor with the "protective goddess and confidante" who comes still later to "lead him aside" at the Sainte-Euverte concert (1:342): the various personifications of the "little phrase" all accentuate their fleeting, transitory character (and one might remember that for Fontanier, genuine personifications are always figures "made only in passing").[11] Like the Wagnerian motifs that intrigue Baudelaire, the "little phrase" is apparently intended to ensure perpetual movement—from one metaphorical "passante" to another, from Baudelaire's text to Proust's, from music to writing. Already at his first encounter with her, therefore, Swann tries to follow the "little phrase" along a path of communication between the region of mobile, musical figuration and the domain of fixed, literal meaning; she seems to lead him from "one of those impressions that may however be the only purely musical ones, without extension [inétendues], entirely original" to a stable understanding of her "extension, symmetrical groupings, written form [or transcription: la graphie]," just as she leads from the dizzying movement of "motifs" to the settled eloquence of the "phrase" (1:206). Given her difficult task of guaranteeing travel between the mobility of music and the immobility of letters, it is not surprising that the "little phrase," however personified, always dresses for walking and that during much of "Un Amour de Swann" she appears only in the "andante" of Vinteuil's sonata.

To show the apparent success of the "little phrase" in this enterprise, the narrator ultimately describes her as an effective translation, using terms much like those in part 1 of Baudelaire's essay. The composer Vinteuil, in his capacity as "explorer of the invisible," has "captured" the phrase and led her back from her original "divine world" to his own sphere: "And one proof that Swann was not mistaken when he believed in the real existence of this phrase is that any slightly refined amateur would have perceived the imposture right away if Vinteuil, having had less power to see and to render her outlines, had tried to dissimulate—by adding here and there some features of his own invention—the lacunas of his vision or the failings of his hand" (1:345). Despite the risk of "lacunas," which both Baudelaire and Proust's narrator agree to be unavoidable, Vinteuil has carried back his "hostage" (1:345) nearly intact and has revived her with great sureness of touch. The "little phrase" is consequently filled with such vitality that it radiates around her, suffuses listeners, and eventually invades their "interior domain"; and with this final crossing of boundaries, claims the narrator, "Vinteuil's phrase had—like such and such a theme from *Tristan* for example, which also represents for us a certain acquisition of sentiment—wedded our mortal condition, taken on something human that was quite touching" (1:344). On some occasions, moreover, the phrase effects a more violent invasion, as when she "shook, like that of a medium, the truly possessed body of the violinist" (1:346). But this kind of incarnation, in which the musical phrase irresistibly appropriates its human listeners from the inside, affects Swann differently. Without apparent violence, the "little phrase" pervades him with "the possibility of a sort of rejuvenation" or "renewal" (1:207, 233); it seems to offer him the energy necessary to overcome the "moral dryness [or drought: sécheresse]" (1:208) that chronically keeps him from any serious study of artworks and forces him to comment only on their most superficial details. In other words, if Swann can allow the "little phrase" to inhabit both mind and senses, he may be able to close the interior gap that isolates his artistic feeling from his critical judgment. Such an integration would permit Swann not merely to return to his work on Ver Meer, but above all to become both the active creator and the subtle interpreter of his relationship with Odette, with whom he falls in love as he would with a work of art.[12] Enlivening Swann from within, the "little phrase" promises to unite Swann with Odette after the manner of an artist uniting critical insight with creative energy.

It is perhaps not an accident, however, that when Odette tries to confirm the unifying power of the "little phrase" by crying, "That one is *our* piece" (1:215), the crucial pronoun [*notre*] intended to overcome all distances between Swann, Odette, and the music appears as one of the rare instances of italics in "Un Amour de Swann." By means of her exclamation, Odette prevents Swann from listening to any other part of Vinteuil's sonata and thus from following the "little phrase" as it attempts to circulate freely between musical contexts, between artistic feeling and graphic understanding, between Odette and Swann. As a result, Swann is always dimly aware of an uncrossable distance and a paralyzing fixity that might at any time keep him from participating in the music's mobility: "And even, suffering to think, at the moment when [the little phrase] passed so close and yet so infinitely far away, that although it spoke to them [Swann and Odette], it did not know them, [Swann] almost regretted that it had a meaning, an intrinsic and unchanging beauty [that was] unfamiliar to them" (1:215). The "little phrase" thus carries within it a latent threat of paralysis and separation, a threat that is never completely hidden. On the same occasion that Swann tries to meet the phrase/"promeneuse" on her mountain path, for example, he is distracted by M. de Forcheville's bad pun about Vinteuil's "Rattlesonata" [Serpent à Sonates], made even worse by the doctor Cottard's inability to understand it (1:259–60); like the Wagner motifs that sometimes "wend their way through the opera like a venomous serpent" (Liszt) or paralyze the music with "rattlesnake" poison (Nietzsche),[13] the "little phrase" may be associated with immobility and isolation as easily as with their opposites. Ultimately, therefore, the "little phrase" is an inscrutable and unreliable guide across any distances between musical and textual figuration or between artistic appreciation and critical interpretation. Proust's narrator evokes these related, unbridgeable distances with particular skill in one paragraph devoted to the increasing gulf between Odette and Swann. Whereas Odette once agreed with the general sentiment among Swann's acquaintances that "he's not really handsome, if you like, but he's chic: that toupet, that monocle, that smile!" she later

> looked at that head which had only aged a little from worrying (but about which everyone now thought, by virtue of the same aptitude that allows one to discover the intentions of a symphonic piece whose program one has read, and the resemblances of a child when one knows its parentage: "He's not positively ugly if you like, but he's ridiculous: that monocle, that toupet, that smile!", concretizing in their suggestible imagination the immaterial demarcation that separates at a distance of several months the head of a cherished lover from the head of a cuckold). (1:314–15)

Just as an impartial observer may find the genetic links between a child and his parents to be entirely invisible, so a detached listener may find no smooth or "natural" paths running between a symphony and its program; even should these paths actually exist, they may remain undiscoverable or unfit for travel. Similarly, neither Odette nor Swann can force a passage across the "immaterial demarcation" separating faces from minds; and the "little phrase," however much she may intensify their gaze across it, cannot lead over the "gaping opening" (1:360) that widens between them.

THE WAGNERIAN VOLCANO

Much of Swann's musical experience reappears, transmuted but easily recognizable, in the intricate relations developed later in the *Recherche* between Vinteuil's music, Albertine, and the narrator. But if, for example, the narrator recounts his impressions as a listener at the Verdurin concert in such a way as to recall Swann at the Sainte-Euverte soiree, he also portrays himself as being much more persistently concerned than Swann with several questions regarding Vinteuil. In particular, the narrator is fascinated by everything that has to do with the transmission or the dissemination of Vinteuil's works. His obsessive interest extends not only to the particular network of homosexual relations that permits the transformation of these works from indecipherable manuscripts into acclaimed performances, but also to broader problems of identity and historicity: he repeatedly asks what it is that sets Vinteuil's works apart from those of all other composers, what constitutes the unique quality of Vinteuil's genius, and what circumstances might favor the future survival of his compositions. Strikingly, it is with a meditation on precisely such questions as these that Baudelaire ends his Wagner essay; and it is clear that for Baudelaire, as for Proust's narrator, the search for answers is bound up with his own future as both a listener and a writer. But Baudelaire, whose manner becomes increasingly condensed and abrupt as his essay nears its conclusion, does not explore his final questions as patiently or as thoroughly as he might, so that it is helpful to follow an analysis of part 4 with some reflections on Proust's *Recherche*.

After declaring at the end of part 3 that he is "constrained to tighten the limits of the study" (¶46), Baudelaire plunges into the last and shortest section of *Richard Wagner* as follows:

> One can always set momentarily aside [faire abstraction de] the systematic part that every great, self-willed artist unavoidably introduces into

all his works; it remains, in that case, to search out and verify by what personal quality of his own he distinguishes himself from others. An artist, a man truly worthy of that great name, must possess something essentially *sui generis*, by virtue of which he is *himself* and not another. From this point of view, artists can be compared to varied flavors, and the repertoire of human metaphors is perhaps not vast enough to furnish the approximate definition of all known artists and of all *possible* artists. (¶47)

Baudelaire proposes in this manner to lead his readers through the concluding stage of the project announced in the first sentence of his essay. The *I*, which he earlier claimed to be the only adequate guide during a search for the temporal and conceptual "beginning" of the Wagner question, now approaches its final task: it must find a way to formulate, in writing, the unique "something" by virtue of which Wagner "is *himself* and not another." To effect this encounter between *I* and *himself* [*je* and *lui*], Baudelaire claims to need two separate strategies or procedures. He intends first to remove from view everything that methodically connects Wagner with other composers, everything learned, borrowed, or imitated from other artists. Secondly, Baudelaire aims to arrive at an "approximate definition" of whatever it is that remains once Wagner has been isolated from these outside methods and influences. If Baudelaire pursues the latter goal with some trepidation, this is apparently because he is not sure it can ever be wholly accomplished; the only way to "define" the individuality (the nonanalyzable "flavor") of an artist, he maintains, is not with explicit statements, but rather with metaphors whose powers of evocation may well prove too limited and imprecise for the present task. In his capacity as critical guide accompanying readers toward the specificity of Wagner's genius, therefore, Baudelaire finds himself in an awkward cleft: he wants on the one hand to block or erase all paths leading outward from Wagner's compositions to the systems or methods of other artists; but he wants on the other hand to discover and widen any paths leading inward to the domain of Wagner's works by way of metaphor. What Baudelaire fails to ask is whether these two kinds of paths are in fact distinct and separable, whether those leading outward can be made abstract enough to disregard ("faire abstraction") and whether those leading inward can be rendered concrete enough to follow meaningfully.

Baudelaire at first makes this distinction seem completely unproblematic. He asserts that Wagner is neatly divisible into "two men . . . , the man of order and the passionate man," and that it is solely "the passionate man, the man of feeling who is in question here" (¶47). While "the man of order" in Wagner methodically adapts or assimilates ideas from elsewhere, "the man of sentiment" stands alone and apart. Baudelaire next claims, however, that the originality of this second Wagner consists not in any substantive or qualitative difference of emotion that separates him from other composers, but in the sheer, unquantifiable excess of passion that he "inscribes so ardently" in his works:

> [I]n the voluptuous and orgiastic part of the overture to *Tannhäuser,* the artist had put as much force, developed as much energy as in the painting of mysticity that characterizes the overture to *Lohengrin.* The same ambition in the one as in the other, the same titanic climb and also the same refinements and the same subtlety. What thus seems to me above all to mark the music of this master in an unforgettable way is its nervous intensity, its violence of passion and of willpower. That music expresses with the most suave or the most strident voice all that is most hidden in the human heart. (¶47)

Initially, then, it would seem that Baudelaire wants to define Wagner's genius by means of a now familiar metaphor that personifies his music in comparison with that of other composers. If other music "voices" human passions, then Wagner's does so hyperbolically; it speaks with excessive intensity, and it chooses only those passions that have been most deeply hidden. But Baudelaire in fact extends this metaphoric path further, or else climbs higher along it. Starting from the sentiment Wagner "inscribes so ardently" and passing through his "titanic climb," Baudelaire arrives a page later at a point where the "voice" of Wagner's music issues in letters of fire from the surreal mouth of a volcano: "I love those excesses of health, those overflowings of willpower that inscribe themselves in works like fiery bitumen in the soil of a volcano" (¶47). Rather evocatively anticipating the vapor-spewing crevices and fire-encircled rocks of *Der Ring des Nibelungen* at Bayreuth, Baudelaire ascribes to Wagnerian art the over-whelming grandeur of a volcano. Baudelaire's final metaphor for Wagner's genius is thus a mountainous landmark that is completely unmistakable, but that can only be viewed from a great distance. This landmark bears a suggestive resemblance to the inspiring "height" from which Baudelaire intends, earlier in his essay, to survey the musical "paths" of Wagnerian opera; but the volcano of part 4, surrounded by flowing paths of hot metal, apparently cannot even be approached, much less climbed. The volcano metaphor implies, therefore, that the passionate excess of Wagner's art not only distinguishes it from the work of other artists, but also protects it against the incursions of critical writing. If Wagner is a volcano in eruption, then any closer approach to it is presumably blocked; Baudelaire suggests with this metaphor that, just as he feared, the "repertory of human meta-phors" will not give his writing access to the isolated region of Wagner's music. Consequently, part 4 reintroduces the threatening possibility first presented at the opening of part 1, the possibility that Baudelaire's inten-tion to "climb back . . . to the beginning of the question" (¶1), to clamber from his own essay to Wagner's music along a path of rhetorical strategies, is doomed to failure.

As if to ward off this recurrent possibility, however, Baudelaire tries to contend that the Wagnerian volcano is not entirely unapproachable. Just before he proposes the volcano metaphor, Baudelaire writes: "Everything implied by the words: *willpower, desire, concentration, nervous intensity, explo-sion,* is felt and guessed in his works. I do not believe I am deluding myself or deceiving anyone by asserting that I see there the principal characteris-tics of the phenomenon that we call *genius;* or at least, that in the analysis of all that we have until now legitimately called *genius,* one rediscovers the aforementioned characteristics" (¶47). Having declared a page earlier that the uniqueness of Wagner's genius—its "something essentially *sui generis*"—lay in its excess of emotional intensity, Baudelaire now declares that such excess characterizes all artistic genius in general. He betrays a certain veiled awareness of this contradiction in the contrast between, on the one hand, the emphasis he gives to both "*génie*" and "*sui generis*" as well as to his enumeration of their various attributes and, on the other hand, the apologetic tone he adopts at the same time ("I do not believe I am deluding myself . . ."). But Baudelaire nonetheless allows this contradiction to encroach upon the image of the volcano, weakening its impact and lessening its singularity. The full sentence that introduces the volcano metaphor reads as follows: "I love those excesses of health, those overflowings of willpower that inscribe themselves in works like fiery bitumen in the soil of a volcano, and that, in ordinary life, often mark the phase, full of delight, following after a great moral or physical crisis" (¶47). The explosive excess of Wagner's music is thus analogous to one of the normal and expected upheavals of everyday life or to what Baudelaire calls in his next paragraph the "familiar course of all human affairs" (¶48). Rather than distinguishing Wagner from other artists of genius, the excessive passion of his music brings him closer to them; it involves him in something much like the normal pattern of creation and crisis that Baudelaire attributes in part 2 to all great artists. Even further, the volcano metaphor now threatens to remove Wagner altogether from the realm of art by placing his work on a level with the upsets and recoveries of "ordinary life." Neither the excessive character of Wagner's genius nor Baudelaire's attempt to figure that excess suffices to set Wagner apart, to establish his absolute uniqueness: excess, which Baudelaire takes to be the "quality of his own" that isolates Wagner's music, seems instead to be the most available means of access to it.

But this brings Baudelaire and his readers to an impasse. Although eager to demonstrate Wagner's unapproachable individuality, Baudelaire finds no way to write about it that does not somehow emphasize its affinity either with all artistic genius or with the nonartistic and the commonplace. Like the molten paths that engrave themselves on a volcano's sides only by flowing outward from it, Baudelaire's metaphor leads his readers as much toward other domains as toward Wagner's. In other words, Baudelaire's metaphoric writing veers away from Wagner's specific genius as surely as would a methodical analysis of "the systematic part" of his works; despite his announced intention, Baudelaire is unable to keep these two kinds of discourse entirely apart.[14] This failure becomes even more evident when he tries to reaffirm their separation by means of a historical comparison. Wagner's specificity, claims Baudelaire, is not only qualitative, but also temporal: "An ideal ambition presides, it is true, over all his compositions;

but if, by the choice of his subjects and his dramatic method, Wagner draws close to antiquity, by the passionate energy of his expression he is at the moment the truest representative of modern nature. And all the skillful knowledge [science], all the efforts, all the combinations of this rich mind are only, truth to tell, the very humble and very zealous servants of this irresistible passion" (¶47). In terms that bring to mind his discussion of Constantin Guys in *Le Peintre de la vie moderne,* Baudelaire proposes to define the excessive intensity of Wagner's art as an essential characteristic of modernity in general.[15] This of course reduces Wagner once more to the status of a type, an exemplary "representative" of all modern artists rather than an artist sui generis. In addition, this passage implies that however much Baudelaire may want to dissociate them for the sake of his argument, Wagner's borrowed, subservient "method" never actually parts company with his sharply individual "expression" and therefore cannot be arbitrarily discounted. That Baudelaire is unable to "set momentarily aside" Wagner's classical method becomes still more graphically clear in the following paragraph, where he reiterates that "Wagner . . . had found in the past the first elements of *the base on which to establish his ideal*" (¶48). While these italics add little to the eloquence of the passage surrounding them and seem intended mainly to signal that this phrase is freely quoted a second time from Wagner's *Lettre sur la musique* (see ¶22), they also serve immediately to recall the visual emphasis laid a little earlier on the typical signs of Wagner's modernity: "*volonté, désir, concentration, intensité nerveuse, explosion.*" As if to arrest the radically individual and uniquely modern dynamism of Wagner's genius, the italics bind it firmly to an ideal methodically adopted from the past.[16]

Perhaps partly because of this failure to isolate and to define the quality that makes Wagner "*himself* and not another," the final two paragraphs of part 4 are uneasy in tone. Baudelaire devotes them to a brief meditation on the future reception of Wagner's works, but he does so cautiously and somewhat hesitantly. Citing Gluck, Hugo, and Delacroix as examples, he ventures the obvious remark that "we have seen many things formerly declared absurd, that have later become models adopted by the crowd" (¶48); and he concludes that even if Wagner is currently ill received in France, circumstances are more than likely to change. But Baudelaire is unwilling to go very far beyond this conventional observation: he insists at first, mildly, that "it is impossible to prophesy anything precise" (¶48) and later, more vehemently, that "the success or failure of *Tannhäuser* can prove absolutely nothing, nor even determine any number whatever of favorable or unfavorable chances in the future" (¶49). Baudelaire thus concludes his essay with an allusion to chance that is considerably bleaker than the one at its beginning. Part 1 of *Richard Wagner* opened with the hopeful assertion that its writer, while not an "expert in probability," nonetheless had "some chance" of overcoming the distance between his writing and the "question" of Wagner's music—some chance of effecting an encounter between an *I* [*je*] who unites his own discourse with that of his readers and a *him* [*lui*] who represents Wagner's musical genius. Here at the end of part 4, the same writer is reluctant even to speculate about the nature of future encounters between Wagner's works and either the comments of "the crowd" or the critiques of "men of letters" (¶48). Although by no means willing to declare such encounters impossible, Baudelaire tacitly concedes that his own gamble on the possibility of travel between music and letters has not entirely paid off. His parting attempt to locate the specificity of Wagner's genius is less than a success, just as the other paths of writing he has followed have not led as far as hoped toward Wagner's music. Baudelaire has kept this music figuratively in view throughout his essay, but he has not literally approached it.

THE REMAINING GAP

It is particularly interesting to read Proust's *Recherche* together with part 4 of *Richard Wagner*, because Proust is one of the future "men of letters" about whose encounter with Wagner's music Baudelaire felt unable to "prophesy anything precise." Despite his reticence, however, Baudelaire was a surprisingly exact foreseer, not so much of Proust's views on Wagner as of his more general attempts to enter into the territory of modern music. Proust extends his meditation on the recognition and definition of musical genius over the course of several interrelated episodes scattered among various sections of the novel; his narrator returns at intervals to the problem of what makes Vinteuil's art not only individual and unique, but also historically "durable" (3:758). Throughout a certain ensemble of passages from the *Recherche,* therefore, Proust gradually elaborates the questions raised somewhat elliptically at the end of Baudelaire's essay, transporting them at the same time into the domain of fictional narrative. But even though Proust's narrator appears on at least one occasion to have partially resolved the difficulty that defeated Baudelaire—that is, the difficulty of locating the precise difference that sets each great artist apart— the narrator himself denounces this success as an illusion. Like Baudelaire, Proust arrives at an impasse from which neither the present, enigmatic uniqueness nor the future, uncertain reception of Vinteuil's music can be closely studied.

Already in "Combray," before any of Vinteuil's compositions have ever been heard, Proust makes it clear that the paths of access to the isolated realm of his music are also paths of emotional excess. For the young protagonist, Vinteuil's music has little intrinsic character and no aesthetic value apart from the excessive behavior associated with it. Left unperformed during the composer's lifetime because of his excessive modesty and untranscribed at his death because of the excessive shame inflicted on him by his daughter, Vinteuil's works appear to his neighbors less as the artistic expression than as the crude, unmediated product of extreme passion: they seem only to be the "poor little pieces of an old piano teacher . . . [that] had hardly any value in themselves, but that we did not scorn because they had so much for him, [since] they had been his reason for living before he sacrificed them to his daughter" (1:158). As long as Vinteuil's compositions present themselves as rudimentary signifiers of extremity or excess with no independent worth or identity, they cannot be experienced directly, as music. The protagonist's nearest possible approach to them involves a literal climb onto the hill behind Montjouvain, a lookout point from which he can gaze down onto the scene of Vinteuil's drawing room. The first time he does this (1:111), the hero sees only the pathetically exaggerated sense of decorum that prevents Vinteuil from playing one of his own compositions for his visitors. The hero's second view into Montjouvain some years later is more revealing: he witnesses a sadistic scene during which Mlle Vinteuil and her lesbian friend profane a picture of the composer, a scene of such excessive cruelty that it should have been viewed "by the footlights of the boulevard theaters rather than under the lamp of a country house" (1:161). This staging of sadistic excess, according to the narrator, transports "the aesthetic of melodrama" into the Vinteuil home: just when the composer's music would seem to be most completely forgotten and inaccessible, it reenters the scene in a disguised and exaggerated form, like the music used to heighten emotion and emphasize moments of crisis during the performance of melodramas.[17]

Even while he associates it with scenes of excess, however, Proust's narrator shows that Vinteuil's music is at the same time indissociable from the everyday or the commonplace. The protagonist's first view into Montjouvain is possible only because of the ordinary customs of social life in Combray; having accompanied his parents on a polite visit, he is allowed to remain outside rather than sit through the conversation indoors. The second Montjouvain scene arises from a less stereotypical occasion, but it is still bound up with everyday routines. The narrator describes it immediately after recalling the frustration of his solitary walks in the surrounding countryside, a frustration that results from his inability to encounter en route a woman passerby [passante] who, appearing as a "necessary and natural product of this soil," would have made visible to him "the individual life of the place" or "the profound flavor of the country" (1:155). In the perpetual absence of such a "passante," the whole region around Montjouvain loses its identifiable uniqueness; like the images on a backdrop when seen from close by, the woods and paths take on the banal, reproducible aspect of "trees painted on the canvas of a panorama" (1:156). As though trying to recover his view of the individuality of the landscape, the narrator turns at this moment to the story of his second climb to the observation post behind Vinteuil's house. Reflecting on what he saw from there, the narrator stresses both its practiced, repeatable quality and its unremarkable setting: the atrocity of the scene belongs to everyday life at Montjouvain (the sadistic "ritual profanations" give "a foundation in life to the aesthetic of melodrama" [1:161]). As in Baudelaire's text on Wagner, it is precisely the intensity associated with Vinteuil's music, its distinctive affinity with excess, that tends to submerge it among the common rituals of daily living; whether politely hidden during social calls or savagely profaned during love scenes, Vinteuil's compositions are strangely difficult to distinguish from their habitual surroundings.

Later in the *Recherche,* once he has become familiar with Vinteuil's sonata and wants to establish its uniqueness, the narrator tries to deny the connections between this music and the routines, however excessive, of ordinary life. His effort to set Vinteuil apart first becomes explicit in *La Prisonnière,* during the passage devoted to his interval of waiting between Françoise's departure for the Trocadéro and her return with Albertine. To while away the time, the narrator begins to play through Vinteuil's sonata; and despite his constant preoccupation with the relations between Albertine and Mlle Vinteuil, he claims that the music reminds him not of his experiences at Montjouvain, but rather of his walks in the region of Guermantes. He recalls that during those walks, he had despaired of ever discovering a sufficiently extraordinary subject for the works of literature he hoped to write (1:170), and he now wonders whether Vinteuil possessed the radical originality that he himself lacks:

> Every great artist seems, in fact, so different from the others, and gives us so strongly that sensation of individuality that we seek in vain in everyday existence! At the moment when I thought that, a measure from the Sonata struck me, a measure that I nonetheless knew well. . . . In playing that measure, and even though Vinteuil was in the midst of expressing there a dream that would have remained altogether foreign to Wagner, I could not stop myself from murmuring: "*Tristan,*" with the smile worn by the friend of a family rediscovering something of the grandfather in an intonation, a gesture of the grandson who never knew him. (3:664)

At the exact instant that he declares Vinteuil's sonata to be entirely unique, the hero finds himself abruptly forced to recognize its resemblance to Wagner's *Tristan und Isolde.*[18] He may succeed temporarily in isolating Vinteuil's sonata from "everyday existence"; but like Baudelaire, who contradictorily attempts to define Wagner's individuality while identifying it with artistic genius in general, Proust's hero is unable to assert the specificity of Vinteuil's genius without simultaneously likening him to another artist. This likeness, admits the protagonist, is distant; but it is nonetheless striking enough to lead part of his attention away from Vinteuil and toward Wagner.

After recounting his discovery of their likeness, Proust's narrator begins to meditate on the exact nature of Vinteuil's resemblance to Wagner. It might be roughly defined, he decides, as a compositional method common to them both, a recognizable manner of achieving the complex interconnection of parts throughout their work. The narrator heavily stresses the notion that this interconnection occurs at once within and between the different creations of each composer: he dwells, among other examples, on both the motivic relations within a single act of *Tristan und Isolde* and the more extensive but less deliberately intended relations between various Wagner operas.[19] On another occasion near the end of *La Prisonnière,* the narrator resumes and prolongs this same discussion, reemphasizing that while the interrelated parts of any particular artist's oeuvre form a "unique world," the technique of creating such interrelations is common to all great artists and furnishes "the most authentic proof of genius" in general (3:877). During both these meditations, however, the narrator betrays a certain uneasiness in the inescapable presence of all these large- and small-scale interconnections. Despite the reassuringly specific identity they seem to confer, the narrator hints that they pervade the art of Wagner and Vinteuil almost to excess; he refers to "the monotony of Vinteuil's works" (3:877) as well as to "the reprise less of a motif than of a neuralgic attack" in *Tristan* (3:665).[20] To illustrate further this threat of excessive uniformity or of painful insistence, the narrator evokes a passage from the third act of *Tristan,* in which Wagner introduces a new motif and skillfully combines it with those already present. Even if this compositional virtuosity does not arise from mechanical "systematizations" or from "the artificial development of a thesis," it still disturbs the narrator: "But then, as much as by the identity I had noticed a moment ago between Vinteuil's phrase and Wagner's, I was troubled by this vulcanian skill [or cleverness: habileté]. Could that be what gave to great artists the illusion of a fundamental, irreducible originality, in appearance the reflection of a more than human reality, in fact the product of industrious labor?" (3:667). As with the volcanic energy that Baudelaire attributes to Wagner, this "vulcanian skill" paradoxically isolates each composer and at the same time connects him with all other great artists. Wagner's apparently superhuman facility in the construction of motivic pathways seems to make him as unique and as unapproachable as a volcano surrounded by rivers of "fiery bitumen" (¶47); yet this outpouring of genius is also what brings him into intimate contact with Vinteuil. The narrator's misgivings, therefore, mark the difficulty involved both in gaining access to Vinteuil's genius and in defining what makes it sui generis.

The narrator returns to the "monotony" (3:767) of Vinteuil's works during his long account of the septet performed at the Verdurin concert (3:749–70). This time, however, he is explicitly determined to convince himself and his readers of the absolute uniqueness of Vinteuil's music. Although he now acknowledges that appearances are against him in this matter, he argues that they are deceptive: "Those phrases [in Vinteuil's works], musicographers could perfectly well discover their alliances [apparentement], their genealogy, in the works of other great musicians, but only for reasons of minor importance, exterior resemblances, analogies ingeniously found by reasoning rather than felt by direct impression. The one [i.e., the impression] given by Vinteuil's phrases was different from any other, as if, despite the conclusions that seem to be drawn from science, the individual existed" (3:760). It is undoubtedly possible, claims the narrator, to force a passage between works by Vinteuil and works by other composers, but only by dint of laborious circumlocution; the ingenious methods of "musicographers" cannot seriously infringe upon the individuality of Vinteuil's genius. The phrases of his music lead by smooth, natural routes toward a remote, "unsuspected universe" (3:759) or an "unknown homeland" (3:761), a region that belongs solely to Vinteuil; any other paths connected with his music are artificial, secondary, stopgap constructions.[21] Like Baudelaire, but with a subtler touch, Proust's narrator tries further to accentuate Vinteuil's originality in historical terms:

> For together with more profound gifts, Vinteuil joined that . . . of using colors not only so stable but so personal as well that, no more than time spoils their freshness, students who imitate their discoverer, and even masters who surpass him, do not make their originality pale. . . . Each timbre was underlined by a color that all the rules in the world, learned by the most knowledgeable musicians, could not imitate, so that Vinteuil,

although a man of his time and settled into his rank in musical evolution, would always leave it and rise to the head as soon as anyone played one of his productions, which would owe its appearance of having blossomed after those of more recent musicians to this character, apparently contradictory and in fact deceptive, of durable novelty. (3:758)

As before, the narrator concedes that Vinteuil's music cannot remain completely isolated, that it cannot totally avoid absorption into the systems of imitators and into the ordered structures of "musical evolution." Whereas Baudelaire in part 4 insists on trying to separate Wagner's entanglements with history from his radically original modernity, the narrator freely admits that the two are intertwined in the case of Vinteuil. But he then proceeds to suggest that in spite—or perhaps because—of its involvement with history, its unresisting availability for absorption and imitation, Vinteuil's music retains a kind of temporal mobility that protects its uniqueness after all. It is paradoxically able, claims the narrator, both to let the music of later masters surpass it and to reassert its insurmountable originality each time it is performed. Consequently, even though it allows "musicographers" to map out its place in music history, Vinteuil's music also continues to travel—whenever it is played—along a path of "durable novelty" that prevents it from becoming trapped within a permanent configuration of masterpieces.

Proust's narrator thus seems to have found a way past part of Baudelaire's difficulty: he believes it is possible somehow to locate Vinteuil's specific genius without tackling the hopeless task of isolating him from all other composers, past or future. But as is suggested by the slightly awkward mixture of metaphors in the passage quoted above ("colors" repeatedly "blossoming" at "the head" of music's evolution), there remains the problem of fashioning a language that will adequately represent the specificity of Vinteuil's art. Just as Baudelaire is somewhat dubious about his search for a metaphor capable of evoking Wagner's "quality of his own," the narrator is openly skeptical of his own writing about Vinteuil; he claims in the course of the septet episode that complete access to music in general is no longer possible, since "humanity has set off down other roads, those of spoken and written language" (3:763), and that Vinteuil's music in particular cannot be fully translated "into human language" (3:760).

In several ways, however, the narrator confronts this problem most revealingly not during his septet meditation, but rather during a scene from earlier in the *Recherche*. Near the beginning of *À l'ombre des jeunes filles en fleurs*, he describes his first hearing of Vinteuil's sonata (1:520–25); the scene occurs in the Swann drawing room, where Odette plays part of the sonata on the piano. Once she has finished, Swann embarks on a lengthy, metaphorical evocation of the music:

> [T]here is in it the whole static side of moonlight, which is the essential side . . . since moonlight can prevent the leaves from stirring. That's what is so well painted in this little phrase, the Bois de Boulogne fallen into catalepsy. At the seaside it's even more striking, because there are the faint responses of the waves that one hears very well, naturally, since nothing else can move. In Paris it's the contrary; at most one notices those strange glimmers on the monuments, that sky lit as if by a fire with no colors and no danger, that kind of immense, guessed-at news item. But in Vinteuil's little phrase, and moreover in the whole Sonata, that's not it; it [the scene] takes place in the Bois, in the gruppetto one distinctly hears the voice of someone who says: "One could almost read one's newspaper." (1:523–24)

In this passage, Swann's misinterpretation of the sonata seems evident. Not only does he overlook all the connotations of wandering mobility that have accompanied the "little phrase" since "Combray," but he also appears to mistake the kind of excess inherent in Vinteuil's genius: instead of passionate agitation or volatile intensity, he perceives only stillness exaggerated to the point of paralysis. Yet Swann's interpretive deafness is only partial; it distorts, but does not altogether miss, both the explosive heightening of feeling that the narrator earlier associated with melodrama and the active, expansive uniformity that he will later attribute to the "vulcanian skill" of composers such as Vinteuil and Wagner. Swann's "sky lit as if by a fire with no colors and no danger" might in fact serve as a distant, inverted variant of the Wagnerian volcano in Baudelaire's essay, rather as though Swann were witnessing the explosion of Vinteuil's music from so far away that he could see its violence vaguely figured in the sky, but not its concrete traces on the ground below. Swann would like, moreover, to remove himself even further from the music, since he insists that it does

not in fact evoke a sudden and bizarre "fire," but rather an ordinary evening in the park; instead of deciphering fiery trails inscribed on a volcano,
Swann listens to the sonata just as he might skim a "news item" in a journal by moonlight. Swann's metaphoric interpretation of the sonata thus
widens rather than narrows the gap between Vinteuil's music and figural
discourse about this music. When he distances and distorts the rhetoric
used by Proust's narrator in other discussions of Vinteuil, Swann unknow-
ingly retreats from the specificity of the composer's genius. And when he
reduces the volcanic intensity of the music to the status of a headline dimly
perceived in a newspaper, Swann only increases the gulf between his language and the music: by (mis)taking a musical meditation for a journalistic
event, he emphasizes that even a "long-meditated work of *circumstance*"[22]
is unlikely to overcome the separation between music and writing.

Following Swann's remarks about the sonata, the narrator confirms that
they involve distortion and misrepresentation, that they "might have been
able to distort, for later on, [his] comprehension of the sonata, music not
being exclusive enough to rule out absolutely what one suggests that we
should find in it" (1:524). But the narrator offers no "corrected" version of
his own; although he continues recounting his conversation with Swann
about the music, he merely returns to the triviality of Swann's impressions.
The "little phrase," concludes the narrator, recalls nothing more to Swann
than the simplest images from evenings long past spent with the Verdurin
coterie in various parks: "Instead of the profound meaning that he had so
often asked of it, what it [the little phrase] brought back to Swann were
those leafy branches arranged, entwined, painted around it (and which it
gave him the desire to see again because it seemed to him to be inside them
like a soul)" (1:524). Between the "little phrase" and Swann's nature metaphors there remains a gap like the unavoidable interval between the central,
"inside" staff of a thyrsus and the leafy vines "arranged, entwined, painted
around it." Much like Baudelaire in his summary of *Tannhäuser,* Proust's
narrator reports on Swann's commentary in a way that clearly suggests the
image of the thyrsus without naming or lingering over it; as if obeying,
in spite of himself, the silencing power Swann attributes to the moonlight,
he allows the harmonizing implications of the thyrsus—music sheltered
intimately within the encircling words, art interlaced with criticism—to

remain unsaid. Still without offering any solution of his own, therefore, the narrator stresses once again the separation between Vinteuil's music and the figural language Swann traces around it.

In this fashion, moreover, the narrator illustrates a general predicament he has formulated in the preceding paragraph, a dilemma that touches, first, on the problem of finding an immediate path between music and language and, second, on the problem of keeping this path open for future readers and listeners. Swann, whose attempted evocation of the sonata fails to overcome the former difficulty, is also unable to solve the latter one by guiding the narrator in his subsequent efforts to cross the gap between music and language. But even if the first problem could be solved, declares the narrator, the second would remain intractable and would always turn writing on music into a gamble: "[T]o be obliged, for a work of art, to add into the total [calculation] of its beauty the factor of time mixes into our judgment something just as chancy and thereby just as devoid of real interest as any prophecy, the nonrealization of which will in no way imply the prophet's mediocrity of mind, for that which calls possibilities into existence or excludes them from it is not necessarily within the competence of genius; one can have had some [genius] and yet not have believed in the future of railroads, nor of airplanes" (1:523).

Like Baudelaire in the final paragraphs of part 4, then, Proust's narrator is acutely aware of the risk inherent in any form of travel between musical works and critical writing, especially writing that is intended either to give or to remove future access to the music. But whereas the narrator flatly denies the "interest" of so uncertain an enterprise as foretelling either the future development of transportation or the future reception of artworks, Baudelaire remains passionately interested in it. With a gambler's mixture of bravado and uncertainty, he concludes his essay as follows:

> I heard it said recently that if Wagner obtained a dazzling success with his drama, it would be a purely individual accident, and that his method would have no subsequent influence at all on the destinies and the transformations of lyric drama. I believe myself authorized, by the study of the past, that is, of the eternal, to predict the absolute contrary, namely, that a complete failure does not in any manner destroy the possibility of new attempts in the same direction, and that in the very near future

one might well see not only new authors, but even previously recognized ones profiting in some measure from ideas put forth by Wagner, and passing happily through the breach opened by him. In what history did one ever read that great causes were lost in a single encounter? (¶49)

Whatever Baudelaire's luck as a prophet foreseeing Wagner's ultimate success in France, his skill in evoking his own situation as a writer on Wagner's music is considerable. The "breach" that appears at the culmination of the passage just quoted might represent Baudelaire's own perspective as well as that of other "authors"—poets, opera composers, or critics. In the light of what precedes it in *Richard Wagner et "Tannhäuser" à Paris*, this image of an open breach loses some of its quality as a cliché and serves as an emblem for the relation between Baudelaire's writing and Wagner's music. These two remain apart from each other at the end of the essay, despite Baudelaire's various rhetorical efforts—translation, personification, quotation, digression, metaphor—to bring them together. But their isolation is not so complete that it shuts off all hope of eventual contact; they are instead separated as if by a wall with a gap in it or by a mountain pass that is for the moment too steep to descend, but that affords a magnificent view. While Baudelaire admits that future attempts to move across the breach between music and writing will be a gamble as risky as his own, he denies that the odds are insurmountable. Perhaps more important, he raises the possibility that the view from the breach may be at least as beautiful as the passage through it, just as certain paintings are more "melodious" (2:425) when seen from too far away. If the literal distance between music and letters can be frustrating, the figurative distance between them can be proportionately rewarding. It is part of Baudelaire's individual genius that without departing from the domain of letters, he leads his readers to admire the faraway figures in Wagner's musical countryside: "[I]s it not more convenient, for certain minds, to judge the beauty of a landscape by placing themselves on a height than by traveling successively over all the paths that furrow it?" (¶31).

APPENDIX 1: *Richard Wagner et "Tannhäuser" à Paris*
by Charles Baudelaire

EDITORIAL NOTE: The following text was first published on April 1, 1861, in the *Revue européenne*. It was subsequently reprinted in three installments (April 14 and 21, May 5, 1861) in *La Presse théâtrale et musicale;* both these journals entitled it simply "Richard Wagner." At about the same time, the publisher Dentu reprinted the text, together with an added section called "Encore quelques mots," as a small independent volume. Bearing the title *Richard Wagner et "Tannhäuser" à Paris,* this volume was registered with the *Bibliographie de la France* on May 4, 1861. The text was not republished again during Baudelaire's lifetime, but it appeared posthumously in the collection of his essays entitled *L'Art romantique* (Paris: Michel Lévy Frères, 1868). The present edition of *Richard Wagner et "Tannhäuser" à Paris* takes the Dentu volume as its basis. I have silently corrected occasional typographical errors (*eu* instead of *en,* for instance), but I have not altered repeated or systematic particularities of spelling (Tannhaüser, poëme and poëte, Listz, rhythme, etc.) and of punctuation (especially hyphens, dashes, and ellipses); these give something of the original text's flavor without making it difficult to read. One footnote appeared in the original (in ¶31); I have indicated it and added others to point out the rare differences between the 1861 Dentu text and the 1868 version in *L'Art romantique.* Also added are paragraph numbers, in order to facilitate the frequent reference made to this edition in my preceding essay.

Richard Wagner et *Tannhäuser* à Paris

I

¶1 Remontons, s'il vous plaît, à treize mois en arrière, au commencement de la question, et qu'il me soit permis, dans cette appréciation, de parler souvent en mon nom personnel. Ce *Je,* accusé justement d'impertinence dans beaucoup de cas, implique cependant une grande modestie; il enferme l'écrivain dans les limites les plus strictes de la sincérité. En réduisant sa tâche, il la rend plus facile. Enfin, il n'est pas nécessaire d'être un probabiliste bien consommé pour acquérir la certitude que cette sincérité trouvera des amis parmi les lecteurs impartiaux; il y a évidemment quelques chances pour que le critique ingénu, en ne racontant que ses propres impressions, raconte aussi celles de quelques partisans inconnus.

¶2 Donc, il y a treize mois, ce fut une grande rumeur dans Paris. Un compositeur allemand, qui avait vécu longtemps chez nous, à notre insu, pauvre, inconnu, par de misérables besognes, mais que, depuis quinze ans déjà, le public allemand célébrait comme un homme de génie, revenait dans la ville, jadis témoin de ses jeunes misères, soumettre ses œuvres à notre jugement. Paris avait jusque-là peu entendu parler de Wagner; on savait vaguement qu'au-delà du Rhin s'agitait la question d'une réforme dans le drame lyrique, et que Listz avait adopté avec ardeur les opinions du réformateur. M. Fétis avait lancé contre lui une espèce de réquisitoire, et les personnes curieuses de feuilleter les numéros de la *Revue et Gazette musicale de Paris,* pourront vérifier une fois de plus que les écrivains qui se vantent de professer les opinions les plus sages, les plus classiques, ne se piquent guère de sagesse ni de mesure, ni même de vulgaire politesse, dans la critique des opinions qui leur sont contraires. Les articles de M. Fétis ne sont guère qu'une diatribe affligeante; mais l'exaspération du vieux dilettantiste servait seulement à prouver l'importance des œuvres qu'il vouait à l'anathème et au ridicule. D'ailleurs, depuis treize mois, pendant lesquels la curiosité publique ne s'est pas ralentie, Richard Wagner a essuyé bien d'autres injures. Il y a quelques années, au retour d'un voyage en Allemagne, Théophile Gautier, très-ému par une représentation de *Tannhaüser,* avait cependant, dans le *Moniteur,* traduit ses impressions avec cette certitude plastique qui donne un charme irrésistible à tous ses écrits. Mais ces documents divers, tombant à de lointains intervalles, avaient glissé sur l'esprit de la foule.

¶3 Aussitôt que les affiches annoncèrent que Richard Wagner ferait entendre dans la salle des Italiens des fragments de ses compositions, un fait amusant se produisit, que nous avons déjà vu, et qui prouve le besoin instinctif, précipité, des Français, de prendre sur toute chose leur parti avant d'avoir délibéré ou examiné. Les uns annoncèrent des merveilles, et les autres se mirent à dénigrer à outrance des œuvres qu'ils n'avaient pas encore entendues. Encore aujourd'hui dure cette situation bouffonne, et l'on peut dire que jamais sujet inconnu ne fut tant discuté. Bref, les concerts de Wagner s'annonçaient comme une véritable bataille de doctrines, comme une de ces solennelles crises de l'art, une de ces mêlées où critiques, artistes et public ont coutume de jeter confusément toutes leurs passions, crises heureuses qui dénotent la santé et la richesse dans la vie intellectuelle d'une nation, et que nous avions, pour ainsi dire, désapprises depuis les grands jours de Victor Hugo. J'emprunte les lignes suivantes au feuilleton de M. Berlioz (9 février 1860): «Le foyer du Théâtre-Italien était curieux à observer le soir du premier concert. C'étaient des fureurs, des cris, des discussions qui semblaient toujours sur le point de dégénérer en voies de fait.» Sans la présence du souverain, le même scandale aurait pu se produire, il y a quelques jours, à l'Opéra, surtout avec un public *plus vrai*. Je me souviens d'avoir vu, à la fin d'une des répétitions générales, un des critiques parisiens accrédités, planté prétentieusement devant le bureau du contrôle, faisant face à la foule au point d'en gêner l'issue, et s'exerçant à rire comme un maniaque, comme un de ces infortunés qui, dans les maisons de santé, sont appelés des *agités*. Ce pauvre homme, croyant son visage connu de toute la foule, avait l'air de dire: «Voyez comme je ris, moi, le célèbre S...! Ainsi ayez soin de conformer votre jugement au mien.» Dans le feuilleton auquel je faisais tout à l'heure allusion, M. Berlioz, qui montra cependant beaucoup moins de chaleur qu'on aurait pu en attendre de sa part, ajoutait: «Ce qui se débite alors de non-sens, d'absurdités et même de mensonges est vraiment prodigieux, et prouve avec évidence que, chez nous au moins, lorsqu'il s'agit d'apprécier une musique différente de celle qui court les rues, la passion, le parti pris prennent seuls la parole et empêchent le bon sens et le bon goût de parler.»

¶4 Wagner avait été audacieux: le programme de son concert ne comprenait ni solos d'instruments, ni chansons, ni aucune des exhibitions si chères à un public amoureux des virtuoses et de leurs tours de force. Rien que des morceaux d'ensemble, chœurs ou symphonies. La lutte fut violente, il est vrai; mais le public, étant abandonné à lui-même, prit feu à quelques-uns de ces irrésistibles morceaux dont la pensée était pour lui plus nettement exprimée, et la musique de Wagner triompha par sa propre force. L'ouverture de *Tannhaüser,* la marche pompeuse du deuxième acte, l'ouverture de *Lohengrin* particulièrement, la *musique de noces* et l'*épithalame* furent magnifiquement acclamés. Beaucoup de choses restaient obscures sans doute, mais les esprits impartiaux se disaient: «Puisque ces compositions sont faites pour la scène, il faut attendre; les choses non suffisamment définies seront expliquées par la plastique.» En attendant, il restait avéré que, comme symphoniste, comme artiste traduisant par les milles combinaisons du son les tumultes de l'âme humaine, Richard Wagner était à la hauteur de ce qu'il y a de plus élevé, aussi grand, certes, que les plus grands.

¶5 J'ai souvent entendu dire que la musique ne pouvait pas se vanter de traduire quoi que ce soit avec certitude, comme fait la parole ou la peinture. Cela est vrai dans une certaine proportion, mais n'est pas tout à fait vrai. Elle traduit à sa manière, et par les moyens qui lui sont propres. Dans la musique, comme dans la peinture et même dans la parole écrite, qui est cependant le plus positif des arts, il y a toujours une lacune complétée par l'imagination de l'auditeur.

¶6 Ce sont dans doute ces considérations qui ont poussé Wagner à considérer l'art dramatique, c'est-à-dire la réunion, la *coïncidence* de plusieurs arts, comme l'art par excellence, le plus synthétique et le plus parfait. Or, si nous écartons un instant le secours de la plastique, du décor, de l'incorporation des types rêvés dans des comédiens vivants et même de la parole chantée, il reste encore incontestable que plus la musique est éloquente, plus la suggestion est rapide et juste, et plus il y a de chances pour que les hommes sensibles conçoivent des idées en rapport avec celles qui inspiraient l'artiste. Je prends tout de suite un exemple, la fameuse ouverture de *Lohengrin,* dont M. Berlioz a écrit un magnifique éloge en style technique; mais je veux me contenter ici d'en vérifier la valeur par les suggestions qu'elle procure.

¶7 Je lis dans le programme distribué à cette époque au Théâtre-Italien: «Dès les premières mesures, l'âme du pieux solitaire qui attend le vase sacré *plonge dans les espaces infinis.* Il voit se former peu à peu une apparition étrange qui prend un corps, une figure. Cette apparition se précise davantage, et *la troupe miraculeuse des anges,* portant au milieu d'eux la coupe sacrée, passe devant lui. Le saint cortége approche; le cœur de l'élu de Dieu s'exalte peu à peu; il s'élargit, il se dilate; d'ineffables aspirations s'éveillent en lui; *il cède à une béatitude croissante,* en se trouvant toujours rapproché de *la lumineuse apparition,* et quand enfin le Saint-Graal lui-même apparaît au milieu du cortége sacré, *il s'abîme dans une adoration extatique, comme si le monde entier eût soudainement disparu.*

¶8 «Cependant le Saint-Graal répand ses bénédictions sur le saint en prière et le consacre son chevalier. Puis *les flammes brûlantes adoucissent progressivement leur éclat;* dans sa sainte allégresse, la troupe des anges, souriant à la terre qu'elle abandonne, regagne les célestes hauteurs. Elle a laissé le Saint-Graal à la garde des hommes purs, *dans le cœur desquels la divine liqueur s'est répandue,* et l'auguste troupe s'évanouit *dans les profondeurs de l'espace,* de la même manière qu'elle en était sortie.»

¶9 Le lecteur comprendra tout à l'heure pourquoi je souligne ces passages. Je prends maintenant le livre de Listz, et je l'ouvre à la page où l'imagination de l'illustre pianiste (qui est un artiste et un philosophe) traduit à sa manière le même morceau:

¶10 «Cette introduction renferme et révèle *l'élément mystique,* toujours présent et toujours caché dans la pièce... Pour apprendre l'inénarrable puissance de ce secret, Wagner nous montre d'abord *la beauté ineffable du sanctuaire,* habité par un Dieu qui venge les opprimés, et ne demande qu'*amour et foi* à ses fidèles. Il nous initie au Saint-Graal; il fait miroiter à nos yeux le temple de bois incorruptible, aux murs odorants, aux portes d'*or,* aux solives d'*asbeste,* aux colonnes d'*opale,* aux parois de *cymophane,* dont les splendides portiques ne sont approchés que de ceux qui ont le cœur élevé et les mains pures. Il ne nous le fait point apercevoir dans son imposante et réelle structure, mais, comme ménageant nos faibles sens, il nous le montre d'abord reflété dans *quelque onde azurée,* ou reproduit *par quelque nuage irisé.*

¶11 «C'est au commencement une *large nappe dormante* de mélodie, *un éther vaporeux qui s'étend,* pour que le tableau sacré s'y dessine à nos yeux profanes; effet exclusivement confié aux violons, divisés en huit pupitres différents, qui, après plusieurs mesures de sons harmoniques, continuent dans les plus hautes notes de leurs registres. Le motif est ensuite repris par les instruments à vent les plus doux; les cors et les bassons, en s'y joignant, préparent l'entrée des trompettes et des trombones, qui répètent la mélodie pour la quatrième fois, *avec un éclat éblouissant de coloris,* comme si dans cet instant unique l'édifice saint *avait brillé* devant *nos regards aveuglés, dans toute sa magnificence lumineuse et radiante.* Mais *le vif étincellement,* amené par degrés à *cette intensité de rayonnement solaire,* s'éteint avec rapidité, comme une *lueur céleste.* La *transparente vapeur* des nuées se referme, la vision disparaît peu à peu dans le même encens *diapré* au milieu duquel elle est apparue, et le morceau se termine par les premières six mesures, devenues *plus éthérées encore.* Son caractère d'*idéale mysticité* est surtout rendu sensible par le *pianissimo* toujours conservé dans l'orchestre, et qu'interrompt à peine le court moment où les *cuivres* font *resplendir* les merveilleuses lignes du seul motif de cette introduction. Telle est l'image qui, à l'audition de ce sublime *adagio,* se présente d'abord à nos sens émus.»

¶12 M'est-il permis à moi-même de raconter, de traduire avec des paroles la traduction inévitable que mon imagination fit du même morceau,[1] lorsque je l'entendis pour la première fois, les yeux fermés, et que je me sentis pour ainsi dire enlevé de terre? Je n'oserais certes pas parler avec complaisance de mes *rêveries,* s'il n'était pas utile de les joindre ici aux *rêveries* précédentes. Le lecteur sait quel but nous poursuivons: démontrer que la véritable musique suggère des idées analogues dans des cerveaux différents. D'ailleurs, il ne serait pas ridicule ici de raisonner *à priori,* sans analyse et sans comparaisons; car ce qui serait vraiment surprenant, c'est que le son *ne pût pas* suggérer la couleur, que les couleurs *ne pussent pas* donner l'idée d'une mélodie, et que le son et la couleur fussent impropres à traduire des idées; les choses s'étant toujours exprimées par une analogie réciproque, depuis le jour où Dieu a proféré le monde comme une complexe et indivisible totalité.

> La nature est un temple où de vivants piliers
> Laissent parfois sortir de confuses paroles;
> L'homme y passe à travers des forêts de symboles
> Qui l'observent avec des regards familiers.

> Comme de longs échos qui de loin se confondent,

Dans une ténébreuse et profonde unité,
Vaste comme la nuit et comme la clarté,
Les parfums, les couleurs et les sons se répondent.

¶13 Je poursuis donc. Je me souviens que, dès les premières mesures, je subis une de ces impressions heureuses que presque tous les hommes imaginatifs ont connues, par le rêve, dans le sommeil. Je me sentis délivré *des liens de la pesanteur,* et je retrouvai par le souvenir l'extraordinaire *volupté* qui circule dans *les lieux hauts* (notons en passant que je ne connaissais pas le programme cité tout à l'heure). Ensuite je me peignis involontairement l'état délicieux d'un homme en proie à une grande rêverie dans une solitude absolue, mais une solitude avec *un immense hori-zon* et une *large lumière diffuse; l'immensité* sans autre décor qu'elle-même. Bientôt j'éprouvai la sensation d'une *clarté* plus vive, *d'une intensité de lumière* croissant avec une telle rapidité, que les nuances fournies par le dictionnaire ne suffiraient pas à exprimer *ce surcroît toujours renaissant d'ardeur et de blancheur.* Alors je conçus pleine-ment l'idée d'une âme se mouvant dans un milieu lumineux, d'une extase *faite de volupté et de connaissance,* et planant au-dessus et bien loin du monde naturel.

¶14 De ces trois traductions, vous pourriez noter facilement les différences. Wagner indique *une troupe d'anges qui apporte un vase sacré;*[2] Listz voit *un monument miraculeusement beau,* qui se reflète dans un mirage vaporeux. Ma rêverie est beau-coup moins illustrée d'objets matériels: elle est plus vague et plus abstraite. Mais l'important est ici de s'attacher aux ressemblances. Peu nombreuses, elles consti-tueraient encore une preuve suffisante; mais, par bonheur, elles sont nombreuses et saisissantes jusqu'au superflu. Dans les trois traductions nous trouvons la sensa-tion de la *béatitude spirituelle et physique;* de *l'isolement;* de la contemplation de *quelque chose infiniment grand et infiniment beau;* d'*une lumière intense* qui réjouit *les yeux et l'âme jusqu'à la pamoison;* et enfin la sensation de *l'espace étendu jusqu'aux dernières limites concevables.*

¶15 Aucun musicien n'excelle, comme Wagner, à *peindre* l'espace et la pro-fondeur, matériels et spirituels. C'est une remarque que plusieurs esprits, et des meilleurs, n'ont pu s'empêcher de faire en plusieurs occasions. Il possède l'art de traduire, par des gradations subtiles, tout ce qu'il y a d'excessif, d'immense, d'ambitieux, dans l'homme spirituel et naturel. Il semble parfois, en écoutant cette musique ardente et despotique, qu'on retrouve peintes sur le fond des ténèbres, déchiré par la rêverie, les vertigineuses conceptions de l'opium.

¶16 A partir de ce moment, c'est-à-dire du premier concert, je fus possédé du désir d'entrer plus avant dans l'intelligence de ces œuvres singulières. J'avais subi (du moins cela m'apparaissait ainsi) une opération spirituelle, une révélation. Ma volupté avait été si forte et si terrible, que je ne pouvais m'empêcher d'y vouloir retourner sans cesse. Dans ce que j'avais éprouvé, il entrait sans doute beaucoup de ce que Weber et Beethoven m'avaient déjà fait connaître, mais aussi quelque chose de nouveau que j'étais impuissant à définir, et cette impuissance me causait une colère et une curiosité mêlées d'un bizarre délice. Pendant plusieurs jours, pendant longtemps, je me dis: «Où pourrai-je bien entendre ce soir de la musique de Wagner?» Ceux de mes amis qui possédaient un piano furent plus d'une fois mes martyrs. Bientôt, comme il en est de toute nouveauté, des morceaux symphoniques de Wagner retentirent dans les casinos ouverts tous les soirs à une foule amoureuse de voluptés triviales. La majesté fulgurante de cette musique tombait là comme le tonnerre dans un mauvais lieu. Le bruit s'en répandit vite, et nous eûmes souvent le spectacle comique d'hommes graves et délicats subissant le contact des cohues malsaines, pour jouir, en attendant mieux, de la marche solennelle des *Invités au Wartburg* ou des majestueuses noces de *Lohengrin*.

¶17 Cependant, des répétitions fréquentes des mêmes phrases mélodiques, dans des morceaux tirés du même opéra, impliquaient des intentions mystérieuses et une méthode qui m'étaient inconnues. Je résolus de m'informer du pourquoi, et de transformer ma volupté en connaissance avant qu'une représentation scénique vînt me fournir une élucidation parfaite. J'interrogeai les amis et les ennemis. Je mâchai l'indigeste et abominable pamphlet de M. Fétis. Je lus le livre de Listz, et enfin je me procurai, à défaut de *l'Art et la Révolution* et de *l'Œuvre d'art de l'avenir,* ouvrages non traduits, celui intitulé: *Opéra et Drame,* traduit en anglais.

II

¶18 Les plaisanteries françaises allaient toujours leur train, et le journalisme vulgaire opérait sans trêve ses gamineries professionnelles. Comme Wagner n'avait jamais cessé de répéter que la musique (dramatique) devait *parler* le sentiment, s'adapter au sentiment avec la même exactitude que la parole, mais évidemment d'une autre manière, c'est-à-dire exprimer la partie indéfinie du sentiment que la parole, trop positive, ne peut pas rendre (en quoi il ne disait rien qui ne fût accepté par tous les esprits sensés), une foule de gens, persuadés par les plaisants du feuilleton, s'imaginèrent que le maître attribuait à la musique la puissance d'exprimer la forme positive des choses, c'est-à-dire qu'il intervertissait les rôles et les fonctions. Il serait aussi inutile qu'ennuyeux de dénombrer tous les quolibets fondés sur cette fausseté, qui venant, tantôt de la malveillance, tantôt de l'ignorance, avaient pour résultat d'égarer à l'avance l'opinion du public. Mais, à Paris plus qu'ailleurs, il est impossible d'arrêter une plume qui se croit amusante. La curiosité générale, étant attirée vers Wagner, engendra des articles et des brochures qui nous initièrent à sa vie, à ses longs efforts et à tous ses tourments. Parmi ces documents forts connus aujourd'hui, je n'en veux extraire que ceux qui me paraissent plus propres à éclairer et à définir la nature et le caractère du maître. Celui qui a écrit que *l'homme, qui n'a pas été, dès son berceau, doté par une fée de l'esprit de mécontentement de tout ce qui existe, n'arrivera jamais à la découverte du nouveau,* devait indubitablement trouver dans les conflits de la vie plus de douleurs que tout autre. C'est de cette facilité à souffrir, commune à tous les artistes et d'autant plus grande que leur instinct du juste et du beau est plus prononcé, que je tire l'explication des opinions révolutionnaires de Wagner. Aigri par tant de mécomptes, déçu par tant de rêves, il dut, à un certain moment, par suite d'une erreur excusable dans un esprit sensible et nerveux à l'excès, établir une complicité idéale entre la mauvaise musique et les mauvais gouvernements. Possédé du désir suprême de voir l'idéal dans l'art dominer définitivement la routine, il a pu (c'est une illusion essentiellement humaine) espérer que des révolutions dans l'ordre politique favoriseraient la cause de la révolution dans l'art. Le succès de Wagner lui-même a donné tort à ses prévisions et à ses espérances; car il a fallu en France l'ordre d'un *despote* pour faire exécuter l'œuvre d'un révolutionnaire. Ainsi nous avons déjà vu à Paris l'évolution romantique favorisée par la monarchie, pendant que les libéraux et les républicains restaient opiniâtrement attachés aux routines de la littérature dite classique.

¶19 Je vois, par les notes que lui-même il a fournies sur sa jeunesse, que tout enfant il vivait au sein du théâtre, fréquentait les coulisses et composait des comédies. La musique de Weber et, plus tard, celle de Beethoven, agirent sur son esprit avec une force irrésistible, et bientôt, les années et les études s'accumulant, il lui fut impossible de ne pas penser d'une manière double, poétiquement et musicalement, de ne pas entrevoir toute idée sous deux formes simultanées, l'un des deux arts commençant sa fonction là où s'arrêtent les limites de l'autre. L'instinct dramatique, qui occupait une si grande place dans ses facultés, devait le pousser à se révolter contre toutes les frivolités, les platitudes et les absurdités des pièces faites pour la musique. Ainsi la Providence qui préside aux révolutions de l'art mûrissait dans un jeune cerveau allemand le problème qui avait tant agité le dix-huitième siècle. Quiconque a lu avec attention la *Lettre sur la musique,* qui sert de préface à *Quatre poëmes d'opéras traduits en prose française,* ne peut conserver à cet égard aucun doute. Les noms de Gluck et de Méhul y sont cités souvent avec une sympathie passionnée. N'en déplaise à M. Fétis, qui veut absolument établir pour l'éternité la prédominance de la musique dans le drame lyrique, l'opinion d'esprits tels que Gluck, Diderot, Voltaire et Gœthe n'est pas à dédaigner. Si ces deux derniers ont démenti plus tard leurs théories de prédilection, ce n'a été chez eux qu'un acte de

découragement et de désespoir. En feuilletant la *Lettre sur la musique,* je sentais re-
vivre dans mons esprit, comme par un phénomène d'écho mnémonique, différents
passages de Diderot qui affirment que la vraie musique dramatique ne peut pas
être autre chose que le cri ou le soupir de la passion noté et rhythmé. Les mêmes
problèmes scientifiques, poétiques, artistiques, se reproduisent sans cesse à travers
les âges, et Wagner ne se donne pas pour un inventeur, mais simplement pour le
confirmateur d'une ancienne idée qui sera sans doute, plus d'une fois encore, alter-
nativement vaincue et victorieuse. Toutes ces questions sont en vérité extrêmement
simples, et il n'est pas peu surprenant de voir se révolter contre les théories de
la musique de l'avenir (pour me servir d'une locution aussi inexacte qu'accréditée)
ceux-là même que nous avons entendus si souvent se plaindre des tortures infligées
à tout esprit raisonnable par la routine du livret ordinaire d'opéra.

¶20 Dans cette même *Lettre sur la musique,* où l'auteur donne une analyse très-
brève et très-limpide de ses trois anciens ouvrages, *l'Art et la Révolution, l'Œuvre
d'art de l'avenir* et *Opéra et Drame,* nous trouvons une préoccupation très-vive du
théâtre grec, tout à fait naturelle, inévitable même chez un dramaturge musicien qui
devait chercher dans le passé la légitimation de son dégoût du présent et des con-
seils secourables pour l'établissement des conditions nouvelles du drame lyrique.
Dans sa lettre à Berlioz, il disait déjà, il y a plus d'un an: «Je me demandai quelles
devaient être les conditions de l'art pour qu'il pût inspirer au public un inviolable
respect, et, afin de ne point m'aventurer trop dans l'examen de cette question,
je fus chercher mon point de départ dans la Grèce ancienne. J'y rencontrai tout
d'abord l'œuvre artistique par excellence, le *drame,* dans lequel l'idée, quelque profonde qu'elle soit, peut se manifester avec le plus de clarté et de la manière la
plus universellement intelligible. Nous nous étonnons à bon droit aujourd'hui que
trente mille Grecs aient pu suivre avec un intérêt soutenu la représentation des
tragédies d'Eschyle; mais si nous recherchons le moyen par lequel on obtenait de
pareils résultats, nous trouvons que c'est par l'alliance de tous les arts concourant
ensemble au même but, c'est-à-dire à la production de l'œuvre artistique la plus
parfaite et la seule vraie. Ceci me conduisit à étudier les rapports des diverses
branches de l'art entre elles, et, après avoir saisi la relation qui existe entre la *plastique* et la *mimique,* j'examinai celle qui se trouve entre la musique et la poésie: de
cet examen jaillirent soudain des clartés qui dissipèrent complétement l'obscurité
qui m'avait jusqu'alors inquiété.»

¶21 «Je reconnus, en effet, que précisément là où l'un de ces arts atteignait à
des limites infranchissables, commençait aussitôt, avec la plus rigoureuse exactitude, la sphère d'action de l'autre; que, conséquemment, par l'union intime de
ces deux arts, on exprimerait avec la clarté la plus satisfaisante ce que ne pou-

vait exprimer chacun d'eux isolément; que, par contraire, toute tentative de rendre avec les moyens de l'un ce qui ne saurait être rendu que par les deux ensemble devait fatalement conduire à l'obscurité, à la confusion d'abord, et ensuite à la dégénérescence et à la corruption de chaque art en particulier.»

¶22 Et dans la préface de son dernier livre, il revient en ces termes sur le même sujet: «J'avais trouvé dans quelques rares créations d'artistes une base réelle où asseoir mon idéal dramatique et musical; maintenant l'histoire m'offrait à son tour le modèle et le type des relations idéales du théâtre et de la vie publique telles que je les concevais. Je le trouvais, ce modèle, dans le théâtre de l'ancienne Athènes: là, le théâtre n'ouvrait son enceinte qu'à de certaines solennités où s'accomplissait une fête religieuse qu'accompagnaient les jouissances de l'art. Les hommes les plus distingués de l'État prenaient à ces solennités une part directe comme poëtes ou directeurs; ils paraissaient comme les prêtres aux yeux de la population assemblée de la cité et du pays, et cette population était remplie d'une si haute attente de la sublimité des œuvres qui allaient être représentées devant elle, que les poëmes les plus profonds, ceux d'un Eschyle et d'un Sophocle, pouvaient être proposés au peuple et assurés d'être parfaitement entendus.»

¶23 Ce goût absolu, despotique, d'un idéal dramatique, où tout, depuis une déclamation notée et soulignée par la musique avec tant de soin qu'il est impossible au chanteur de s'en écarter en aucune syllabe, véritable arabesque de sons dessinée par la passion, jusqu'aux soins les plus minutieux, relatifs aux décors et à la mise en scène, où tous les détails, dis-je, doivent sans cesse concourir à une totalité d'effet, a fait la destinée de Wagner. C'était en lui comme une postulation perpétuelle. Depuis le jour où il s'est dégagé des vieilles routines du livret et où il a courageusement renié son *Rienzi,* opéra de jeunesse qui avait été honoré d'un grand succès, il a marché, sans dévier d'une ligne, vers cet impérieux idéal. C'est donc sans étonnement que j'ai trouvé dans ceux de ses ouvrages qui sont traduits, particulièrement dans *Tannhaüser, Lohengrin* et *le Vaisseau fantôme,* une méthode de construction excellente, un esprit d'ordre et de division qui rappelle l'architecture des tragédies antiques. Mais les phénomènes et les idées qui se produisent périodiquement à travers les âges empruntent toujours à chaque résurrection le caractère complémentaire de la variante et de la circonstance. La radieuse Vénus antique, l'Aphrodite née de la blanche écume, n'a pas impunément traversé les horrifiques ténèbres du moyen âge. Elle n'habite plus l'Olympe ni les rives d'un archipel parfumé. Elle est retirée au fond d'une caverne, magnifique, il est vrai, mais illuminée par des feux qui ne sont pas ceux du bienveillant Phœbus. En descendant sous terre, Vénus s'est rapprochée de l'enfer, et elle va sans doute, à de certaines solennités abominables, rendre régulièrement hommage à l'Archidémon, prince de la chair et seigneur du péché. De même, les poëmes de Wagner, bien qu'ils révèlent un goût sincère et une parfaite intelligence de la beauté classique, participent aussi, dans une forte dose, de l'esprit romantique. S'ils font rêver à la majesté de Sophocle et d'Eschyle, ils contraignent en même temps l'esprit à se souvenir des *Mystères* de l'époque la plus plastiquement catholique. Ils ressemblent à ces grandes visions que le moyen âge étalait sur les murs de ses églises ou tissait dans ses magnifiques tapisseries. Ils ont un aspect général décidément légendaire. *Le Tannhaüser,* légende; *le Lohengrin,* légende; légende, *le Vaisseau fantôme.* Et ce n'est pas seulement une propension naturelle à tout esprit poétique qui a conduit Wagner vers cette apparente spécialité; c'est un parti pris formel puisé dans l'étude des conditions les plus favorables du drame lyrique.

¶24 Lui-même, il a pris soin d'élucider la question dans ses livres. Tous les sujets, en effet, ne sont pas également propres à fournir un vaste drame doué d'un caractère d'universalité. Il y aurait évidemment un immense danger à traduire en fresque le délicieux et le plus parfait tableau de genre. C'est surtout dans le cœur universel de l'homme et dans l'histoire de ce cœur que le poëte dramatique trouvera des tableaux universellement intelligibles. Pour construire en pleine liberté le drame idéal, il sera prudent d'éliminer toutes les difficultés qui pourraient naître de détails techniques, politiques ou même trop positivement historiques. Je laisse la parole au maître lui-même: «Le seul tableau de la vie humaine qui soit appelé poétique est celui où les motifs qui n'ont de sens que pour l'intelligence abstraite font place aux mobiles purement humains qui gouvernent le cœur. Cette tendance (celle relative à l'invention du sujet poétique) est la loi souveraine qui préside à la forme et à la représentation poétique... L'arrangement rhythmique et l'ornement (presque musical) de la rime sont pour le poëte des moyens d'assurer au vers, à la phrase, une puissance qui captive comme par un charme et gouverne à son gré le sentiment. Essentielle au poëte, cette tendance le conduit jusqu'à la limite de son art, limite que touche immédiatement la musique, et, par conséquent, l'œuvre la plus complète du poëte devrait être celle qui, dans son dernier achèvement, serait une parfaite musique.

¶25 «De là, je me voyais nécessairement amené à désigner le *mythe* comme matière idéale du poëte. Le mythe est le poëme primitif et anonyme du peuple, et nous le trouvons à toutes les époques repris, remanié sans cesse à nouveau par les grands poëtes des périodes cultivées. Dans le mythe, en effet, les relations humaines dépouillent presque complétement leur forme conventionnelle et intelligible seulement à la raison abstraite; elles montrent ce que la vie a de vraiment humain, d'éternellement compréhensible, et le montrent sous cette forme concrète, exclusive de toute imitation, laquelle donne à tous les vrais mythes leur caractère individuel que vous reconnaissez au premier coup d'œil.»

¶26 Et ailleurs, reprenant le même thème, il dit: «Je quittai une fois pour toutes le terrain de l'histoire et m'établis sur celui de la légende... Tout le détail nécessaire pour décrire et représenter le fait historique et ses accidents, tout le détail qu'exige, pour être parfaitement comprise, une époque spéciale et reculée de l'histoire, et que les auteurs contemporains de drames et de romans historiques déduisent, par cette raison, d'une manière si circonstanciée, je pouvais le laisser de côté... La légende, à quelque époque et à quelque nation qu'elle appartienne, a l'avantage de comprendre exclusivement ce que cette époque et cette nation ont de purement humain, et de le présenter sous une forme originale très-saillante, et dès lors intelligible au premier coup d'œil. Une ballade, un refrain populaire, suffisent pour vous représenter en un instant ce caractère sous les traits les plus arrêtés et les plus frappants... Le caractère de la scène et le ton de la légende contribuent ensemble à jeter l'esprit dans cet état de *rêve* qui le porte bientôt jusqu'à la pleine *clairvoyance,* et l'esprit découvre alors un nouvel enchaînement des phénomènes du monde, que ses yeux ne pouvaient apercevoir dans l'état de veille ordinaire...»

¶27 Comment Wagner ne comprendrait-il pas admirablement le caractère sacré, divin du mythe, lui qui est à la fois poëte et critique? J'ai entendu beaucoup de personnes tirer de l'étendue même de ses facultés et de sa haute intelligence critique une raison de défiance relativement à son génie musical, et je crois que l'occasion est ici propice pour réfuter une erreur très-commune, dont la principale racine est peut-être le plus laid des sentiments humains, l'envie. «Un homme qui raisonne tant de son art ne peut pas produire naturellement de belles œuvres,» disent quelques-uns qui dépouillent ainsi le génie de sa rationalité, et lui assignent une fonction purement instinctive et pour ainsi dire végétale. D'autres veulent considérer Wagner comme un théoricien qui n'aurait produit des opéras que pour vérifier à *posteriori* la valeur de ses propres théories. Non-seulement ceci est parfaitement faux, puisque le maître a commencé tout jeune, comme on le sait, par produire des essais poétiques et musicaux d'une nature variée, et qu'il n'est arrivé que progressivement à se faire un idéal de drame lyrique, mais c'est même une chose absolument impossible. Ce serait un événement tout nouveau dans l'histoire des arts qu'un critique se faisant poëte, un renversement de toutes les lois psychiques, une monstruosité; au contraire, tous les grands poëtes deviennent naturellement, fatalement, critiques. Je plains les poëtes que guide le seul instinct; je les crois incomplets. Dans la vie spirituelle des premiers, une crise se fait infailliblement, où ils veulent raisonner leur art, découvrir les lois obscures en vertu desquelles ils ont produit, et tirer de cette étude une série de préceptes dont le but divin est l'infaillibilité dans la production poétique. Il serait prodigieux qu'un critique devînt poëte, et il est impossible qu'un poëte ne contienne pas un critique. Le lecteur ne sera donc pas étonné que je considère le poëte comme le meilleur de tous les critiques. Les gens qui reprochent au musicien Wagner d'avoir écrit des livres sur la philosophie de son art et qui en tirent le soupçon que sa musique n'est pas un produit naturel, spontané, devraient nier également que Vinci, Hogarth, Reynolds, aient pu faire de bonnes peintures, simplement parce qu'ils ont déduit et analysé les principes de leur art. Qui parle mieux de la peinture que notre grand Delacroix? Diderot, Gœthe, Shakespeare, autant de producteurs, autant d'admirables critiques. La poésie a existé, s'est affirmée la première, et elle a engendré l'étude des règles. Telle est l'histoire incontestée du travail humain. Or, comme chacun est le diminutif de tout le monde, comme l'histoire d'un cerveau individuel représente en petit l'histoire du cerveau universel, il serait juste et naturel de supposer (à défaut des preuves qui existent) que l'élaboration des pensées de Wagner a été analogue au travail de l'humanité.

III

¶28 *Tannhaüser* représente la lutte des deux principes qui ont choisi le cœur humain pour principal champ de bataille, c'est-à-dire de la chair avec l'esprit, de l'enfer avec le ciel, de Satan avec Dieu. Et cette dualité est représentée tout de suite, par l'ouverture, avec une incomparable habileté. Que n'a-t-on pas déjà écrit sur ce morceau? Cependant il est présumable qu'il fournira encore matière à bien des thèses et des commentaires éloquents; car c'est le propre des œuvres vraiment artistiques d'être une source inépuisable de suggestions. L'ouverture, dis-je, résume donc la pensée du drame par deux chants, le chant religieux et le chant voluptueux, qui, pour me servir de l'expression de Listz, «sont ici posés comme deux termes, et qui, dans le finale, trouvent leur équation.» Le *chant des pèlerins* apparaît le premier, avec l'autorité de la loi suprême, comme marquant tout de suite le véritable sens de la vie, le but de l'universel pèlerinage, c'est-à-dire Dieu. Mais comme le sens intime de Dieu est bientôt noyé dans toute conscience par les concupiscences de la chair, le chant représentatif de la sainteté est peu à peu submergé par les soupirs de la volupté. La vraie, la terrible, l'universelle Vénus se dresse déjà dans toutes les imaginations. Et que celui qui n'a pas encore entendu la merveilleuse ouverture de *Tannhaüser* ne se figure pas ici un chant d'amoureux vulgaires, essayant de tuer le temps sous les tonnelles, les accents d'une troupe enivrée jetant à Dieu son défi dans la langue d'Horace. Il s'agit d'autre chose, à la fois plus vrai et plus sinistre. Langueurs, délices mêlées de fièvre et coupées d'angoisses, retours incessants vers une volupté qui promet d'éteindre, mais n'éteint jamais la soif; palpitations furieuses du cœur et des sens, ordres impérieux de la chair, tout le dictionnaire des onomatopées de l'amour se fait entendre ici. Enfin le thème religieux reprend peu à peu son empire, lentement, par gradations, et absorbe l'autre dans une victoire paisible, glorieuse, comme celle de l'être irrésistible sur l'être maladif et désordonné, de saint Michel sur Lucifer.

¶29 Au commencement de cette étude, j'ai noté la puissance avec laquelle Wagner, dans l'ouverture de *Lohengrin*, avait exprimé les ardeurs de la mysticité, les appétitions de l'esprit vers le Dieu incommunicable. Dans l'ouverture de *Tannhäuser*, dans la lutte des deux principes contraires, il ne s'est pas montré moins subtil ni moins puissant. Où donc le maître a-t-il puisé ce chant furieux de la chair, cette connaissance absolue de la partie diabolique de l'homme? Dès les premières mesures, les nerfs vibrent à l'unisson de la mélodie;[3] toute chair qui se souvient se met à trembler. Tout cerveau bien conformé porte en lui deux infinis, le ciel et l'enfer, et dans toute image de l'un de ces infinis il reconnaît subitement la moitié de lui-même. Aux titillations sataniques d'un vague amour succèdent bientôt des entraînements, des éblouissements, des cris de victoire, des gémissements de gratitude, et puis des hurlements de férocité, des reproches de victimes et des hosannahs impies de sacrificateurs, comme si la barbarie devait toujours prendre sa place dans le drame de l'amour, et la jouissance charnelle conduire, par une logique satanique inéluctable, aux délices du crime. Quand le thème religieux, faisant invasion à travers le mal déchaîné, vient peu à peu rétablir l'ordre et reprendre l'ascendant, quand il se dresse de nouveau, avec toute sa solide beauté, au-dessus de ce chaos de voluptés agonisantes, toute l'âme éprouve comme un rafraîchissement, une béatitude de rédemption; sentiment ineffable qui se reproduira au commencement du deuxième tableau, quand Tannhäuser, échappé de la grotte de Vénus, se retrouvera dans la vie véritable, entre le son religieux des cloches natales, la chanson naïve du pâtre, l'hymne des pèlerins et la croix plantée sur la route, emblème de toutes ces croix qu'il faut traîner sur toutes les routes. Dans ce dernier cas, il y a une puissance de contraste qui agit irrésistiblement sur l'esprit et qui fait penser à la manière large et aisée de Shakespeare. Tout à l'heure nous étions dans les profondeurs de la terre (Vénus, comme nous l'avons dit, habite auprès de l'enfer), respirant une atmosphère parfumée, mais étouffante, éclairée par une lumière rose qui ne venait pas du soleil; nous étions semblables au chevalier Tannhäuser lui-même, qui, saturé de délices énervantes, *aspire à la douleur!* cri sublime que tous les critiques jurés admireraient dans Corneille, mais qu'aucun ne voudra peut-être voir dans Wagner. Enfin nous sommes replacés sur la terre; nous en aspirons l'air frais, nous en acceptons les joies avec reconnaissance, les douleurs avec humilité. La pauvre humanité est rendue à sa patrie.

¶30 Tout à l'heure, en essayant de décrire la partie voluptueuse de l'ouverture, je priais le lecteur de détourner sa pensée des hymnes vulgaires de l'amour, tels que les peut concevoir un galant en belle humeur; en effet, il n'y a ici rien de trivial; c'est plutôt le débordement d'une nature énergique, qui verse dans le mal toutes les forces dues à la culture du bien; c'est l'amour effréné, immense, chaotique, élevé jusqu'à la hauteur d'une contre-religion, d'une religion satanique. Ainsi, le compositeur, dans la traduction musicale, a échappé à cette vulgarité qui accompagne trop souvent la peinture du sentiment le plus *populaire*,—j'allais dire populacier,— et pour cela il lui a suffi de peindre l'excès dans le désir et dans l'énergie, l'ambition indomptable, immodérée, d'une âme sensible qui s'est trompée de voie. De même, dans la représentation plastique de l'idée, il s'est dégagé heureusement de la fastidieuse foule des victimes, des Elvires innombrables. L'idée pure, incarnée dans l'unique Vénus, parle bien plus haut et avec bien plus d'éloquence. Nous ne voyons pas ici un libertin ordinaire, *voltigeant de belle en belle,* mais l'homme général, universel, vivant morganatiquement avec l'Idéal absolu de la volupté, avec la Reine de toutes les diablesses, de toutes les faunesses et de toutes les satyresses, reléguées sous terre depuis la mort du grand Pan, c'est-à-dire avec l'indestructible et irrésistible Vénus.

¶31 Une main mieux exercée que la mienne dans l'analyse des ouvrages lyriques présentera, ici même, au lecteur, un compte rendu technique et complet de cet étrange et méconnu *Tannhäuser*;[4] je dois donc me borner à des vues générales qui, pour rapides qu'elles soient, n'en sont pas moins utiles. D'ailleurs, n'est-il pas plus commode, pour certains esprits, de juger de la beauté d'un paysage en se plaçant sur une hauteur, qu'en parcourant successivement tous les sentiers qui le sillonnent?

¶32 Je tiens seulement à faire observer, à la grande louange de Wagner, que, malgré l'importance très-juste qu'il donne au poëme dramatique, l'ouverture de *Tannhäuser,* comme celle de *Lohengrin,* est parfaitement intelligible, même à celui qui ne connaîtrait pas le livret; et ensuite, que cette ouverture contient nonseulement l'idée mère, la dualité psychique constituant le drame, mais encore les formules principales, nettement accentuées, destinées à peindre les sentiments généraux exprimés dans la suite de l'œuvre, ainsi que le démontrent les retours forcés de la mélodie diaboliquement voluptueuse et du motif religieux ou *Chant des pèlerins,* toutes les fois que l'action le demande. Quant à la grande marche du second acte, elle a conquis depuis longtemps le suffrage des esprits les plus rebelles, et l'on peut lui appliquer le même éloge qu'aux deux ouvertures dont j'ai parlé, à savoir d'exprimer de la manière la plus visible, la plus colorée, la plus représentative, ce qu'elle veut exprimer. Qui donc, en entendant ces accents si riches et si fiers, ce rhythme pompeux, élégamment cadencé, ces fanfares royales, pourrait se figurer autre chose qu'une pompe féodale, une défilade d'hommes héroïques, dans des vêtements éclatants, tous de haute stature, tous de grande volonté et de foi naïve, aussi magnifiques dans leurs plaisirs que terribles dans leurs guerres?

¶33 Que dirons-nous du récit de Tannhaüser, de son voyage à Rome, où la beauté littéraire est si admirablement complétée et soutenue par la mélopée, que les deux éléments ne font plus qu'un inséparable tout? On craignait la longueur de ce morceau, et, cependant, le récit contient, comme on l'a vu, une puissance dramatique invincible. La tristesse, l'accablement du pécheur pendant son rude voyage, son allégresse en voyant le suprême pontife qui délie les péchés, son désespoir quand celui-ci lui montre le caractère irréparable de son crime, et enfin le sentiment presque ineffable, tant il est terrible, de la joie dans la damnation; tout est dit, exprimé, traduit, par la parole et la musique, d'une manière si positive qu'il est presque impossible de concevoir une autre manière de le dire. On comprend bien alors qu'un pareil malheur ne puisse être réparé que par un miracle, et on excuse l'infortuné chevalier de chercher encore le sentier mystérieux qui conduit à la grotte, pour retrouver au moins les grâces de l'enfer auprès de sa diabolique épouse.

¶34 Le drame de *Lohengrin* porte, comme celui de *Tannhaüser,* le caractère sacré, mystérieux et pourtant universellement intelligible de la légende. Une jeune princesse, accusée d'un crime abominable, du meurtre de son frère, ne possède aucun moyen de prouver son innocence. Sa cause sera jugée par le jugement de Dieu. Aucun chevalier présent ne descend pour elle sur le terrain; mais elle a confiance dans une vision singulière; un guerrier inconnu est venu la visiter en rêve. C'est ce chevalier-là qui prendra sa défense. En effet, au moment suprême et comme chacun la juge coupable, une nacelle approche du rivage, tirée par un cygne attelé d'une chaîne d'or. Lohengrin, chevalier du Saint-Graal, protecteur des innocents, défenseur des faibles, a entendu l'invocation du fond de la retraite merveilleuse où est précieusement conservé cette coupe divine, deux fois consacrée par la sainte Cène et par le sang de Notre Seigneur, que Joseph d'Arimathie y recueillit tout ruisselant de sa plaie. Lohengrin, fils de Parcival, descend de la nacelle, revêtu d'une armure d'argent, le casque en tête, le bouclier sur l'épaule, une petite trompe d'or au côté, appuyé sur son épée. «Si je remporte pour toi la victoire, dit Lohengrin à Elsa, veux-tu que je sois ton époux?... Elsa, si tu veux que je m'appelle ton époux... il faut que tu me fasses une promesse: Jamais tu ne m'interrogeras, jamais tu ne chercheras à savoir ni de quelles contrées j'arrive, ni quel est mon nom et ma nature.» Et Elsa: «Jamais, seigneur, tu n'entendras de moi cette question.» Et, comme Lohengrin répète solennellement la formule de la promesse, Elsa répond: «Mon bouclier, mon ange, mon sauveur! toi qui crois fermement à mon innocence, pourrait-il y avoir un doute plus criminel que de n'avoir pas foi en toi? Comme tu me défends dans ma détresse, de même je garderai fidèlement la loi que tu m'imposes.» Et Lohengrin, la serrant dans ses bras, s'écrie: «Elsa, je t'aime!» Il y a là une beauté de dialogue comme il s'en trouve fréquemment dans les drames de Wagner, toute trempée de magie primitive, toute grandie par le sentiment idéal, et dont la solennité ne diminue en rien la grâce naturelle.

¶35 L'innocence d'Elsa est proclamée par la victoire de Lohengrin; la magicienne Ortrude et Frédéric, deux méchants intéressés à la condamnation d'Elsa, parviennent à exciter en elle la curiosité féminine, à flétrir sa joie par le doute, et l'obsèdent maintenant jusqu'à ce qu'elle viole son serment et exige de son époux l'aveu de son origine. Le doute a tué la foi, et la foi disparue emporte avec elle le bonheur. Lohengrin punit par la mort Frédéric d'un guet-apens que celui-ci lui a tendu, et devant le roi, les guerriers et le peuple assemblés, déclare enfin sa véritable origine: «...Quiconque est choisi pour servir le Graal est aussitôt revêtu d'une puissance surnaturelle; même celui qui est envoyé par lui dans une tèrre lointaine, chargé de la mission de défendre le droit de la vertu, n'est pas dépouillé de sa force sacrée autant que reste inconnue sa qualité de chevalier du Graal; mais telle est la nature de cette vertu du Saint-Graal, que, dévoilée, elle fuit aussitôt les regards profanes; c'est pourquoi vous ne devez concevoir nul doute sur son chevalier; s'il est reconnu par vous, il lui faut vous quitter sur-le-champ. Écoutez maintenant comment il récompense la question interdite! Je vous ai été envoyé par le Graal; mon père, Parcival, porte sa couronne; moi, son chevalier, j'ai nom Lohengrin.» Le cygne reparaît sur la rive pour remmener le chevalier vers sa miraculeuse patrie. La magicienne, dans l'infatuation de sa haine, dévoile que le cygne n'est autre que le frère d'Elsa, emprisonné par elle dans un enchantement. Lohengrin monte dans la nacelle après avoir adressé au Saint-Graal une fervente prière. Une colombe prend la place du cygne, et Godefroi, duc de Brabant, reparaît. Le chevalier est retourné vers le mont Salvat. Elsa qui a douté, Elsa qui a voulu savoir, examiner, contrôler, Elsa a perdu son bonheur. L'idéal est envolé.

¶36 Le lecteur a sans doute remarqué dans cette légende une frappante analogie avec le mythe de la Psyché antique, qui, elle aussi, fut victime de la démoniaque curiosité, et, ne voulant pas respecter l'incognito de son divin époux, perdit, en pénétrant le mystère, toute sa félicité. Elsa prête l'oreille à Ortrude, comme Ève au serpent. L'Ève éternelle tombe dans l'éternel piége. Les nations et les races se transmettent-elles des fables, comme les hommes se lèguent des héritages, des patrimoines ou des secrets scientifiques? On serait tenté de le croire, tant est frappante l'analogie morale qui marque les mythes et les légendes éclos dans différentes contrées. Mais cette explication est trop simple pour séduire longtemps un esprit philosophique. L'allégorie créée par le peuple ne peut pas être comparée à ces semences qu'un cultivateur communique fraternellement à un autre qui les veut acclimater dans son pays. Rien de ce qui est éternel et universel n'a besoin d'être acclimaté. Cette analogie morale dont je parlais est comme l'estampille divine de toutes les fables populaires. Ce sera bien, si l'on veut, le signe d'une origine unique, la preuve d'une parenté irréfragable, mais à la condition que l'on ne cherche cette origine que dans le principe absolu et l'origine commune de tous les êtres. Tel mythe peut être considéré comme frère d'un autre, de la même façon que le nègre est dit le frère du blanc. Je ne nie pas, en de certains cas, la fraternité ni la filiation; je crois seulement que dans beaucoup d'autres l'esprit pourrait être induit en erreur par la ressemblance des surfaces ou même par l'analogie morale, et que, pour reprendre notre métaphore végétale, le mythe est un arbre qui croît partout, en tout climat, sous tout soleil, spontanément et sans boutures. Les religions et les poésies des quatre parties du monde nous fournissent sur ce sujet des preuves surabondantes. Comme le péché est partout, la rédemption est partout; le mythe partout. Rien de plus cosmopolite que l'Éternel. Qu'on veuille bien me pardonner cette digression qui s'est ouverte devant moi avec une attraction irrésistible. Je reviens à l'auteur de *Lohengrin*.

¶37 On dirait que Wagner aime d'un amour de prédilection les pompes féodales, les assemblées homériques où gît une accumulation de force vitale, les foules enthousiasmées, réservoir.d'électricité humaine, d'où le style héroïque jaillit avec une impétuosité naturelle. La musique de noces et l'épithalame de *Lohengrin* font un digne pendant à l'introduction des invités au Wartburg dans *Tannhäuser,* plus majestueux encore peut-être et plus véhément. Cependant le maître, toujours plein de goût et attentif aux nuances, n'a pas représenté ici la turbulence qu'en pareil cas manifesterait une foule roturière. Même à l'apogée de son plus violent tumulte, la musique n'exprime qu'un délire de gens accoutumés aux règles de l'étiquette; c'est une cour qui s'amuse, et son ivresse la plus vive garde encore le rhythme de la décence. La joie clapoteuse de la foule alterne avec l'épithalame, doux, tendre et solennel; la tourmente de l'allégresse publique contraste à plusieurs reprises avec l'hymne discret et attendri qui célèbre l'union d'Elsa et de Lohengrin.

¶38 J'ai déjà parlé de certaines phrases mélodiques dont le retour assidu, dans différents morceaux tirés de la même œuvre, avait vivement intrigué mon oreille, lors du premier concert offert par Wagner dans la salle des Italiens. Nous avons observé que, dans *Tannhaüser,* la récurrence des deux thèmes principaux, le motif religieux et le chant de la volupté, servait à réveiller l'attention du public et à le replacer dans un état analogue à la situation actuelle. Dans *Lohengrin,* ce système mnémonique est appliqué beaucoup plus minutieusement. Chaque personnage est, pour ainsi dire, blasonné par la mélodie qui représente son caractère moral et le rôle qu'il est appelé à jouer dans la fable. Ici je laisse humblement la parole à Listz, dont, par occasion, je recommande le livre (*Lohengrin et Tannhaüser*) à tous les amateurs de l'art profond et raffiné, et qui sait, malgré cette langue un peu bizarre qu'il affecte, espèce d'idiome composé d'extraits de plusieurs langues, traduire avec un charme infini toute la rhétorique du maître:

¶39 «Le spectateur, préparé et résigné à ne chercher *aucun de ces morceaux détachés, qui, engrenés l'un après l'autre sur le fil de quelque intrigue, composent la substance de nos opéras habituels,* pourra trouver un singulier intérêt à suivre durant trois actes la combinaison profondément réfléchie, étonnamment habile et poétiquement intelligente, avec laquelle Wagner, *au moyen de plusieurs phrases principales,* a serré *un noeud mélodique* qui constitue tout son drame. Les replis que font ces phrases, en se liant et s'entrelaçant autour des paroles du poëme, sont d'un effet émouvant au dernier point. Mais si, après en avoir été frappé et impressionné à la représentation, on veut encore se rendre mieux compte de ce qui a si vivement affecté, et étudier la partition de cette œuvre d'un genre si neuf, on reste étonné de toutes les intentions et nuances qu'elle renferme et qu'on ne saurait immédiatement saisir. Quels sont les drames et les épopées de grands poëtes qu'il ne faille pas longtemps étudier pour se rendre maître de toute leur signification?

¶40 «Wagner, par un procédé qu'il applique d'une manière tout à fait imprévue, réussit à étendre l'empire et les prétentions de la musique. Peu content du pouvoir qu'elle exerce sur les cœurs en y réveillant toute la gamme des sentiments humains, il lui rend possible d'inciter nos idées, de s'adresser à notre pensée, de faire appel à notre réflexion, et la dote d'un sens moral et intellectuel... Il dessine mélodiquement le caractère de ses personnages et de leurs passions principales, et ces mélodies se font jour, *dans le chant ou dans l'accompagnement,* chaque fois que les passions et les sentiments qu'elles expriment sont mis en jeu. Cette persistance systématique est jointe à un art de distribution qui offrirait, par la finesse des aperçus psychologiques, poétiques et philosophiques dont il fait preuve, un intérêt de haute curiosité à ceux aussi pour qui les croches et doubles-croches sont lettres mortes et purs hiéroglyphes. Wagner, forçant notre méditation et notre mémoire à un si constant exercice, arrache, par cela seul, l'action de la musique au domaine des vagues attendrissements et ajoute à ses charmes quelques-uns des plaisirs de l'esprit. Par cette méthode qui complique les faciles jouissances procurées par *une série de chants rarement apparentés entre eux,* il demande une singulière attention du public; mais en même temps il prépare de plus parfaites émotions à ceux qui savent les goûter. Ses mélodies sont en quelque sorte *des personnifications d'idées;* leur retour annonce celui des sentiments que les paroles qu'on prononce n'indiquent point explicitement; c'est à elles que Wagner confie de nous révéler tous les secrets des cœurs. Il est des phrases, celle, par exemple, de la première scène du second acte, qui traversent l'opéra comme un serpent venimeux, s'enroulant autour des victimes et fuyant devant leurs saints défenseurs; il en est, comme celle de l'introduction, qui ne reviennent que rarement, avec les suprêmes et divines révélations. Les situations ou les personnages de quelque importance sont tous musicalement exprimés par une mélodie qui en devient le constant symbole. Or, comme ces mélodies sont d'une rare beauté, nous dirons à ceux qui, dans l'examen d'une partition, se bornent à juger des rapports de croches et doubles-croches entre elles, que même si la musique de cet opéra devait être privée de son beau texte, elle serait encore une production de premier ordre.»

¶41 En effet, sans poésie, la musique de Wagner serait encore une œuvre poétique, étant douée de toutes les qualités qui constituent une poésie bien faite; explicative par elle-même, tant toutes choses y sont bien unies, conjointes, réciproquement adaptées, et, s'il est permis de faire un barbarisme pour exprimer le superlatif d'une qualité, prudemment *concaténées.*

¶42 *Le Vaisseau fantôme,* ou *le Hollandais volant,* est l'histoire si populaire de ce Juif errant de l'Océan, pour qui cependant une condition de rédemption a été obtenue par un ange secourable: *Si le capitaine, qui mettra pied à terre tous les sept ans, rencontre une femme fidèle, il sera sauvé.*[5] L'infortuné, repoussé par la tempête à chaque fois qu'il voulait doubler un cap dangereux, s'était écrié une fois: «Je passerai cette infranchissable barrière, dussé-je lutter toute l'éternité!» Et l'éternité avait accepté le défi de l'audacieux navigateur. Depuis lors, le fatal navire s'était montré çà et là, dans différentes plages, courant sus à la tempête avec le désespoir d'un guerrier qui cherche la mort; mais toujours la tempête l'épargnait, et le pirate lui-même se sauvait devant lui en faisant le signe de la croix. Les premières paroles du Hollandais, après que son vaisseau est arrivé au mouillage, sont sinistres et solennelles: «Le terme est passé; il s'est encore écoulé sept années! La mer me jette à terre avec dégoût... Ah! orgueilleux Océan! dans peu de jours il te faudra me porter encore!... Nulle part une tombe! nulle part la mort! telle est ma terrible sentence de damnation... Jour du jugement, jour suprême, quand luiras-tu dans ma nuit?...» A côté du terrible vaisseau un navire norwégien a jeté l'ancre; les deux capitaines lient connaissance, et le Hollandais demande au Norwégien «de lui accorder pour quelques jours l'abri de sa maison... de lui donner une nouvelle patrie.» Il lui offre des richesses énormes dont celui-ci s'éblouit, et enfin lui dit brusquement: «As-tu une fille?... Qu'elle soit ma femme!... Jamais je n'atteindrai ma patrie. A quoi me sert donc d'amasser des richesses? Laisse-toi convaincre, consens à cette alliance et prends tous mes trésors.»—«J'ai une fille, belle, pleine de fidélité, de tendresse, de dévouement pour moi.»—«Qu'elle conserve toujours à son père cette tendresse filiale, qu'elle lui soit fidèle; elle sera aussi fidèle à son époux.»—«Tu me donnes des joyaux, des perles inestimables; mais le joyau le plus précieux, c'est une femme fidèle.»—«C'est toi qui me le donnes?... Verrai-je ta fille dès aujourd'hui?»

¶43 Dans la chambre du Norwégien, plusieurs jeunes filles s'entretiennent du *Hollandais volant,* et Senta, possédée d'une idée fixe, les yeux toujours tendus vers un portrait mystérieux, chante la ballade qui retrace la damnation du navigateur: «Avez-vous rencontré en mer le navire à la voile rouge de sang, au mât noir? A bord, l'homme pâle, le maître du vaisseau, veille sans relâche. Il vole et fuit, sans terme, sans relâche, sans repos. Un jour pourtant l'homme peut rencontrer la délivrance, s'il trouve sur terre une femme qui lui soit fidèle jusque dans la mort... Priez le ciel que bientôt une femme lui garde sa foi!—Par un vent contraire, dans une tempête furieuse, il voulut autrefois doubler un cap; il blasphéma dans sa folle audace: Je n'y renoncerais pas de l'éternité! Satan l'a entendu, il l'a pris au mot! Et maintenant son arrêt est d'errer à travers la mer, sans relâche, sans repos!... Mais pour que l'infortuné puisse rencontrer encore la délivrance sur terre, un ange de Dieu lui annonce d'où peut lui venir le salut. Ah! puisses-tu le trouver, pâle navigateur! Priez le ciel que bientôt une femme lui garde cette foi!—Tous les sept ans, il jette l'ancre, et, pour chercher une femme, il descend à terre. Il a courtisé tous les sept ans, et jamais encore il n'a trouvé une femme fidèle... Les voiles au vent! levez l'ancre! Faux amour, faux serments! Alerte! en mer! sans relâche, sans repos!» Et, tout d'un coup, sortant d'un abîme de rêverie, Senta inspirée s'écrie: «Que je sois celle qui te délivrera par sa fidélité! Puisse l'ange de Dieu me montrer à toi! C'est par moi que tu obtiendras le salut!» L'esprit de la jeune fille est attiré magnétiquement par le malheur; son vrai fiancé, c'est le capitaine damné que l'amour seul peut racheter.

¶44 Enfin, le Hollandais paraît, présenté par le père de Senta; il est bien l'homme du portrait, la figure légendaire suspendue au mur. Quand le Hollandais, semblable au terrible Melmoth qu'attendrit la destinée d'Immalée, sa victime, veut la détourner d'un dévouement trop périlleux, quand le damné plein de pitié repousse l'instrument du salut, quand, remontant en toute hâte sur son navire, il la veut laisser au bonheur de la famille et de l'amour vulgaire, celle-ci résiste et s'obstine à le suivre: «Je te connais bien! je connais ta destinée! Je te connaissais lorsque je t'ai vu pour la première fois!» Et lui, espérant l'épouvanter: «Interroge les mers de toutes les zones, interroge le navigateur qui a sillonné l'Océan dans tous les sens; il connaît ce vaisseau, l'effroi des hommes pieux: on me nomme le *Hollandais volant!*» Elle répond, poursuivant de son dévouement et de ses cris le navire qui s'éloigne: «Gloire à ton ange libérateur! gloire à sa loi! Regarde, et vois si je te suis fidèle jusqu'à la mort!» Et elle se précipite à la mer. Le navire s'engloutit. Deux formes aériennes s'élèvent au-dessus des flots: c'est le Hollandais et Senta transfigurés.

¶45 Aimer le malheureux pour son malheur est une idée trop grande pour tomber ailleurs que dans un cœur ingénu, et c'est certainement une très-belle pensée que d'avoir suspendu le rachat d'un maudit à l'imagination passionnée d'une jeune fille. Tout le drame est traité d'une main sûre, avec une manière directe; chaque situation, abordée franchement; et le type de Senta porte en lui une grandeur surnaturelle et romanesque qui enchante et fait peur. La simplicité extrême du poëme augmente l'intensité de l'effet. Chaque chose est à sa place, tout est bien ordonné et de juste dimension. L'ouverture, que nous avons entendue au concert du Théâtre-Italien, est lugubre et profonde comme l'Océan, le vent et les ténèbres.

¶46 Je suis contraint de resserrer les bornes de cette étude, et je crois que j'en ai dit assez (aujourd'hui du moins) pour faire comprendre à un lecteur non prévenu les tendances et la forme dramatique de Wagner. Outre *Rienzi, le Hollandais volant, Tannhäuser* et *Lohengrin,* il a composé *Tristan et Isolde,* et quatre autres opéras formant une tétralogie, dont le sujet est tiré des Niebelungen, sans compter ses nombreuses œuvres critiques. Tels sont les travaux de cet homme dont la personne et les ambitions idéales ont défrayé si longtemps la badauderie parisienne et dont la plaisanterie facile a fait journellement sa proie pendant plus d'un an.

IV

¶47 On peut toujours faire momentanément abstraction de la partie systématique que tout grand artiste volontaire introduit fatalement dans toutes ses œuvres; il reste, dans ce cas, à chercher et à vérifier par quelle qualité propre, personnelle, il se distingue des autres. Un artiste, un homme vraiment digne de ce grand nom, doit posséder quelque chose d'essentiellement *sui generis,* par la grâce de quoi il est *lui* et non un autre. A ce point de vue, les artistes peuvent être comparés à des saveurs variées, et le répertoire des métaphores humaines n'est peut-être pas assez vaste pour fournir la définition approximative de tous les artistes connus et de tous les artistes *possibles.* Nous avons déjà, je crois, noté deux hommes dans Richard Wagner, l'homme d'ordre et l'homme passionné. C'est de l'homme passionné, de l'homme de sentiment qu'il est ici question. Dans le moindre de ses morceaux il inscrit si ardemment sa personnalité que cette recherche de sa qualité principale ne sera pas très-difficile à faire. Dès le principe, une considération m'avait vivement frappé; c'est que dans la partie voluptueuse et orgiaque de l'ouverture de *Tann-haüser* l'artiste avait mis autant de force, développé autant d'énergie que dans la peinture de la mysticité qui caractérise l'ouverture de *Lohengrin*. Même ambition dans l'une que dans l'autre, même escalade titanique, et aussi mêmes raffinements et même subtilité. Ce qui me paraît donc avant tout marquer d'une manière inoubliable la musique de ce maître, c'est l'intensité nerveuse, la violence dans la passion et dans la volonté. Cette musique-là exprime avec la voix la plus suave ou la plus stridente tout ce qu'il y a de plus caché dans le cœur de l'homme. Une ambition idéale préside, il est vrai, à toutes ses compositions; mais si, par le choix de ses sujets et sa méthode dramatique, Wagner se rapproche de l'antiquité, par l'énergie passionnée de son expression il est actuellement le représentant le plus vrai de la nature moderne. Et toute la science, tous les efforts, toutes les combinaisons de ce riche esprit ne sont, à vrai dire, que les serviteurs très-humbles et très-zélés de cette irrésistible passion. Il en résulte, dans quelque sujet qu'il traite, une solennité d'accent superlative. Par cette passion il ajoute à chaque chose je ne sais quoi de surhumain; par cette passion il comprend tout et fait tout comprendre. Tout ce qu'impliquent les mots: *volonté, désir, concentration, intensité nerveuse, explosion,* se sent et se fait deviner dans ses œuvres. Je ne crois pas me faire illusion ni tromper personne en affirmant que je vois là les principales caractéristiques du phénomène que nous appelons *génie;* ou du moins, que dans l'analyse de tout ce que nous avons jusqu'ici légitimement appelé *génie* on retrouve lesdites caractéristiques. En matière d'art, j'avoue que je ne hais pas l'outrance; la modération ne m'a jamais semblé le signe d'une nature artistique vigoureuse. J'aime ces excès de santé, ces débordements de volonté qui s'inscrivent dans les œuvres comme le bitume en-flammé dans le sol d'un volcan, et qui, dans la vie ordinaire, marquent souvent la phase, pleine de délices, succédant à une grande crise morale ou physique.

¶48 Quant à la réforme que le maître veut introduire dans l'application de la musique au drame, qu'en arrivera-t-il? Là-dessus, il est impossible de rien prophé-tiser de précis. D'une manière vague et générale, on peut dire, avec le Psalmiste, que, tôt ou tard, ceux qui ont été abaissés seront élevés, que ceux qui ont été élevés seront humiliés, mais rien de plus que ce qui est également applicable au train connu de toutes les affaires humaines. Nous avons vu bien des choses déclarées jadis absurdes, qui sont devenues plus tard des modèles adoptés par la foule. Tout le public actuel se souvient de l'énergique résistance où se heurtèrent, dans le commencement, les drames de Victor Hugo et les peintures d'Eugène Delacroix. D'ailleurs nous avons déjà fait observer que la querelle qui divise maintenant le public était une querelle oubliée et soudainement ravivée, et que Wagner lui-même avait trouvé dans le passé les premiers éléments de *la base pour asseoir son idéal.* Ce qui est bien certain, c'est que sa doctrine est faite pour rallier tous les gens d'esprit fatigués depuis longtemps des erreurs de l'Opéra, et il n'est pas étonnant que les hommes de lettres, en particulier, se soient montrés sympathiques pour un musicien qui se fait gloire d'être poëte et dramaturge. De même les écrivains du dix-huitième siècle avaient acclamé les ouvrages de Gluck, et je ne puis m'empêcher de voir que les personnes qui manifestent le plus de répulsion pour les ouvrages de Wagner montrent aussi une antipathie décidée à l'égard de son précurseur.

¶49 Enfin le succès ou l'insuccès de *Tannhaüser* ne peut absolument rien prouver, ni même déterminer une quantité quelconque de chances favorables ou défavorables dans l'avenir. *Tannhaüser,* en supposant qu'il fût un ouvrage détestable, aurait pu *monter aux nues.* En le supposant parfait, il pourrait révolter. La question, dans le fait, la question de la réformation de l'opéra n'est pas vidée, et la bataille continuera; apaisée, elle recommencera. J'entendais dire récemment que si Wagner obtenait par son drame un éclatant succès, ce serait un accident purement individuel, et que sa méthode n'aurait aucune influence ultérieure sur les destinées et les transformations du drame lyrique. Je me crois autorisé, par l'étude du passé, c'est-à-dire de l'éternel, à préjuger l'absolu contraire, à savoir qu'un échec complet ne détruit en aucune façon la possibilité de tentatives nouvelles dans le même sens, et que dans un avenir très-rapproché on pourrait bien voir non pas seulement des auteurs nouveaux, mais même des hommes anciennement accrédités, profiter, dans une mesure quelconque, des idées émises par Wagner, et passer heureusement à travers la brèche ouverte par lui. Dans quelle histoire a-t-on jamais lu que les grandes causes se perdaient en une seule partie?

18 mars 1861

ENCORE QUELQUES MOTS

¶50 «L'épreuve est faite! La *musique de l'avenir* est enterrée!» s'écrient avec joie tous les siffleurs et cabaleurs. «L'épreuve est faite!» répètent tous les niais du feuilleton. Et tous les badauds leur répondent en choeur, et très-innocemment: «L'épreuve est faite!»

¶51 En effet, une épreuve a été faite, qui se renouvellera encore bien des milliers de fois avant la fin du monde; c'est que, d'abord, toute œuvre grande et sérieuse ne peut pas se loger dans la mémoire humaine ni prendre sa place dans l'histoire sans de vives contestations; ensuite, que dix personnes opiniâtres peuvent, à l'aide de sifflets aigus, dérouter des comédiens, vaincre la bienveillance du public, et pénétrer même de leurs protestations discordantes la voix immense d'un orchestre, cette voix fût-elle égale en puissance à celle de l'Océan. Enfin, un inconvénient des plus intéressants a été vérifié, c'est qu'un système de location qui permet de s'abonner à l'année crée une sorte d'aristocratie, laquelle peut, à un moment donné, pour un motif ou un intérêt quelconque, exclure le vaste public de toute participation au jugement d'une œuvre. Qu'on adopte dans d'autres théâtres, à la Comédie-Française, par exemple, ce même système de location, et nous verrons bientôt, là aussi, se produire les mêmes dangers et les mêmes scandales. Une société restreinte pourra enlever au public immense de Paris le droit d'apprécier un ouvrage dont le jugement appartient à tous.

¶52 Les gens qui se croient débarrassés de Wagner se sont réjouis beaucoup trop vite; nous pouvons le leur affirmer. Je les engage vivement à célébrer moins haut un triomphe qui n'est pas des plus honorables d'ailleurs, et même à se garnir de résignation pour l'avenir.[6] En vérité, ils ne comprennent guères le jeu de bascule des affaires humaines, le flux et le reflux des passions. Ils ignorent aussi de quelle patience et de quelle opiniâtreté la Providence a toujours doué ceux qu'elle investit d'une fonction. Aujourd'hui la réaction est commencée; elle a pris naissance le jour même où la malveillance, la sottise, la routine et l'envie coalisées ont essayé d'enterrer l'ouvrage. L'immensité de l'injustice a engendré mille sympathies, qui maintenant se montrent de tous côtés.

*

¶53 Aux personnes éloignées de Paris, que fascine et intimide cet amas monstrueux d'hommes et de pierres, l'aventure inattendue du drame de *Tannhäuser* doit apparaître comme une énigme. Il serait facile de l'expliquer par la coïncidence malheureuse de plusieurs causes, dont quelques-unes sont étrangères à l'art. Avouons tout de suite la raison principale, dominante: l'opéra de Wagner *est un ouvrage sérieux,* demandant une attention soutenue; on conçoit tout ce que cette condition implique de chances défavorables dans un pays où l'ancienne tragédie réussissait surtout par les facilités qu'elle offrait à la distraction. En Italie, on prend des sorbets et l'on fait des cancans dans les intervalles du drame où la mode ne commande pas les applaudissements; en France, on joue aux cartes. «Vous êtes un impertinent, vous qui voulez me contraindre à prêter à votre œuvre une attention continue,» s'écrie l'abonné récalcitrant, «je veux que vous me fournissiez un plaisir digestif plutôt qu'une occasion d'exercer mon intelligence.» A cette cause principale, il faut en ajouter d'autres qui sont aujourd'hui connues de tout le monde, à Paris du moins. L'ordre impérial, qui fait tant d'honneur au prince, et dont on peut le remercier sincèrement, je crois, sans être accusé de courtisanerie, a ameuté contre l'artiste beaucoup d'envieux et beaucoup de ces badauds qui croient toujours faire acte d'indépendance en aboyant à l'unisson. Le décret qui venait de rendre quelques libertés au journal et à la parole, ouvrait carrière à une turbulence naturelle, longtemps comprimée, qui s'est jetée, comme un animal fou, sur le premier passant venu. Ce passant, c'était le *Tannhaüser,* autorisé par le chef de l'État et protégé ouvertement par la femme d'un ambassadeur étranger. Quelle admirable occasion! Toute une salle française s'est amusée pendant plusieurs heures de la douleur de cette femme, et, chose moins connue, madame Wagner elle-même a été insultée pendant une des représentations. Prodigieux triomphe!

¶54 Une mise en scène plus qu'insuffisante, faite par un ancien vaudevilliste (vous figurez-vous les *Burgraves* mis en scène par M. Clairville?); une exécution molle et incorrecte de la part de l'orchestre; un ténor allemand, sur qui on fondait les principales espérances, et qui se met à chanter faux avec une assiduité déplorable; une Vénus endormie, habillée d'un paquet de chiffons blancs, et qui n'avait pas plus l'air de descendre de l'Olympe que d'être née de l'imagination chatoyante d'un artiste du moyen âge; toutes les places livrées, pour deux représentations, à une foule de personnes hostiles ou, du moins, indifférentes à toute aspiration idéale, toutes ces choses doivent être également prises en considération. Seuls (et l'occasion naturelle s'offre ici de les remercier), mademoiselle Sax et Morelli ont fait tête à l'orage. Il ne serait pas convenable de ne louer que leur talent; il faut aussi vanter leur bravoure. Ils ont résisté à la déroute; ils sont restés, sans broncher un instant, fidèles au compositeur. Morelli, avec l'admirable souplesse italienne, s'est conformé humblement au style et au goût de l'auteur, et les personnes qui ont eu souvent le loisir de l'étudier disent que cette docilité lui a profité, et qu'il n'a jamais paru dans un aussi beau jour que sous le personnage de Wolfram. Mais que dirons-nous de M. Niemann, de ses faiblesses, de ses pamoisons, de ses mauvaises humeurs d'enfant gâté, nous qui avons assisté à des tempêtes théâtrales, où des hommes tels que Frédérick et Rouvière, et Bignon lui-même, quoique moins autorisé par la célébrité, bravaient ouvertement l'erreur du public, jouaient avec d'autant plus de zèle qu'il se montrait plus injuste, et faisaient constamment cause commune avec l'auteur?—Enfin, la question du ballet, élevée à la hauteur d'une question vitale et agitée pendant plusieurs mois, n'a pas peu contribué à l'émeute. «Un opéra sans ballet! qu'est-ce que cela?» disait la routine. «Qu'est-ce que cela?» disaient les entreteneurs de filles. «Prenez garde!» disait lui-même à l'auteur le ministre alarmé. On a fait manœuvrer sur la scène, en manière de consolation, des régiments prussiens en jupes courtes, avec les gestes mécaniques d'une école militaire; et une partie du public disait, voyant toutes ces jambes et illusionné par une mauvaise mise en scène: «Voilà un mauvais ballet et une musique qui n'est pas faite pour la danse.» Le bon sens répondait: «Ce n'est pas un ballet; mais ce devrait être une bacchanale, une orgie, comme l'indique la musique, et comme ont su quelquefois en représenter la Porte-Saint-Martin, l'Ambigu, l'Odéon, et même des théâtres inférieurs, mais comme n'en peut pas figurer l'Opéra, qui ne sait rien faire du tout.» Ainsi, ce n'est pas une raison littéraire, mais simplement l'inhabileté des machinistes, qui a nécessité la suppression de tout un tableau (la nouvelle apparition de Vénus).

¶55 Que les hommes qui peuvent se donner le luxe d'une maîtresse parmi les danseuses de l'Opéra, désirent qu'on mette le plus souvent possible en lumière les talents et les beautés de leur emplette, c'est là certes un sentiment presque paternel que tout le monde comprend et excuse facilement; mais que ces mêmes hommes, sans se soucier de la curiosité publique et des plaisirs d'autrui, rendent impossible l'exécution d'un ouvrage qui leur déplaît parce qu'il ne satisfait pas aux exigences de leur protectorat, voilà ce qui est intolérable. Gardez votre harem et conservez-en religieusement les traditions; mais faites-nous donner un théâtre où ceux qui ne pensent pas comme vous pourront trouver d'autres plaisirs mieux accommodés à leur goût. Ainsi nous serons débarrassés de vous, et vous de nous, et chacun sera content.

*

¶56 On espérait arracher à ces enragés leur victime en la présentant au public un dimanche, c'est-à-dire un jour où les abonnés et le Jockey-Club abandonnent volontiers la salle à une foule qui profite de la place libre et du loisir. Mais ils avaient fait ce raisonnement assez juste: «Si nous permettons que le succès ait lieu aujourd'hui, l'administration en tirera un prétexte suffisant pour nous imposer l'ouvrage pendant trente jours.» Et ils sont revenus à la charge, armés de toutes pièces, c'est-à-dire des instruments homicides confectionnés à l'avance. Le public, le public entier, a lutté pendant deux actes, et dans sa bienveillance, doublée par l'indignation, il applaudissait non-seulement les beautés irrésistibles, mais même les passages qui l'étonnaient et le déroutaient, soit qu'ils fussent obscurcis par une exécution trouble, soit qu'ils eussent besoin, pour être appréciés, d'un impossible recueillement. Mais ces tempêtes de colère ou d'enthousiasme amenaient immédiatement une réaction non moins violente et beaucoup moins fatigante pour les opposants. Alors ce même public, espérant que l'émeute lui saurait gré de sa mansuétude, se taisait, voulant avant toute chose connaître et juger. Mais les *quelques* sifflets ont *courageusement* persisté, *sans motif et sans interruption;* l'admirable récit du voyage à Rome n'a pas été entendu (chanté même? je n'en sais rien) et tout le troisième acte a été submergé dans le tumulte.

¶57 Dans la presse, aucune résistance, aucune protestation, excepté celle de M. Franck Marie, dans *la Patrie.* M. Berlioz a évité de dire son avis; courage négatif. Remercions-le de n'avoir pas ajouté à l'injure universelle. Et puis alors, un immense tourbillon d'imitation a entraîné toutes les plumes, a fait délirer toutes les langues, semblable à ce singulier esprit qui fait dans les foules des miracles alternatifs de bravoure et de couardise; le courage collectif et la lâcheté collective; l'enthousiasme français et la panique gauloise.

¶58 Le *Tannhaüser* n'avait même pas été entendu.

*

¶59 Aussi, de tous côtés, abondent maintenant les plaintes; chacun voudrait voir l'ouvrage de Wagner, et chacun crie à la tyrannie. Mais l'administration a baissé la tête devant quelques conspirateurs, et on rend l'argent déjà déposé pour les représentations suivantes. Ainsi, spectacle inouï, s'il en peut exister toutefois de plus scandaleux que celui auquel nous avons assisté, nous voyons aujourd'hui une direction vaincue, qui, malgré les encouragements du public, renonce à continuer des représentations des plus fructueuses.

¶60 Il paraît d'ailleurs que l'accident se propage, et que le public n'est plus considéré comme le juge suprême en fait de représentations scéniques. Au moment même où j'écris ces lignes, j'apprends qu'un beau drame, admirablement construit et écrit dans un excellent style, va disparaître, au bout de quelques jours, d'une autre scène où il s'était produit avec éclat et malgré les efforts d'une certaine caste impuissante, qui s'appelait jadis la classe lettrée, et qui est aujourd'hui inférieure en esprit et en délicatesse à un public de port de mer. En vérité, l'auteur est bien fou qui a pu croire que ces gens prendraient feu pour une chose aussi impalpable, aussi gazéiforme que l'*honneur*. Tout au plus sont-ils bons à l'*enterrer*.

¶61 Quelles sont les raisons mystérieuses de cette expulsion? Le succès gênerait-il les opérations futures du directeur? D'inintelligibles considérations officielles auraient-elles forcé sa bonne volonté, violenté ses intérêts? Ou bien faut-il supposer quelque chose de monstrueux, c'est-à-dire qu'un directeur peut feindre, pour se faire valoir, de désirer de bons drames, et ayant enfin atteint son but, retourne bien vite à son véritable goût, qui est celui des imbéciles, évidemment le plus productif? Ce qui est encore plus inexplicable, c'est la faiblesse des critiques (dont quelques-uns sont poëtes), qui caressent leur principal ennemi, et qui, si parfois, dans un accès de bravoure passagère, ils blâment son mercantilisme, n'en persistent pas moins, en une foule de cas, à encourager son commerce par toutes les complaisances.

*

¶62 Pendant tout ce tumulte et devant les déplorables facéties du feuilleton, dont je rougissais, comme un homme délicat d'une saleté commise devant lui, une idée cruelle m'obsédait. Je me souviens que, malgré que j'aie toujours soigneusement étouffé dans mon cœur ce patriotisme exagéré dont les fumées peuvent obscurcir le cerveau, il m'est arrivé, sur des plages lointaines, à des tables d'hôte composées des éléments humains les plus divers, de souffrir horriblement quand j'entendais des voix (équitables ou injustes, qu'importe?) ridiculiser la France. Tout le sentiment filial, philosophiquement comprimé, faisait alors explosion. Quand un déplorable académicien s'est avisé d'introduire, il y a quelques années, dans son discours de réception, une appréciation du génie de Shakespeare, qu'il appelait familièrement le vieux *Williams,* ou le bon *Williams,*—appréciation digne en vérité d'un concierge de la Comédie-Française,—j'ai senti en frissonnant le dommage que ce pédant sans orthographe allait faire à mon pays. En effet, pendant plusieurs jours, tous les journaux anglais se sont amusés de nous, et de la manière la plus navrante. Les littérateurs français, à les entendre, ne savaient même pas l'orthographe du nom de Shakespeare; ils ne comprenaient rien à son génie, et la France abêtie ne connaissait que deux auteurs, Ponsard et Alexandre Dumas fils, *les poëtes favoris du nouvel Empire,* ajoutait *l'Illustrated London News.* Notez que la haine politique combinait son élément avec le patriotisme littéraire outragé.

¶63 Or, pendant les scandales soulevés par l'ouvrage de Wagner, je me disais: «Qu'est-ce que l'Europe va penser de nous, et en Allemagne que dira-t-on de Paris? Voilà une poignée de tapageurs qui nous déshonorent collectivement!» Mais non, cela ne sera pas. Je crois, je sais, je jure que parmi les littérateurs, les artistes et même parmi les gens du monde, il y a encore un bon nombre de personnes bien élevées, douées de justice, et dont l'esprit est toujours libéralement ouvert aux nouveautés qui leur sont offertes. L'Allemagne aurait tort de croire que Paris n'est peuplé que de polissons qui se mouchent avec les doigts, à cette fin de les essuyer sur le dos d'un grand homme qui passe. Une pareille supposition ne serait pas d'une totale impartialité. De tous les côtés, comme je l'ai dit, la réaction s'éveille; des témoignages de sympathie des plus inattendus sont venus encourager l'auteur à persister dans sa destinée. Si les choses continuent ainsi, il est présumable que beaucoup de regrets pourront être prochainement consolés, et que *Tannhäuser* reparaîtra, mais dans un lieu où les abonnés de l'Opéra ne seront pas intéressés à le poursuivre.

*

¶64 Enfin, l'idée est lancée, la trouée est faite; c'est l'important. Plus d'un compositeur français voudra profiter des idées salutaires émises par Wagner. Si peu de temps que l'ouvrage ait paru devant le public, l'ordre de l'Empereur, auquel nous devons de l'avoir entendu, a apporté un grand secours à l'esprit français, esprit logique, amoureux d'ordre, qui reprendra facilement la suite de ses évolutions.

Sous la République et le premier Empire, la musique s'était élevée à une hauteur qui en fit, à défaut de la littérature découragée, une des gloires de ces temps. Le chef du second Empire n'a-t-il été que curieux d'entendre l'œuvre d'un homme dont on parlait chez nos voisins, ou une pensée plus patriotique et plus compréhensive l'excitait-elle? En tout cas, sa simple curiosité nous aura été profitable à tous.

8 avril 1861

Langsam

NOTES

CHAPTER 1: *From an Unsafe Distance*

1. On relations between Baudelaire's Wagner essay and mid-nineteenth-century journalism in general, see Susan Bernstein, "Virtuosity of the Nineteenth Century: Music and Language in Heine, Liszt, and Baudelaire" (Ph.D. diss., Johns Hopkins University, 1991), 484–505.

2. See, in order, Margaret Gilman, *Baudelaire the Critic* (New York: Columbia University Press, 1943; New York: Octagon Press, 1971), 168–84; Philippe Lacoue-Labarthe, *Musica ficta (Figures de Wagner)* (Paris: Christian Bourgois, 1991), 58–62; Lucy Beckett, "Wagner and His Critics," in *The Wagner Companion,* ed. Peter Burbidge and Richard Sutton (New York: Cambridge University Press, 1979), 366; and Theodor W. Adorno, *Versuch über Wagner,* 2d ed. (Frankfurt am Main: Suhrkamp, 1981), 48. Unless otherwise indicated, all translations here and throughout are my own.

3. Charles Baudelaire, *Correspondance,* ed. Claude Pichois and Jean Ziegler, 2 vols. (Paris: Gallimard, Bibliothèque de la Pléiade, 1973), 2:129.

4. Baudelaire described his reaction to the concerts in letters to Wagner and to others. See Baudelaire, *Correspondance,* 1:667, 671–74. Baudelaire subsequently mentioned work on his Wagner article in various letters throughout 1860; see especially Baudelaire, *Correspondance,* 1:6, 13, 35, 58, 63, 69, 101, 102, 105, 110.

5. The essay was printed in the *Revue européenne* on April 1, 1861, and it was reprinted in *La Presse théâtrale et musicale* on April 14, April 21, and May 5, 1861; in both instances, it was entitled "Richard Wagner." The longer title, *Richard Wagner et "Tannhäuser" à Paris,* first appeared when E. Dentu published the essay as a separate brochure at the end of April 1861.

6. See Appendix 1, ¶50–64. Hereafter, all references to paragraphs in the present

edition of *Richard Wagner et "Tannhäuser" à Paris* will appear in parentheses in my text. All translations from Baudelaire's works are my own, although in making them I have occasionally consulted the following: Charles Baudelaire, *The Painter of Modern Life and Other Essays*, trans. and ed. Jonathan Mayne (London: Phaidon Press, 1964; New York: Da Capo, 1986); Charles Baudelaire, *Baudelaire: Selected Writings on Art and Artists*, trans. and intro. P. E. Charvet (Harmondsworth, England: Penguin Books, 1972); Charles Baudelaire, *Baudelaire as a Literary Critic*, trans. and ed. Lois Boe Hyslop and Francis E. Hyslop Jr. (University Park: Pennsylvania State University Press, 1964); Charles Baudelaire, *Baudelaire: The Complete Verse*, trans. and ed. Francis Scarfe, 2 vols. (London: Anvil Press Poetry, 1986). As I have already begun to do above, I will occasionally abbreviate the title of Baudelaire's Wagner essay as *Richard Wagner*.

Baudelaire is fairly accurate in his list of reasons contributing to the *Tannhäuser* fiasco. For more details on Wagner and the Paris Opéra, some good places to begin are Léon Guichard, *La Musique et les lettres en France au temps du wagnérisme* (Paris: Presses Universitaires de France, 1963), 27–44; G. Leprince, *Présence de Wagner* (Paris: Éditions du Vieux Colombier, 1963), 23–43; and Gerald Dale Turbow, "Art and Politics: Wagnerism in France," in *Wagnerism in European Culture and Politics,* ed. David C. Large and William Weber (Ithaca, N.Y.: Cornell University Press, 1984), 134–66.

7. On April 3, 1861, Baudelaire wrote to his mother about his Wagner essay: "It must reappear immediately as a brochure, *with a supplement.* Now this supplement is not done. And it's being demanded for *today" (Correspondance,* 2:143–44).

8. I owe some aspects of this double interpretation to Barbara Johnson's discussion of a similarly negative, rhetorical question in Baudelaire's preface to *Le Spleen de Paris.* See Johnson, *Défigurations du langage poétique* (Paris: Flammarion, 1979), 24–26.

9. Charles Baudelaire, *Œuvres complètes,* ed. Claude Pichois, 2 vols. (Paris: Gallimard, Bibliothèque de la Pléiade, 1983–85), 2:425. Further references to volume and page numbers in this edition will appear in parentheses.

10. Jean-Pierre Richard emphasizes the importance specifically assigned to the observer's distance from landscape painting in Baudelaire's *Salon de 1846:* "[S]pace then plays the role of a sort of resonance chamber in which the various perceptible qualities of a landscape are created and exchanged among themselves [se provoquent et s'échangent]" ("Profondeur de Baudelaire," in *Poésie et profondeur* [Paris: Seuil, 1955], 113).

11. Joycelynne Loncke makes this point in *Baudelaire et la musique* (Paris: Nizet, 1975), 202–3. Juliette Hassine makes it at greater length in her *Essai sur Proust*

et Baudelaire (Paris: Nizet, 1979); see especially her chapter entitled "Les Marines baudelairiennes et les marines proustiennes," 145–80.

12. This reading of "La Musique" draws on two other interpretations of the poem, although the context of each is different from my own. The first is by Sandra L. Bermann in *The Sonnet over Time,* University of North Carolina Studies in Comparative Literature, no. 63 (Chapel Hill: University of North Carolina Press, 1988), 107–11; Bermann analyzes various figural levels at which the poem identifies the poetic self with a ship and the music with the sea. The second interpretation is by Susan Blood, who draws particular attention to the temporal structure proposed by the poem ("souvent" / "D'autres fois"); see "The Ethical Imperative in Baudelaire's Aesthetics" (Ph.D. diss., Johns Hopkins University, 1988), 44–47.

13. This passage is translated and quoted in Carl Dahlhaus, *The Idea of Absolute Music,* trans. Roger Lustig (Chicago: University of Chicago Press, 1989), 24. The original German can be found in Richard Wagner, *Das Kunstwerk der Zukunft,* in *Gesammelte Schriften und Dichtungen,* 4th ed., 10 vols. (Leipzig: C. F. W. Siegel's Musikalienhandlung, 1907), 3:83.

14. Wagner, *Gesammelte Schriften und Dichtungen,* 3:82.

15. Wagner, *Der fliegende Holländer,* act 1, scene 2: "—Wie oft in Meeres tiefsten Schlund / Stürzt' ich voll Sehnsucht mich hinab" (*Gesammelte Schriften und Dichtungen,* 1:260).

16. See E[rnst] T[heodor] A[madeus] Hoffmann, *Sämtliche Werke,* ed. Hartmut Steinecke and Wulf Segebrecht, 6 vols. (Frankfurt am Main: Deutscher Klassiker Verlag, 1993), vol. 2, pt. 1, p. 63. See also E[rnst] T[heodor] A[madeus] Hoffmann, "Pensées extrêmement éparses," in *Contes fantastiques,* trans. [Adolphe-François] Loève-Veimars, intro. and notes José Lambert, 3 vols. (Paris: Flammarion, 1982), 3:417. The Loève-Veimars translation of Hoffmann's works, first published in France from 1830 to 1833, was almost certainly known to Baudelaire.

17. In the original German: "Der Duft der dunkelroten Nelken wirkt mit sonderbarer magischer Gewalt auf mich; unwillkürlich versinke ich in einen träumerischen Zustand une höre dann, wie aus weiter Ferne, die anschwellenden und wieder verfliessenden tiefen Töne des Bassethorns" (Hoffmann, *Sämtliche Werke,* vol. 2, pt. 1, p. 63). Suggestively, Loève-Veimars translated "Nelken" as "soucis," which can mean either "marigolds" or "worries."

18. See François-Joseph Fétis, "Richard Wagner," *Revue et Gazette musicale de Paris* 19, no. 23 (June 6, 1852): 185–87; no. 24 (June 13, 1852): 193–95; no. 25 (June 20, 1852): 201–3; no. 26 (June 27, 1852): 209–11; no. 28 (July 11, 1852): 225–27; no. 30 (July 25, 1852): 242–45; no. 32 (Aug. 8, 1852): 257–59. See also Richard Wagner, *Quatre poèmes d'opéras traduits en prose française, précédés d'une lettre*

sur la musique, French trans. [Paul Amand] Challemel-Lacour (Paris: A. Bourdilliat, 1861), i–lxxiii.

19. In the original: La mélodie en est belle, mais l'harmonie qui devrait la soutenir la heurte et l'entrave. Wagner me semble un être sain de corps et de jambes qui s'entêterait à marcher avec des béquilles. Quoted in J.-P. Moschelès, "Revue de quinzaine," *La Chronique musicale* 4, no. 16 (Nov. 1, 1868): 3. Moschelès attributes this quotation to Eugène Tarbès, who reviewed the performance for *Le Gaulois.*

20. Baron Ernouf, "L'Œuvre de R. Wagner," *Revue comtenporaine* (Feb. 15, 1860): 552. In French: Je l'avouerai franchement: une longue course à travers des landes et des marais, sous un ciel noir, épais, sillonné d'éclairs blafards ne m'aurait pas plus fatigué que l'attention opiniâtre qu'il était de mon devoir de prêter à tous ces morceaux.

21. In the original: Ses harmonies grandioses, ses chants profondément modulés et indéterminés dans leur forme, ses accents tronqués et pourtant sublimes sont comme le souffle du vent qui passe sur une grève déserte. Émile Faure, "Le Premier Concert de Richard Wagner et la presse parisienne," *La Presse théâtrale et musicale* 7, no. 5 (Feb. 5, 1860): 2. This article is a compilation of more or less lengthy quotations from fourteen reviews of the concert. The quotation just given is attributed to Franck-Marie, who wrote for *La Patrie.*

22. Une fois entré dans ce domaine, où tout est inconnu, il ne peut y avoir aucun repos: on est dans l'immensité, on aperçoit dans l'espace des mondes que l'on ne peut atteindre; la vague incertitude qui s'empare de l'âme ne la quitte qu'au moment où, renonçant à des recherches sans résultat, elle revient au positif en remettant le pied sur le monde où elle a été créée et où elle se connaît mieux. Quoted in Émile Faure, "La Presse parisienne et les concerts Wagner," *La Presse théâtrale et musicale* 7, no. 7 (Feb. 19, 1860). The quotation, attributed to M. Simiot, is drawn from a review in *La Causerie.*

23. "[Mozart] serait comparable à ces petits sentiers qui côtoient les rivières et où le promeneur s'égare dans les belles journées de printemps; . . . on avance sans avancer, et l'on s'abîme dans une somnolence contemplative." Charles Grandmougin, *Esquisse sur Richard Wagner* (Paris: Durand, Schœnewerk, 1873), 19–20. Grandmougin's images have much in common with the geographical imagery for music by Haydn, Mozart, and Beethoven in E. T. A. Hoffmann's celebrated essay on Beethoven's Fifth Symphony; for the French version of this essay, see "La Musique instrumentale de Beethoven," in Hoffmann, *Contes fantastiques,* 3:409–15.

24. Grandmougin, *Esquisse,* 20: [O]n éprouve, en l'écoutant, la même impression que lorsqu'on gravit une montagne. La plaine se déroule peu à peu sous nos pieds; l'horizon s'agrandit; . . . et quand nous atteignons le sommet de la montagne, nous

reconnaissons à peine le pays, tant le crescendo de l'ascension en a métamorphosé l'ensemble.

25. Grandmougin, *Esquisse*, 21: [L]es caractères se développent parallèlement et se font mutuellement contraste comme les différentes valeurs de ton d'un tableau.

26. Grandmougin, *Esquisse*, 26: [S]i l'on rattache Wagner à Beethoven, . . . c'est principalement pour avoir transporté la symphonie au théâtre. For a detailed interrogation of Wagner's long-standing reputation as a composer of "symphonic" operas, see Carolyn Abbate, "Opera as Symphony, a Wagnerian Myth," in *Analyzing Opera: Verdi and Wagner*, ed. Carolyn Abbate and Roger Parker (Berkeley and Los Angeles: University of California Press, 1989), 92–124.

27. See Jeffrey Cooper, *The Rise of Instrumental Music and Concert Series in Paris, 1828–1871*, Studies in Musicology, no. 65 (Ann Arbor, Mich.: UMI, 1983), 85–104.

28. For further information on distinctions between concert and opera etiquette in Wagner's time, see William Weber, "Wagner, Wagnerism, and Musical Idealism," in *Wagnerism in European Culture and Politics*, ed. David C. Large and William Weber (Ithaca, N.Y.: Cornell University Press, 1984), 28–71.

29. Edmond Roche, "Richard Wagner: Premier concert à grand orchestre donné, le 25 janvier 1860, au Théâtre Impérial Italien," *La Presse théâtrale et musicale* 7, no. 4 (Jan. 29, 1860): 1. See also Paul Scudo, *L'Année musicale, deuxième année* (Paris: Hachette, 1860), 147, and Hector Berlioz, "Concerts de Richard Wagner: La Musique de l'avenir," in *À travers chants*, ed. Léon Guichard (Paris: Gründ, 1971), 321–22. All these reviews paint much the same picture of the chaos in the halls of the Théâtre-Italien; in his essay, Baudelaire quotes from Berlioz's description (¶3).

30. The quotation is taken from H[enri] Cohen, "Concerts Populaires," *La Chronique musicale* 3, no. 15 (Feb. 1, 1874): 126. For further information on Wagner performances by the Concerts Populaires, see Élisabeth Bernard, "La Vie symphonique à Paris entre 1861 et 1914 suivie d'une étude analytique des programmes des *Concerts Populaires de Musique Classique*, de l'*Association Artistique*, et de la *Société des Nouveaux-Concerts*" (thèse de doctorat, 3e cycle, Université de Paris I, 1976), 25–37, and *Le Chef d'orchestre* (Paris: Éditions La Découverte, 1989), 136–47.

31. Richard Wagner, "Bayreuth," in *Richard Wagner's Prose Works*, trans. William Ashton Ellis, 8 vols. (New York: Broude Brothers, 1966), 5:334; Wagner, *Gesammelte Schriften und Dichtungen*, 9:337.

32. Wagner, "Bayreuth," 5:334–35; Wagner, *Gesammelte Schriften und Dichtungen*, 9:337.

33. Wagner, "Bayreuth," 5:335; Wagner, *Gesammelte Schriften und Dichtungen*, 9:337–38.

34. Wagner, "Bayreuth," 5:336; Wagner, *Gesammelte Schriften und Dichtungen,*
9:339. On the design and construction of the Bayreuth Festival Theater, see
Geoffrey Skelton, "The Idea of Bayreuth," in *The Wagner Companion,* ed.
Peter Burbidge and Richard Sutton (New York: Cambridge University Press, 1979),
389–411, and John Deathridge and Carl Dahlhaus, *The New Grove Wagner* (New
York: W. W. Norton, 1984), 57–66. See also Beat Wyss, *"Ragnarök* of Illusion:
Richard Wagner's 'Mystical Abyss' at Bayreuth," *October* 54 (1990): 57–78. Wyss
notes that an "abyss" hiding the orchestra was first designed (but never built) by
Gottfried Semper for a theater in a remodeled hall of the Munich Glass Palace
(61). Wyss also emphasizes that one important effect of the "optical recession"
built into the Festspielhaus auditorium is "the inescapable, if you will, equality of
central-perspective-for-all," a perspective that "is antithetical to a concept of the
loge theater that accentuates social discrepancies" (74).

35. Robert Hartford, ed., *Bayreuth: The Early Years. An account of the Early Decades
of the Wagner Festival as seen by the Celebrated Visitors & Participants* (Cambridge:
Cambridge University Press, 1980), 54.

36. Hartford, *Bayreuth: The Early Years,* 55.

37. Albert Lavignac, *Le Voyage artistique à Bayreuth,* 4th ed. (Paris: Delagrave,
1900), 1: On va à Bayreuth comme on veut, à pied, à cheval, en voiture, à bicy-
clette, en chemin de fer, et le vrai pèlerin devrait y aller à genoux. Mais la voie la
plus pratique, au moins pour les Français, c'est le chemin de fer.

38. Lavignac, *Le Voyage artistique à Bayreuth,* 3.

39. Lavignac, *Le Voyage artistique à Bayreuth,* v.

CHAPTER 2: *Emphatic Music*

1. Georges Poulet, *La Distance intérieure,* vol. 2 of *Études sur le temps humain*
(1952; Paris: Plon, Rocher, 1976), i. Unless otherwise indicated, all translations are
my own.

2. See Appendix 1, ¶1. All further references to paragraphs in the present edition
of *Richard Wagner et "Tannhäuser" à Paris* will appear in parentheses.

3. My analysis of Baudelaire's *I* owes much to two essays. The first is Emile
Benveniste's "La Nature des pronoms," in *Problèmes de linguistique générale,* 2 vols.
(Paris: Gallimard, 1966), 1:251-57. Among his remarks on the pronoun *I,* Benveniste writes, "If I perceive two successive instances of discourse containing *I,*
proffered by the same voice, nothing yet assures me that one of them is not re-
ported discourse, a quotation in which *I* would be imputable to another" (252).
The second essay is Jacques Derrida's "Signature événement contexte," in *Marges*

de la philosophie (Paris: Minuit, 1972), 365–93. For an analysis that differs from my own, see Philippe Lacoue-Labarthe, "Baudelaire," in *Musica ficta (Figures de Wagner)* (Paris: Christian Bourgois, 1991), 25–90. Lacoue-Labarthe understands Baudelaire's *I* as both "a demand that is made . . . in the name of the subjectivity of him who wants to be, indissociably, poet (writer) and critic" and "a subject who up to a certain point demands *himself* of Wagner" (59–60). See also Susan Bernstein, "Virtuosity of the Nineteenth Century: Music and Language in Heine, Liszt, and Baudelaire" (Ph.D. diss., Johns Hopkins University, 1991), 485–86. For Bernstein, the *I* is at once Baudelaire's "personal voice" and "the monotonously uniform sign of the journalistic reader: the indefinite public, the members of the crowd."

4. Walter Benjamin, *Charles Baudelaire: Ein Lyriker im Zeitalter des Hochkapitalismus,* ed. Rolf Tiedemann (Frankfurt am Main: Suhrkamp, 1974), 131.

5. The full program for each of the three concerts ran as follows: Overture to *Der fliegende Holländer;* Entrance and Chorus of Guests at the Wartburg (act 2), Pilgrimage and Pilgrim's Chorus (act 3), and Overture to *Tannhäuser;* Prelude to *Tristan und Isolde;* Prelude, Betrothal March (act 2), and Wedding Music and Chorus (act 3) from *Lohengrin.* The concerts were performed on January 25, February 1, and February 8, 1860.

6. The program for the Pastoral Symphony was distributed on March 15, 1829 (Programs for the Société des Concerts du Conservatoire, 1828–1913, Bibliothèque Nationale, Département de la Musique, Paris). For details on the program for the *Symphonie fantastique,* see comments by Edward Cone in Hector Berlioz, *Fantastic Symphony: An Authoritative Score, Historical Background, Analysis, Views, and Comments,* ed. Edward T. Cone (New York: W. W. Norton, 1971), 18–35.

7. Cf. Roger Scruton, "Programme Music," in *The New Grove Dictionary of Music and Musicians,* ed. Stanley Sadie, 20 vols. (London: Macmillan, 1980), 15:283–87. Scruton examines some of the drawbacks of a broad definition that would include "all music with extra-musical reference, whether to objective events or subjective feelings"; he prefers to privilege music with a narrative or descriptive intention, thus excluding music intended only to express emotion or to imitate extramusical sounds (284). For more detailed remarks on the concept of musical representation, see Roger Scruton, "Representation in Music," *Journal of the Royal Institute of Philosophy* 51, no. 197 (July 1976): 273–87. For a historical sketch of program music in the first half of the nineteenth century, see Carl Dahlhaus, *Nineteenth-Century Music,* trans. J. Bradford Robinson (Berkeley and Los Angeles: University of California Press, 1989), 88–96, 142–52, 236–44.

8. Zacharie Astruc, "Chronique musicale: Richard Wagner," *Revue internationale* 2 (Feb. 29, 1860): 464.

9. In the original: Dans l'impossibilité de faire entendre en entier ses opéras, l'auteur se permet d'offrir au public quelques lignes d'explications, qui lui feront mieux comprendre le sens des morceaux détachés qu'il lui soumet aujourd'hui. A copy of the program booklet distributed at the Théâtre-Italien is preserved at the Bibliothèque de l'Opéra, Paris, in a bound collection numbered C.5065[(6)].

10. Franz Liszt, "Berlioz und seine 'Harold-Symphonie,'" in *Gesammelte Schriften von Franz Liszt,* ed. L. Ramann, 6 vols. (Leipzig: Breitkopf und Härtel, 1882), 4:21. In the original: [Ein Programm ist] irgend ein der rein-instrumentalen Musik in verständlicher Sprache beigefügtes Vorwort, mit welchem der Komponist bezweckt, die Zuhörer gegenüber seinem Werke vor der Willkür poetischer Auslegung zu bewahren und die Aufmerksamkeit im Voraus auf die poetische Idee des Ganzen, auf einen besonderen Punkt desselben hinzulenken.

11. Rose Rosengard Subotnik suggests, in *Developing Variations: Style and Ideology in Western Music* (Minneapolis: University of Minnesota Press, 1991), that romantic music may have obliged its listeners to make sense of its tonal structures by relating them to "various other, autonomous layers of potential meaning," some of which—like programs—were nonmusical (124). Unlike classical music, Subotnik argues, romantic music does not present itself as a self-sufficient structure that unfolds temporally according to the logic of tonal relations. Instead, each romantic piece appears to constitute a fragmentary, arbitrarily organized structure that cannot be understood from within on the basis of its "tonal unfolding" (122). The romantic listener, therefore, "must be able to refer to what can be imagined as analogous, essentially stylistic structures, both cultural and individual, coexisting outside and yet somehow underneath the music. In making such reference, listeners can develop a type of competence whereby they are able, on the basis of static associations or isolated details, to recognize the musical structure as a whole in the sense that they can identify it" (125). It seems to me that one sign of such competence among general (musically untrained) listeners of Baudelaire's time was their invention of programs for individual pieces.

12. Astruc, "Chronique musicale," 464: Ne sera-t-il plus possible de rêver sur un son? de l'assimiler à une poétique interprétation littéraire? de lui donner, même par la parole, un développement original, en restant, bien entendu, aux limites du vrai? Que faisons-nous tous les jours dans les thèmes innombrables que nous hasardons sur la musique des vieux maîtres?

13. Benveniste notes that the third-person forms of pronouns and verbs, in opposition to forms for the first and second persons, mark an absence or an exclusion from the *je-tu* [I-thou] relation rather than a third participant: "[T]he 'third person' is not a 'person'; it is in fact the verbal form whose function is to express the *non-*

person." One of the consequences is the use of the third person for historical or
fictional narratives that aim to present events as if they were narrating themselves
without the intervention of any storyteller. See Benveniste, *Problèmes de linguistique
générale,* 1:227–31, 239–41.

14. For further discussion on instrumental music that purports to "tell a story"
with the aid of illustrative titles or narrative programs, see Peter Kivy, "Music as
Narration," in *Sound and Semblance: Reflections on Musical Representation* (Princeton:
Princeton University Press, 1984), 159–96. More recently, Carolyn Abbate has published an important study of musical narration; see "Music's Voices" and "What
the Sorcerer Said," in *Unsung Voices: Opera and Musical Narrative in the Nineteenth
Century* (Princeton: Princeton University Press, 1991), 3–60.

15. Louis Lacombe, "Richard Wagner (troisième partie)," *La Presse théâtrale et
musicale* 7, no. 12 (Mar. 25, 1860). In the original: A ces quatre parties viennent s'en
joindre d'autres, puis les instruments à vent entrent un à un, et bientôt toutes les
voix de l'orchestre, s'unissant en un concert harmonieux, ondulent et s'établissent
un moment dans le grave. Lacombe's description of the instrumentation is somewhat inaccurate, since the woodwinds do not enter "one by one." The second
statement of the melody is played by flutes, oboes, and clarinets; the third is given
to French horns, violas, and cellos. Lacombe himself gives no measure numbers; I
have indicated them for convenience.

16. Lacombe, "Richard Wagner (troisième partie)." Lacombe here refers to the
correspondence between mm. 1–6, where sustained A major chords lead into the
first statement of the melody, and mm. 67–75, where similar chords and a fragment
of the melody prepare the closing plagal cadence.

17. Hector Berlioz, "Concerts de Richard Wagner: La Musique de l'avenir," in
À travers chants, ed. Léon Guichard (Paris: Gründ, 1971), 326. Berlioz's article was
originally published in the *Journal des Débats* (Feb. 9, 1860).

18. Berlioz, "Concerts de Richard Wagner," 326.

19. Wagner, Concert Program, 1860, p. 11. The original French reads: Le Saint-
Graal était la coupe dans laquelle le Sauveur avait bu à la dernière Cène et où
Joseph d'Arimathie avait reçu le sang du crucifié. La tradition raconte que le vase
sacré avait été une fois déjà retiré aux hommes indignes, mais que Dieu avait dé-
cidé de le remettre aux mains de quelques privilégiés qui, par leur pureté d'âme,
par la sainteté de leur vie, avaient mérité cet honneur. C'est le retour de [*sic*] Saint-
Graal sur la montagne des saints chevaliers, au milieu d'une troupe d'anges, que
l'introduction du [*sic*] *Lohengrin* a tenté d'exprimer.

20. Charles Baudelaire, *Œuvres complètes,* ed. Claude Pichois, 2 vols. (Paris: Gallimard, Bibliothèque de la Pléiade, 1983–85), 2:165. Further references to volume

and page numbers in this edition of Baudelaire's works will appear in parentheses in my text.

21. Richard Stamelman, "The Shroud of Allegory: Death, Mourning, and Melancholy in Baudelaire's Work," *Texas Studies in Literature and Language* 25, no. 3 (1983): 399. In a study of several of Baudelaire's poems, Stamelman examines how allegory "posits an unbridgeable distance between itself and a referent it can never fully signify or recover" (392). For additional discussion of distance and allegory in Baudelaire's poetic works, see Richard Klein, " 'Bénédiction'/'Perte d'auréole': Parables of Interpretation," *Modern Language Notes* 85, no. 4 (1970): 515–28; see also Nathaniel Wing, "The Danaides Vessel: On Reading Baudelaire's Allegories," in *The Limits of Narrative* (Cambridge: Cambridge University Press, 1986), 8–18.

22. As Claude Pichois explains in a note (Baudelaire, *Œuvres complètes,* 2:1455), Liszt's program first appeared in the *Journal des débats* on October 22, 1850, as part of a long article on the premiere of *Lohengrin* in Weimar. This article reappeared as the first half of a book, Franz Liszt's *"Lohengrin" et "Tannhäuser" de Richard Wagner* (Leipzig: F. A. Brockhaus, 1851; Paris: Adef-Albatros, 1980).

23. Liszt, *"Lohengrin" et "Tannhäuser,"* 64. In a preceding paragraph, Liszt writes that "in this cup, Our Lord consecrated the bread and the wine at the Last Supper, and Joseph of Arimathia gathered in it the blood that flowed from the wound in his side when He was on the cross" (62).

24. It might also be possible to translate the French "tableau sacré" as "sacred scene" or as "sacred tableau," in the sense of a dramatic grouping of motionless figures presented on stage. I much prefer "sacred picture," however, not only because I think Liszt's program implicitly compares the unfolding prelude to a painting at various stages of completion, but also because Liszt uses the French verb "dessiner," which explicitly suggests that the "tableau" is *drawn* on a background surface. Further, the staged scene in a *tableau vivant* traditionally calls for human figures, which are absent from Liszt's program; the only human participants to whom Liszt refers are those watching from the audience.

25. See Antoine Reicha, *Vollständiges Lehrbuch der musikalischen Composition,* translated from the French in parallel columns and annotated by Carl Czerny, 4 vols. (Vienna: Diabelli, 1832), 503–8. With the examples in this passage, Reicha specifically emphasizes that a motif is an eight-bar melody consisting in several one- or two-bar units that may be extracted from the melody and developed throughout the rest of the composition according to detailed rules for repetition and transformation. Cf. Adolf Bernhard Marx, *Die Lehre von der musikalischen Komposition, praktisch theoretisch,* vol. 1 (Leipzig: Breitkopf und Härtel, 1841), 31. Although other theorists from the early nineteenth century, such as Jérome-Joseph de Momigny and

Alexandre Choron, also dealt with these concepts, they did so without using the term *motif;* even Reicha uses the word interchangeably with the word *"thême"* [*sic*].

26. For further background discussion of operatic motifs, see John Warrack, "Leitmotif," in *The New Grove Dictionary of Music and Musicians,* ed. Stanley Sadie, 20 vols. (London: Macmillan, 1980), 10:644–46. For more specific considerations, see, for example, David Charlton, "Motive and Motif: Méhul before 1791," *Music and Letters* 57, no. 4 (1976): 362–69, and Ora Frishberg Saloman, "La Cépède's *La Poétique de la musique* and Le Sueur," *Acta musicologica* 47 (Jan.–June 1975): 144–54.

27. The visual, temporal, compositional, and programmatic connotations of *motif* are admirably synthesized by Jean François Le Sueur in an essay on his *musique motivée,* a series of masses he composed specifically for various festivals of the church year; to explain why congregations would need a written program in order to follow these masses, he writes that "while the Listener seeks [to grasp] the situation and to compare the intentions, the motifs of the Singing and of the Symphony, the passage is already finished; the musical picture has fled during its performance, and leaves you the time neither to reason, nor to seek what it represents" [pendant que l'Auditeur cherche la situation, & à comparer les intentions, les motifs du Chant & de la Symphonie, le passage est déjà fait; le tableau musical a fui pendant l'exécution, & ne vous laisse plus le temps, ni de raisonner, ni de chercher ce qu'il représente]. See *Exposé d'une musique une, imitative, et propre à chaque solemnité, où l'on donne une Dissertation sur ses effets, & le Plan d'une Musique particulière à la Solemnité de la Pentecôte* (Paris: Veuve Hérissant, 1787), 3. See also Dahlhaus, *Nineteenth-Century Music,* 142–52, 236–44; Dahlhaus claims in particular that for romantic composers, " 'motive' refers not only to the musical germ-cell that serves as the starting point of a piece of music, but also to what Wagner called the aesthetic raison d'être behind this cell" (144).

28. Alfred Lorenz, "Der musikalische Aufbau von Wagners *Lohengrin,*" in *Bayreuther Festspielführer,* ed. Otto Strobel (Bayreuth: Georg Niehrenheim, 1936), 189–97.

29. Lorenz, "Der musikalische Aufbau," 195.

30. The measure numbers that appear here are those indicated by Lorenz in his article.

31. Jean-Jacques Rousseau, *Les Rêveries du promeneur solitaire* (Paris: Garnier-Flammarion, 1964), 41.

32. My reading of the word "translate" ("traduire") as a metaphor in Baudelaire's essay owes part of its form to Derrida's discussion of translation (*Übersetzung*) as a metaphor in Freud's writing. See Jacques Derrida, "Freud et la scène de l'écriture," in *L'Écriture et la différence* (Paris: Seuil, 1967), 312–13. For related

discussions of translation as a metaphor in Baudelaire, see Michele Hannoosh, "Painting as Translation in Baudelaire's Art Criticism," *Forum for Modern Language Studies* 22, no. 1 (1986): 22–33, and Mira Levy-Bloch, "La Traduction chez Baudelaire: Les Trois Imaginations du poète-traducteur," *Nineteenth-Century French Studies* 20, nos. 3–4 (1992): 361–79.

33. The term *programmatic sonnet* is borrowed from Paul de Man's essay "Anthropomorphism and Trope in the Lyric," in *The Rhetoric of Romanticism* (New York: Columbia University Press, 1984), 243.

34. When *Richard Wagner* was reprinted posthumously in *L'Art romantique* (1868), this became "render [rendre] with words" instead of "translate [traduire] with words."

35. I draw here on Benveniste's discussion of the simple past tense in *Problèmes de linguistique générale,* 1:239–45; as he analyzes it, the simple past is "the time of the event outside of the person of a narrator" (241).

36. Theodor W. Adorno, *Versuch über Wagner,* 2d ed. (Frankfurt am Main: Suhrkamp, 1981), 48. All translations from this work are my own, although I referred in making them to a translation by Rodney Livingstone under the title *In Search of Wagner* (London: NLB, 1981).

37. Adorno, *Versuch,* 39.

38. Adorno's discussion of the prelude may be found on pp. 49–50 of the *Versuch.* He specifies that he refers to mm. 5–12, but it is probable that he in fact includes the downbeat of m. 13 in the "Thema."

39. Adorno specifies that the melodic hesitation "mirrors" the relation between the first and sixth scale degrees. In traditional harmony, the VI chord may substitute for the I chord because the two differ in only one note and coincide at the crucial lower third of the I chord. In the case of the *Lohengrin* prelude, I (A-C♯-E) shares two pitches with VI (F♯-A-C♯), so that VI may substitute for I in the harmony of the theme; but the two remaining pitches (E and F♯) are precisely the ones that alternate in the melody.

40. Adorno, *Versuch,* 48.

41. Paul de Man, "The Rhetoric of Temporality," in *Blindness and Insight: Essays in the Rhetoric of Contemporary Criticism,* 2d ed., rev., Theory and History of Literature, vol. 7 (Minneapolis: University of Minnesota Press, 1983), 225. De Man makes this point in other essays as well; see, notably, "Pascal's Allegory of Persuasion," in *Allegory and Representation: Selected Papers from the English Institute, 1979–1980,* edited with preface by Stephen J. Greenblatt (Baltimore: Johns Hopkins University Press, 1981), 1: "Allegory is sequential and narrative, yet the topic of its narration

is not necessarily temporal at all, thus raising the question of the referential status of a text whose semantic function, though strongly in evidence, is not primarily determined by mimetic moments."

42. In fact, "*adagio*" is the only word in the program that Liszt himself put in italics. See Liszt, *"Lohengrin" et "Tannhäuser,"* 66.

43. Bernstein also remarks briefly on the relation that the italics create between music and figurative language: "[M]usic signifies the adherence of communicated sense to the material expanse of its signifiers in general. . . . This materially-bound experiential level affects the one who receives it; it does not communicate conceptually. This sense of music thus characterizes not only poetic language, but more generally, the persuasive action of text on reader. Baudelaire's underlining, spacing, and quotation marks operate musically; they are, shall we say, 'prosaic' counterparts to the specifically poetic traits of language traditionally identified with music" ("Virtuosity of the Nineteenth Century," 507).

From a different angle, Lacoue-Labarthe also suggests, in *Musica ficta,* that Baudelaire linked typographical features with musical motifs. Lacoue-Labarthe argues first that Baudelaire surreptitiously regards motivic transformation in Wagner's music as proof that music is not superior to poetry (as Wagner claims in his *Lettre sur la musique),* but rather inseparable from it. In part 3 of his essay, Baudelaire borrows from Liszt an explanation of how the Wagnerian leitmotiv, by associating characters and situations with recurring melodies, can engage in a certain process of signification. Lacoue-Labarthe then speculates that for Baudelaire, music thereby holds the power "*to type* [*typer*], in the sense that this word, in Greek, designates the imprint, the mark imprinted by a seal, the stamp [la frappe]" (88). Lacoue-Labarthe adds that "the type [le type] is also the character—or the *letter.* If one reflects that the letter, in archaic Greek (that of Democritus, for example), could equally well be expressed as *rhuthmos,* one begins to muse [rêver]" (89).

It should also be noted that Barbara Johnson analyzes another, somewhat similar instance in which Baudelaire uses italics to explore the connections between literal writing and figurative language; see "Disfiguring Poetic Language," in *A World of Difference* (Baltimore: Johns Hopkins University Press, 1987), 100–115. When he partially italicizes the expression *"tuer* le Temps" [*to kill* Time] in the prose poem "Le Galant Tireur," Baudelaire "restores to a dead figure the original impact that has been lost through linguistic habit. The italics give back to the verb *to kill* all its literality. . . . Thus, paradoxically, it is through the verb *to kill* that the 'dead' figure is resuscitated" (106–7).

44. Gautier remarks that Baudelaire "had italics and capital letters in his voice"

[avait dans la voix des italiques et des majuscules initiales]. See Théophile Gautier, "Charles Baudelaire," preface to *Œuvres complètes,* by Charles Baudelaire, 7 vols. (Paris: Michel Lévy Frères, 1869), 1:5.

45. My argument here is related to one of Jacques Derrida's starting points in *De la grammatologie* (Paris: Minuit, 1967). In a section of his first chapter, subtitled "Le Programme," Derrida notes that "one now tends to say 'writing' for . . . everything that can give rise to an inscription in general, whether or not it is literal and even if what it distributes in space is foreign to the order of the voice: cinematography, choreography, certainly, but also pictural, musical, sculptural 'writing,' etc." (19).

CHAPTER 3: *Music in Person*

1. See Appendix 1, ¶16. All subsequent references to paragraphs in the present edition of *Richard Wagner et "Tannhäuser" à Paris* will be given in parentheses. All translations of this and other texts are my own unless otherwise noted.

2. Charles Baudelaire, *Œuvres complètes,* ed. Claude Pichois, 2 vols. (Paris: Gallimard, Bibliothèque de la Pléiade, 1983–85), 2:1452–53. Further references to volume and page numbers in this edition will appear parenthetically in the main text.

3. For a more extended interpretation of this passage from Baudelaire's letter, see Philippe Lacoue-Labarthe, *Musica ficta (Figures de Wagner)* (Paris: Christian Bourgois, 1991), 60–68. Lacoue-Labarthe analyzes the passage as an important instance of "the motif of *anamnesis*" in Baudelaire's writing (61).

4. Baudelaire writes to Wagner: "I would still have hesitated for a long time to reveal my admiration to you in a letter, if my eyes had not fallen every day on unworthy, ridiculous articles, in which every possible effort was made to slander your genius" (*Œuvres complètes,* 2:1452).

5. In *Musica ficta,* Lacoue-Labarthe emphasizes such excess; he claims that in Baudelaire's view it prevents Wagner's music from translating anything purely or simply human: "[M]usical meaningfulness [significance] . . . refers less to the soul in excess than to the body in excess, that is, to the flesh, which moreover does not in any way lack soul. . . . In this moment the perceptible passes beyond itself, the *phusis* is transcended—and Baudelaire is right to speak of 'supernature' " (81–82).

6. Cf. Baudelaire's *Un Mangeur d'opium* (1:480). Baudelaire here evokes a "fertile canvas [or background: toile] of shadows" like the "background [fond] of shadows" in the above quotation. He notes that as De Quincey's opium addiction progressed, he was "cruelly tormented" by the images that continually appeared on this shadowy background and that he was unable either to suppress or to interpret.

7. At the end of part 1 (¶17), Baudelaire claims that he was unable to read

Wagner's *Die Kunst und die Revolution* or his *Das Kunstwerk der Zukunft,* since neither had been translated into French. Baudelaire apparently succeeded, however, in reading an English translation of *Oper und Drama,* published serially in a London journal entitled the *Musical World* between May 19, 1855, and April 26, 1856 (*Œuvres complètes,* 2:1462–63 n. 3).

8. Susan Bernstein rightly stresses that Baudelaire was heavily dependent on press reports and reviews for his own acquaintance with Wagner's work ("Virtuosity of the Nineteenth Century: Music and Language in Heine, Liszt, and Baudelaire" [Ph.D. diss., Johns Hopkins University, 1991], 487–500, 538–39).

9. Bernstein claims, to the contrary, that "in quoting, [Baudelaire] renounces the ability to speak," although he also "seems to gain authority by citation" because of the readers' impression that Wagner himself is speaking within the essay: "As Baudelaire carries out this transcription, or scriptural translation—carrying over—[of] a piece of a foreign text into his own, thus deflecting from the voice of a *Je,* the device is obscured and we seem to read Wagner; Baudelaire seems to say, to add, nothing" ("Virtuosity of the Nineteenth Century," 554–55). For me, this is inconsistent with Baudelaire's claim, in the first paragraph of the essay, to speak for and with others at precisely the same time that he speaks for himself.

10. For two other approaches to the question of personification or prosopopoeia in discourse on music, see Fred Everett Maus, "Music as Drama," *Music Theory Spectrum* 10 (1988): 56–73, and Carolyn Abbate, "Music's Voices," in *Unsung Voices: Opera and Musical Narrative in the Nineteenth Century* (Princeton: Princeton University Press, 1991), 3–29. Strikingly different from each other, both studies have helped to shape my thinking on this topic.

11. Baudelaire does not at first identify the source of this paraphrase, but he indicates a few sentences later that it is based on Wagner's *Lettre sur la musique,* one of the works from which Baudelaire thereafter quotes extensively.

12. This letter appeared in the *Journal des Débats* on February 22, 1860; Berlioz's review had been published in the *Journal des Débats* on February 9, 1860. This review may also be found in Hector Berlioz, *À travers chants,* ed. Léon Guichard (Paris: Gründ, 1971), 321–33.

13. The italics this time are not added by Baudelaire; they appear in the *Journal des Débats.* However, they are absent from the German version of this letter to Berlioz, printed in Richard Wagner, *Gesammelte Schriften und Dichtungen,* 4th ed., 10 vols. (Leipzig: C. F. W. Siegel's Musikalienhandlung, 1907), 7:82–86.

14. Richard Wagner, *Quatre poèmes d'opéras traduits en prose française, précédés d'une lettre sur la musique,* French trans. [Paul Amand] Challemel-Lacour (Paris: A. Bourdilliat, 1861). Although the date printed in the book is 1861, Claude Pichois

observes that it was actually published in December 1860 (Baudelaire, *Œuvres complètes*, 2:1457). Included were the librettos—in prose translations—for *Le Vaisseau fantôme*, *Tannhäuser*, *Lohengrin*, and *Tristan et Iseult*. The German version of the introductory *Lettre* may be found in Wagner, *Gesammelte Schriften und Dichtungen*, 7:87–137.

15. I borrow the hyphenated "person-ify" from Barbara Johnson, "Apostrophe, Animation, Abortion," in *A World of Difference* (Baltimore: Johns Hopkins University Press, 1987), 191.

16. The passage given above appears in Wagner's *Lettre sur la musique*, xvii–xviii.

17. Wagner, *Lettre sur la musique*, xxv. Both sentences form part of a much larger discussion of the poet's role in the composition of an opera and appear within long passages punctuated by numerous semicolons. The first precedes Baudelaire's quotation: "I looked for the meaning of these obstinate hopes; I found the explanation, it seemed to me, in a penchant that is natural to the poet and that for him dominates the conception as well as the form; this penchant is to use the instrument of abstract ideas, language, in such a way that it acts upon feeling itself. This tendency is manifest in the invention of the poetic subject; the only picture . . ." The second, replaced by an ellipsis in Baudelaire's essay, reads: "The poet seeks, in his language, to substitute for the abstract and conventional value of words their tangible and primeval meaning; the rhythmic arrangement . . ."

18. See also Richard Wagner, *Gesammelte Schriften und Dichtungen*, 4:30–53. In part 2, section 2, of *Oper und Drama*, Wagner argues in much more detail for his belief that the purpose of myth is to represent all perceptible phenomena in the form of individual and specific human beings; he writes, for example, that "just as the human form is the most comprehensible [to human understanding], so also is the essence of natural phenomena, which humankind has not yet recognized in their real form [Wirklichkeit], comprehensible only through condensation into human form" (4:32).

19. While analyzing several passages from Wagner's *Lettre sur la musique*, including the one that forms Baudelaire's third quotation, Philippe Lacoue-Labarthe emphasizes its frequent allusions to processes of absorption and dissolution: "[I]t is obviously always the same chemical or chemical-physiological metaphor, whenever it is not, as in numerous examples one could find, openly sexual" (*Musica ficta*, 54). Wagner's prose writings do offer many other images of physical incorporation and transformation; one of the best known is the recurrent image of a poetic seed implanted in the womb of music and later brought forth as drama (see, for example, Frank W. Glass, *The Fertilizing Seed: Wagner's Concept of the Poetic Intent* [Ann Arbor, Mich.: UMI, 1983], and Jean-Jacques Nattiez, *Wagner Androgyne:*

A Study in Interpretation, trans. Stewart Spencer [Princeton: Princeton University Press, 1993]). On the specific incorporation of music into live characters on stage, see Leo Treitler, "Mozart and the Idea of Absolute Music," in *Music and the Historical Imagination* (Cambridge: Harvard University Press, 1989), 176–214; Treitler relates concepts of absolute music among German romantic critics to "Wagner's concept of opera, the idea that the musical expression constitutes the substance, the innermost essence of the drama that is made visible and concretized by the words and stage action" (212).

Baudelaire was, of course, also known for his metaphors of absorption and incorporation, particularly those in *Les Paradis artificiels.* See Joshua Wilner, "Music without Rhythm: Incorporation and Intoxication in the Prose of Baudelaire and De Quincey," (Ph.D. diss., Yale University, 1980).

20. The various sentences combined to make this quotation may be found in the *Lettre sur la musique,* xlviii–xlix. In Wagner's text, only "*clairvoyance*" is italicized.

21. Pierre Fontanier, *Les Figures du discours,* intro. Gérard Genette (Paris: Flammarion, 1977), 111. Fontanier's emphasis.

22. Fontanier, *Les Figures du discours,* 111.

23. Fontanier, *Les Figures du discours,* 113.

24. Fontanier, *Les Figures du discours,* 111.

25. Paul de Man, "Anthropomorphism and Trope in the Lyric," in *The Rhetoric of Romanticism* (New York: Columbia University Press, 1984), 241. De Man's emphasis.

26. See Cynthia Chase, "Giving a Face to a Name: De Man's Figures," in *Decomposing Figures: Rhetorical Readings in the Romantic Tradition* (Baltimore: Johns Hopkins University Press, 1986), 83. In her gloss on the passage from "Anthropomorphism and Trope in the Lyric" quoted above, Chase emphasizes that anthropomorphism not only identifies something in the natural or inanimate world as a human being, but also tries to confirm that humanity is a natural, unquestionable part of that world: "Taking the natural as human, it takes the human as given. This is to take the human as natural, to create a naturalness of man from which man and nature in effect disappear as the distinction between them is effaced." In the terms of Baudelaire's essay, anthropomorphism allows listeners to think that music becomes a more natural presence among them when it is incarnated in a human being.

27. My argument here is in some respects similar to one put forth by Timothy Raser in his paper "Reference and Citation in Baudelaire's Art Criticism," presented at the Seventeenth Annual Colloquium in Nineteenth-Century French Studies, New Orleans, Oct. 18, 1991. Raser explores relations between quotation

and prosopopoeia in Baudelaire's art criticism; he suggests that both work—in somewhat different ways—to create a Barthesian "effet de réel" whose aim is to render Baudelaire's text transparent, thus affording readers a direct view of the paintings and their meaning.

28. Antoine Compagnon, *La Seconde Main, ou le travail de la citation* (Paris: Seuil, 1979), 31. Compagnon specifies that quotations acquire this autonomous status only because of their "metonymic canonization," which allows the single term *quotation* to denote the acts of both excision and insertion, as well as the textual fragment itself: "The amalgam, in quotation, of two manipulations and the object manipulated has the effect of making a wholly cultural procedure look natural. It subsumes the manipulations beneath the object, masking them behind it. . . . To naturalize quotation is to claim that it goes without saying [or goes on its own: va de soi], like an automobile" (30–31).

29. Baudelaire refers here to the 1860 concerts, and he exaggerates in declaring that they prominently featured motifs whose recurrence united different extracts from the same opera. Of the four operas involved, only *Tannhäuser* and *Lohengrin* were represented by more than a single extract; of these, only *Tannhäuser* presented the same motif in two of its three excerpts (the overture and the opening of act 3). Wagner, moreover, signaled this particular recurrence in his program booklet, so that Baudelaire probably—and suggestively—derived his fascination as much from reading about motifs as from hearing them.

30. As Claude Pichois states (Baudelaire, *Œuvres complètes*, 2:1465), Baudelaire's description of *Tannhäuser* recalls his famous passage from *Mon cœur mis à nu:* "There is in everyone, at all times, two simultaneous postulations, one toward God, the other toward Satan" (1:682–83). Baudelaire's quotation of Liszt comes from Franz Liszt, *"Lohengrin" et "Tannhäuser" de Richard Wagner* (Leipzig: F. A. Brockhaus, 1850; Paris: Adef-Albatros, 1980), 146; further references to this work will appear in parentheses in the text. In this and other passages from part 3, Baudelaire's interest in the relation between overtures and operas calls for further discussion; see chapter 4 below.

31. Cf. Lacoue-Labarthe, *Musica ficta*, 80: when Baudelaire talks about *Tannhäuser*, "it is the demoniac, satanic, carnal theme that holds all his attention—and first of all his attention as a writer. . . . [W]hat he tries to write, for himself, is the 'chaos of dying, voluptuous pleasures,' that *emotion* [*émoi*] itself, in its literal sense, or that ecstasy. On the other hand, when he comes to the second theme, to the 'bliss of redemption,' he restricts himself to speaking, from a certain distance (and in a slightly conventional way), of 'ineffable feeling' and he falls back, in the style of simple description, on the indications of the libretto: he recounts."

32. Richard Wagner, "De l'ouverture," *Revue et Gazette musicale* 10, 14, and 17 (Jan. 1841); reprinted in *Œuvres en prose*, French trans. J.-G. Prod'homme, 13 vols. (Paris: Delagrave, 1907), 1:231–49. Further references to this edition will appear in parentheses in the text. This essay belongs to a series of articles that Wagner published (in French) while living in Paris from 1839 to 1842. For the German version, see Wagner, *Gesammelte Schriften und Dichtungen*, 1:194–206. In this article, Wagner discusses most of the overtures played by the Société des Concerts du Conservatoire in 1839 and 1840; see Reinhard Strohm, "Gedanken zu Wagners Opernouvertüren," in *Wagnerliteratur-Wagnerforschung*, ed. Carl Dahlhaus and Egon Voss (Mainz: B. Schott, 1985), 70.

33. This passage appears in Liszt's *"Lohengrin" et "Tannhäuser,"* 67–69. Baudelaire is responsible for all the italics in the quotation, as well as for the ellipsis in the middle of the second paragraph.

34. *Nœud* is the French word for both the coil of a single snake and the entangled mass of snakes in a nest (*nœud de vipères*).

35. It should be noted that others besides Liszt applied the term *personification* to Wagner's motifs. In a review of Wagner's Paris concerts in 1860, Ernest Reyer wrote: "And I was struck by the beauty, the richness, the sonority of this orchestra, in which every instrument has a role, a personification that begins when such and such a character is mute or disappears" [Et j'ai été frappé de la beauté, de la richesse, de la sonorité de cet orchestre, dans lequel chaque instrument a un rôle, une personnification qui commence quand tel personnage est muet ou disparaît] (quoted in Émile Faure, "La Presse parisienne et les concerts Wagner," *La Presse théâtrale et musicale* 7, no. 6 [Feb. 12, 1860]). Since Reyer, like Baudelaire, could not have derived this impression of the motifs solely from attendance at the concerts, it is likely that he too had read about them; his use of the term *personification* may in fact have been borrowed from Liszt.

36. The last phrase quoted (from p. 50) is part of Liszt's translation of the poem written by Franz Dingelstedt and recited at the unveiling of Herder's statue on August 28, 1850.

37. The implications of this passage are greater than my interpretation here shows, since Baudelaire evokes "phantoms of stone" in several of his works. See Graham Robb, "Baudelaire and the Ghosts of Stone," *Romance Notes* 25, no. 2 (1984): 137–44.

38. Zacharie Astruc similarly noted these complementary dangers in his review of the 1860 concerts: "I spoke of eloquence; Richard Wagner is above all eloquent—not only in the general aspect of his work—but further in the diverse parts that compose it, in the infinite details that give it vast, complicated, pene-

trating life. . . . In Wagner, obscurity applies to the whole, never to the detail
that is very perceptible, but that can in the long run tire a mind that is not sufficiently thoughtful" [J'ai parlé d'éloquence; Richard Wagner est surtout éloquent—
non pas seulement dans la physionomie générale de son œuvre—mais encore
dans les diverses parties qui la composent, dans les infinis détails qui lui donnent
sa vie compliquée, large, pénétrante. . . . Chez Wagner, l'obscurité s'applique à
l'ensemble, jamais au détail qui se perçoit fort bien, mais peut fatiguer à la longue
un cerveau qui n'est point suffisamment réfléchi] ("Chronique musicale: Richard
Wagner," *Revue internationale* 2 [Feb. 29, 1860]: 467). For a useful historical outline
of the uneasy relation between parts (or details) and wholes within the general
metaphor of the artwork as a live organism, see Ruth A. Solie, "The Living Work:
Organicism and Musical Analysis," *19th-Century Music* 4, no. 2 (1980): 147–56.

39. On the strangeness of Liszt's discourse, both as quoted in Baudelaire's essay
and elsewhere, see Bernstein, "Virtuosity of the Nineteenth Century," 235–426,
573–95.

40. See Henri Thomas, "Nietzsche et Baudelaire," in *La Chasse aux trésors* (Paris:
Gallimard, 1961), 141. Thomas points out a fragment from 1883 in which Nietzsche
writes: "Baudelaire, a sort of Richard Wagner without the music." In a similar
fragment from 1885, according to Thomas, Nietzsche suggests that "as [Baude-
laire] was in his time the first prophet and advocate of Delacroix, he is perhaps the
first Wagnerian in Paris." In 1885, Nietzsche had not yet seen any evidence that
Baudelaire actually knew about Wagner.

41. From a letter Nietzsche wrote to Peter Gast on February 26, 1888, published
in Nietzsche's *Werke in Drei Bänden,* ed. Karl Schlechta (Munich: Carl Hanser, 1973),
3:1280. Nietzsche tells in this letter about his accidental discovery, in Baudelaire's
Œuvres posthumes, that Baudelaire had written about Wagner and corresponded
briefly with him.

42. Thomas, "Nietzsche et Baudelaire," 141.

43. Friedrich Nietzsche, *Die Geburt der Tragödie,* in *Sämtliche Werke: Kritische Studienausgabe in 15 Bänden,* ed. Giorgio Colli and Mazzino Montinari (Munich: Deutscher Taschenbuch; Berlin: Walter de Gruyter, 1980), 1:25–26. Translated by Walter
Kaufmann under the title *The Birth of Tragedy,* in *The Birth of Tragedy and The Case
of Wagner* (New York: Random House, 1967), 33. Unless otherwise indicated, all
translations of Nietzsche's works quoted in the following discussion are Walter
Kaufmann's. All references to the original works come from the edition just cited.

44. Nietzsche, *Birth,* 33; *Sämtliche Werke,* 1:25. Nietzsche is responsible for all
italics that appear in this and other quotations drawn from his works. On relations
between Nietzsche's metaphor of coupling and Wagner's favored image of a sexual

union between poetry (taken as masculine) and music (taken as feminine), see Nattiez, *Wagner Androgyne* (trans. Spencer), 156–62.

45. Nietzsche, *Birth*, 33; *Sämtliche Werke*, 1:25.

46. Nietzsche, *Birth*, 41, 43; *Sämtliche Werke*, 1:35–36.

47. Nietzsche, *Birth*, 33; *Sämtliche Werke*, 1:26. For a detailed study of the relations between the Apollinian and the Dionysian as states or impulses of nature and as forms of art, see John Sallis, *Crossings: Nietzsche and the Space of Tragedy* (Chicago: University of Chicago Press, 1991), 9–75.

48. Nietzsche, *Birth*, 38; *Sämtliche Werke*, 1:30.

49. Nietzsche, *Birth*, 37; *Sämtliche Werke*, 1:30.

50. I have borrowed the translation of this passage from Paul de Man, "Rhetoric of Tropes (Nietzsche)," in *Allegories of Reading: Figural Language in Rousseau, Nietzsche, Rilke, and Proust* (New Haven: Yale University Press, 1979), 110–11. See also Nietzsche, *Sämtliche Werke*, 1:880.

51. De Man, *Rhetoric of Romanticism*, 241.

52. Nietzsche, *Birth*, 54; *Sämtliche Werke*, 1:50.

53. Nietzsche, *Birth*, 63–64; *Sämtliche Werke*, 1:60–61.

54. Nietzsche specifies in *The Birth of Tragedy* that "all the celebrated figures of the Greek stage—Prometheus, Oedipus, etc.—are mere masks of this original hero, Dionysus" (73); *Sämtliche Werke*, 1:71.

55. Nietzsche, *Birth*, 127; *Sämtliche Werke*, 1:136.

56. Nietzsche, *Birth*, 28; *Sämtliche Werke*, 1:137.

57. Friedrich Nietzsche, *Twilight of the Idols*, in *The Portable Nietzsche*, trans. and ed. Walter Kaufmann (New York: Viking, 1954), 519; see also *Sämtliche Werke*, 6:117.

58. Nietzsche, *Twilight*, 519–20; *Sämtliche Werke*, 6:117–18.

59. Nietzsche, *Twilight*, 520; *Sämtliche Werke*, 6:118.

60. Nietzsche, *Twilight*, 466; *Sämtliche Werke*, 6:58.

61. Friedrich Nietzsche, *The Case of Wagner*, in *The Birth of Tragedy and The Case of Wagner*, 157; *Sämtliche Werke*, 6:13.

62. Nietzsche, *Case*, 157; *Sämtliche Werke*, 6:13–14.

63. Nietzsche, *Case*, 164; *Sämtliche Werke*, 6:21.

64. Nietzsche, *Case*, 160; *Sämtliche Werke*, 6:16.

65. Nietzsche, *Case*, 192; *Sämtliche Werke*, 6:52–53.

66. Nietzsche, *Case*, 166; *Sämtliche Werke*, 6:23.

67. Nietzsche, *Case*, 177; *Sämtliche Werke*, 6:35.

68. Nietzsche, *Case*, 172; *Sämtliche Werke*, 6:29–30.

69. Nietzsche, *Case*, 170; *Sämtliche Werke*, 6:27.

70. Nietzsche, *Case*, 170; *Sämtliche Werke*, 6:27.

71. Nietzsche, *Case*, 169; *Sämtliche Werke*, 6:26.

72. Nietzsche, *Case*, 167; *Sämtliche Werke*, 6:23.

73. Nietzsche, *Case*, 167; *Sämtliche Werke*, 6:23–24.

74. Friedrich Nietzsche, *Nietzsche contra Wagner*, in *The Portable Nietzsche*, 663–64. As Kaufmann notes on p. 661, the original version of "Where I Admire" is found in section 87 of *The Gay Science*. The final sentences quoted here ("Wagner is one who has suffered deeply . . .") appear only in the later version. See also *Sämtliche Werke*, 6:417–18.

CHAPTER 4: *Openings*

1. See Appendix 1, ¶18 and ¶3. All further references to paragraphs in the present edition will appear in parentheses.

2. Susan Bernstein points out, in "Virtuosity of the Nineteenth Century: Music and Language in Heine, Liszt, and Baudelaire" (Ph.D. diss., Johns Hopkins University, 1991), that journalism almost inevitably confuses this sequence: "From the point of view of journalistic reception, however, the point of which is to communicate what is absent, or give access to a foreign sphere otherwise beyond the sphere of individual immediate experience, the report precedes the event it reports, or the translation precedes the original. The false discourse of the public is grounded in this inverted order" (491).

3. On classical representations of Echo, as well as on figurative uses of echoes and echoing in general, see John Hollander, *The Figure of Echo: A Mode of Allusion in Milton and After* (Berkeley and Los Angeles: University of California Press, 1981).

4. Outside his Wagner essay, Baudelaire considers a closely related problem in a famous passage from *Le Peintre de la vie moderne*. When he theorizes an inevitable but incalculable mixture of "an eternal, invariable element" and "a relative, circumstantial element" in all genuine works of art, Baudelaire touches implicitly on the succession of artistic achievements and critical assessments that render the history of art both varied and repetitive. See especially "Le Beau, la mode et le bonheur," from *Le Peintre de la vie moderne*, in Charles Baudelaire, *Œuvres complètes*, ed. Claude Pichois, 2 vols. (Paris: Gallimard, Bibliothèque de la Pléiade, 1983–85), 2:683–86. Further references to volume and page numbers in this edition will appear in parentheses. All translations for this and other works are my own unless otherwise indicated.

5. This line from "Correspondances" (1:11) is quoted with the rest of the quatrains in Baudelaire's Wagner essay (¶12).

6. Baudelaire is not far here from part of the argument Paul de Man presents in "Criticism and Crisis," in *Blindness and Insight: Essays in the Rhetoric of Contemporary Criticism,* 2d ed., rev., Theory and History of Literature, vol. 7. (Minneapolis: University of Minnesota Press, 1983), 3–19. Although he takes Mallarmé rather than Baudelaire as his starting point, de Man emphasizes the crisis involved in artistic self-scrutiny: "We can speak of crisis when a 'separation' takes place, by self-reflection, between what, in literature, is in conformity with the original intent and what has irrevocably fallen away from this source" (8). De Man then argues that all criticism consists to some extent in scrutinizing the relation between an artwork and its original intent; and he concludes, much like Baudelaire, that "the notion of crisis and that of criticism are very closely linked, so much so that one could state that all true criticism occurs in the mode of crisis" (8). I return below to the connections between Baudelaire's essay and the Mallarmé texts discussed by de Man.

7. See Paul Valéry, "Situation de Baudelaire," in *Œuvres complètes,* ed. Jean Hytier, 2 vols. (Paris: Gallimard, Bibliothèque de la Pléiade, 1957), 2:604. While discussing contrasts between Baudelaire and the French romantic poets, Valéry declares that Baudelaire might be called a "classic," that is, a writer who "*carries a critic within himself*" (Valéry's emphasis); and Valéry further claims that "classicism" is always a second stage or posterior development, one that "thus implies voluntary and considered acts that modify a 'natural' production." Valéry does not seem to have Baudelaire's remarks from *Richard Wagner* specifically in mind, although Valéry mentions this essay later in his article (2:611–12).

8. I am aware of two analyses of this passage from Baudelaire's essay that differ from my own. See, first, Mira Levy-Bloch, "La Traduction chez Baudelaire: Les Trois Imaginations du poète-traducteur," *Nineteenth-Century French Studies* 20, nos. 3–4 (1992): 361–79. In an effort to show exactly how, in Baudelaire's view, the imagination translates sensual experience into artworks, Levy-Bloch traces a process with five stages; citing the Wagner essay, she claims that the successful integration of artistic and critical faculties forms the fourth of these stages. See also Bernstein, "Virtuosity of the Nineteenth Century," 592. After quoting part of ¶27, Bernstein suggests that the critical second stage of artistic development represents a "gesture of intellectualization," with which "Baudelaire posits a *crisis* or gap within the artistic life (a *lacuna* marking incompletion, or the possibility of a new addition) which allows him to gain mastery for the position of the poet-critic." Bernstein is right, I think, in thus connecting the work of the Baudelairean translator (as evoked in ¶5) with the development of the artist.

9. In other terms, I suggest that Baudelaire's question ("How could Wagner not

admirably understand . . .") may not be entirely rhetorical; it may need to be read not as a statement that Wagner in fact understands myth, but instead as a genuine question about whether or not Wagner actually achieves the mixture of art and criticism necessary for an understanding of myth. This second reading seems at first unconvincing, because the digression opens with an emphatic defense of Wagner; but in view of what happens later, the second reading cannot be wholly discounted.

10. Baudelaire is of course known for his tendency to appropriate (not to say plagiarize) passages from works that he admired. For a detailed list of his borrowings, see Claude Pichois, "Baudelaire ou la difficulté créatrice," in *Baudelaire, études et témoignages* (Neuchâtel: La Baconnière, 1982), 242–61.

11. Richard Wagner, *Quatre poèmes d'opéras traduits en prose française, précédés d'une lettre sur la musique,* French trans. [Paul Amand] Challemel-Lacour (Paris: A. Bourdilliat, 1861), xli–xlii. Further references to pages in this edition will be cited parenthetically.

12. Wagner repeats this declaration with small variations on pp. xxi, xxxvii–xxxviii, and xlv.

13. For a more detailed reading of the passages on Beethoven from Wagner's *Lettre sur la musique,* see Carolyn Abbate, "Opera as Symphony, a Wagnerian Myth," in *Analyzing Opera: Verdi and Wagner,* ed. Carolyn Abbate and Roger Parker (Berkeley and Los Angeles: University of California Press, 1989), 92–124. In her discussion of *Zukunftsmusik,* the German version of the *Lettre,* Abbate argues that Wagner proposed not simply to combine music such as Beethoven's with rational discourse in the form of a dramatic poem, but—more daringly—to invent a new kind of dramatic poem (characterized both by a rational plot and by "highly repetitive language") that would form a "poetic counterpart" to the thematic relationships of Beethoven symphonies (101–2).

It is interesting to note that for musicologists a generation later, Beethoven's music came to represent the very kind of logic that Wagner denies it in his *Lettre sur la musique.* Hugo Riemann, for instance, theorized the notion of musical logic, which he then applied to Beethoven's music in *Beethovens Streichquartette erläutert* (Berlin: Schlesinger and Lienau, 1910) and in *L. van Beethovens sämtliche Klavier-Solo-Sonaten,* 2 vols. (Berlin: Hesse, 1917).

14. In fact, Baudelaire almost pointedly avoids quoting the sentence in question; for his fourth quotation in part 2, he chooses both the sentence just before this one and the sentence just after it, joining them together with an ellipsis.

15. Jacob Grimm, *Teutonic Mythology,* trans. James Steven Stallybrass, 4 vols. (New York: George Bell, 1883; New York: Dover, 1966), 3:xxv.

16. Grimm, *Teutonic Mythology*, 3:xiii, xxxiv. These quotations may be found in the original German in Jacob Grimm's *Deutsche Mythologie*, ed. Elard Hugo Meyer, 4th ed., 3 vols. (Berlin: Ferd. Dümmler, 1876), 2:xi, xx, xxvi.

17. In Boiste's *Dictionnaire universel*, printed in 1866, the first definition of *fable* is a "thing feigned, invented in order to instruct and amuse," later qualified both as a "fabulous narration" and as "instruction disguised beneath the allegory of an action." Similarly, the primary definition of *légende* is an exemplary "life of the saints." See P. C. D. Boiste, *Dictionnaire universel de la langue française, avec le latin et l'étymologie*, 5th ed. (Paris: Firmin-Didot/Rey et Belhatte, 1866), 303, 424.

18. It should be noted that Baudelaire's second digression also borrows from Franz Liszt, *"Lohengrin" et "Tannhäuser" de Richard Wagner* (Leipzig: F. A. Brockhaus, 1851; Paris: Adef-Albatros, 1980). Liszt points out in some detail the similarity between the story of Elsa and "so many different myths" (99), including the myth of Psyche (104). But he also argues that Wagner is not intellectually interested in these resemblances, since Wagner is "a poet in much too real a sense to want to put *philosophy in action* into his dramas" (101; Liszt's emphasis).

19. Baudelaire's thinking on the origin of myth here closely resembles one of Lévi-Strauss's arguments on the same subject. Just as Baudelaire insists on an origin that seems undeniable, but that cannot be traced or recognized, Lévi-Strauss writes: "[M]ythic thought . . . manifests itself under the guise of an irradiation, with the drawback that the measurement of its directions and their angles encourages one to postulate a common origin: an ideal point where the rays deflected by the structure of the myth would go to rejoin one another if, precisely, they did not come from elsewhere and had not remained parallel for the whole length of their journey." See Claude Lévi-Strauss, *Le Cru et le cuit* (Paris: Plon, 1964), 13–14.

20. Liszt, *"Lohengrin" et "Tannhäuser,"* 147.

21. Liszt, *"Lohengrin" et "Tannhäuser,"* 160.

22. Jean-Jacques Rousseau, *Dictionnaire de la musique*, in *Œuvres complètes*, 8 vols. (Paris: Lefèvre, 1839), 4:587. Rousseau's emphasis.

23. Rousseau, *Œuvres complètes*, 4:587.

24. For a useful sketch of the main positions taken throughout this debate, see Basil Deane, "The French Operatic Overture from Grétry to Berlioz," *Proceedings of the Royal Music Association* 99 (1972–73): 67–80.

25. Le Comte de La Cépède, *La Poëtique de la musique*, 2 vols. (Paris: L'Imprimerie de Monsieur, 1785), 2:1: "What the peristyle, which serves as a vestibule to kings' palaces, is to those grand and superb edifices, the overture is to the tragedy" [Ce que le péristyle, qui sert de vestibule aux palais des rois, est à ces grands & superbes édifices, l'ouverture l'est à la tragédie]. Gérard Genette invokes a closely

related image when he defines the "paratext" in *Seuils* (Paris: Seuil, 1987): "More than a limit or a watertight frontier, what is in question here is a *threshold*, or— a word used by Borges about a preface—a 'vestibule' that offers to everyone the possibility of entering, or of turning back" (7–8).

26. See Genette, *Seuils*, 219: "The major drawback of the preface is that it constitutes an instance of unequal and even shaky communication, since its author offers an advance commentary on a text with which the reader is not yet familiar." Jacques Derrida approaches the same problem from another perspective in *La Dissémination* (Paris: Seuil, 1972), 13: "For the foreword, reformulating a meaning [or an intention to speak: un vouloir-dire] after the fact, the text is an already-written [un écrit]—a past—that, in a false appearance of present time, a hidden and all-powerful author, in full mastery of his product, presents to the reader as her/his future."

27. Nicholas Temperley states that "there was never a time when the concert overture was entirely distinct from the dramatic overture," but he adds that the practice of composing independent overtures gained its first real impetus among German composers between 1805 and 1820 and was subsequently refined by Mendelssohn and Berlioz; see Nicholas Temperley, "Overture," *The New Grove Dictionary of Music and Musicians*, ed. Stanley Sadie, 20 vols. (London: Macmillan, 1980), 14:34–35. In France, independent overtures for wind ensemble came briefly into vogue just after the 1789 revolution, and the separate performance of opera overtures was popularized at the turn of the nineteenth century by concerts given by students of the Conservatoire; see David Charlton, *The Overture in France, 1790–1810*, ser. D, vol. 7 of *The Symphony, 1720–1840*, ed. Barry S. Brook (New York: Garland, 1983), xvii–xviii.

28. Hector Berlioz, *À travers chants*, ed. Léon Guichard (Paris: Gründ, 1971), 176.

29. Richard Wagner, "De l'ouverture," *Revue et Gazette musicale*, January 10, 14, and 17, 1841; reprinted in *Œuvres en prose*, French trans. J.-G. Prod'homme, 13 vols. (Paris: Delagrave, 1907), 1:243, 245.

30. See Susanne Steinbeck, *Die Ouvertüre von Beethoven bis Wagner: Probleme und Lösungen* (Munich: Emil Katzbichler, 1973). Steinbeck examines at length the "continual debate" between the nineteenth-century overture and sonata form (7). After briefly exploring the ways in which the typical design of sonata form (exposition, development, recapitulation) lent itself to dramatic interpretation, Steinbeck notes that the release of tension implicit in the recapitulation often conflicted with the attention-building purposes of the overture. As a result, overture composers continually modified and invented form schemes to suit their own ends (see esp. 7–18).

31. See Richard Wagner, "Über Franz Liszt's Symphonische Dichtungen," in

Gesammelte Schriften und Dichtungen, 4th ed., 10 vols. (Leipzig: C. F. W. Siegel's Musikalienhandlung, 1907), 5:182–98. For a useful discussion of Wagner's successive views on overtures and form, see Thomas S. Grey, "Wagner, the Overture, and the Aesthetics of Musical Form," *19th-Century Music* 12, no. 1 (1988): 3–22.

32. I am summarizing the text in the program booklet of the 1860 concerts, from a copy consulted at the Bibliothèque de l'Opéra in Paris (bound collection C.5065 [6]). This program was first written in German for the Zurich Music Festival of 1852; the original version was slightly longer than the Paris translation, although not substantially different from it. See Wagner, *Gesammelte Schriften und Dichtungen,* 5:177–79.

33. Its absence is all the more noticeable in that Baudelaire must have read Liszt's reference to the "tyrses" [*sic*] carried by Venus's followers in act 1, scene 1 (Liszt, *"Lohengrin" et "Tannhäuser,"* 162).

34. For a summary of Wagner's combination of the Tannhäuser myth with that of the minnesingers' contest at the Wartburg, see Ernest Newman, *The Wagner Operas,* 2 vols. (New York: Harper Colophon, 1983), 1:50–65.

35. In *Un Mangeur d'opium,* Baudelaire writes: "I will no doubt abridge a great deal; De Quincey is essentially digressive; the expression *Humorist* can be more aptly applied to him than to anyone else; in one place, he compares his thought to a thyrsus, a simple rod that derives all its interesting features [physionomie] and all its charm from the complicated foliage that envelops it" (1:444). For further discussion of Baudelaire's preoccupation with the thyrsus, see Melvin Zimmerman, "La Genèse du symbole du thyrse chez Baudelaire," *Bulletin baudelairien* 2, no. 1 (1966): 8–10; see also Marc Eigeldinger, "À propos de l'image du thyrse," *Revue d'histoire littéraire de la France* (Jan.–Feb. 1975): 110–12. Both Zimmerman and Eigeldinger relate Baudelaire's thyrsus to a similar image in *Le Neveu de Rameau,* further suggesting that this is the passage from Diderot to which Baudelaire refers in his Wagner essay (¶19).

36. Although Wagner had finished this revision in time for the Paris performance, it was not used on that occasion; the shortened overture, dovetailed into act 1, scene 1, was not incorporated into the opera until its 1875 performances in Vienna. See Carolyn Abbate, "The Parisian 'Vénus' and the 'Paris' *Tannhäuser,*" *Journal of the American Musicological Society* 36, no. 1 (1983): 73–74.

37. Liszt, *"Lohengrin" et "Tannhäuser,"* 64.

38. Defined as broadly as possible, a prelude is "an instrumental movement intended to precede another movement, a group of movements or a large-scale work"; see Howard Ferguson, "Prelude," in *The New Grove Dictionary of Music and Musicians,* ed. Stanley Sadie, 20 vols. (London: Macmillan, 1980), 15:210–11.

39. Betty Bang Mather and David Lasocki, *The Art of Preluding, 1700–1830* (New

York: McGinnis & Marx Music Publishers, 1984), 6: "James Grassineau's *A Musical Dictionary* (1740) defines a prelude as 'a flourish, or an irregular air.' The word 'flourish' may originally have been borrowed from fencing, for Richard Huloet in his *Abecedarium Anglico Latinum* of 1552 defines it as 'what a master of fence does with his weapon, or a musician in singing, *proludo* [*preludo*].'"

40. Ferguson, "Prelude," 15:211. For a probing discussion on the question of musical autonomy with particular reference to Chopin's Preludes, see Rose Rosengard Subotnik, "On Grounding Chopin," in *Developing Variations: Style and Ideology in Western Music* (Minneapolis: University of Minnesota Press, 1991), 141–65.

41. Steinbeck, *Die Ouvertüre*, 122. In Steinbeck's opinion, the *Vorspiel* is implicated in Wagner's discussion of *Versmelodie* in *Oper und Drama;* both must function within the whole music drama to transform anticipation into memory. Steinbeck writes: "The prelude refers with its leitmotifs to the 'Versmelodie' and awakens a preparatory 'presentiment,' from which the 'reminiscence' will be derived when the motif is taken up again by the orchestra in the course of the drama." The passage from Wagner to which she refers may be found in his *Gesammelte Schriften und Dichtungen*, 4:190.

42. Liszt, *"Lohengrin" et "Tannhäuser,"* 60.

43. Franz Liszt, "Berlioz und seine 'Harold-Symphonie,'" in *Gesammelte Schriften von Franz Liszt*, ed. L. Ramann, 6 vols. (Leipzig: Breitkopf und Härtel, 1882), 4:21, 50. Liszt's definition of a program as a premonitory *Vorwort* is quoted in full in chapter 2 above.

44. Franz Liszt, *Pages romantiques*, ed. Jean Chantavoine (Paris: Éditions d'Aujourd'hui, 1985), 106–7. The passage to which I refer reads as follows: "Few books appear today that are not preceded by a long preface, which is, so to speak, a second book about the book. This precaution, superfluous from many points of view when the book in question is written in ordinary language, is it not an absolute necessity . . . for compositions of the modern school, generally aspiring to become the expression of a clear-cut individuality? Is it not to be regretted, for example, that Beethoven—so difficult to comprehend, and about whose intentions one has such trouble reaching an agreement—did not summarily indicate the intimate thought of several of his great works and the principal modifications of that thought?"

45. Liszt, *Pages romantiques*, 107.

46. Derrida, *La Dissémination*, 27.

47. Steinbeck specifies in greater detail the motivic relations between the prelude and the rest of the opera; see *Die Ouvertüre*, 124–28.

48. Friedrich Nietzsche, *The Birth of Tragedy and The Case of Wagner*, trans. Walter

Kaufmann (New York: Random House, 1967), 161; see also Nietzsche's *Sämtliche Werke: Kritische Studienausgabe in 15 Bänden,* ed. Giorgio Colli and Mazzino Montinari (Munich: Deutscher Taschenbuch; Berlin: Walter de Gruyter, 1980), 6:17: "Der Lohengrin enthält eine feierliche In-Acht-Erklärung des Forschens und Fragens."

49. Theodor W. Adorno, *Versuch über Wagner,* 2d ed. (Frankfurt am Main: Suhrkamp, 1981), 116–17.

50. It might be objected here that *Lohengrin*'s two evil characters, the politically ambitious Telramund and his sorceress wife Ortrud, in fact subject Lohengrin and his origins to stringent interrogation. This questioning and the music associated with it—notably the motifs that so impressed Liszt, winding through act 2 "comme un serpent venimeux" (¶40)—would seem to give listeners some critical distance from which to examine Lohengrin's demand for secrecy. But both Telramund and Ortrud are consistently presented as guilty of either cruelty or conspiracy, which weakens the force of their criticism. Moreover, their motifs enter the opera only after the prelude has already begun positioning listeners with respect to Elsa's guilt and Lohengrin's innocence, so that the later motifs' power to question is somewhat diluted by the prelude's ambiguous power either to inculpate or to exonerate listeners in advance.

51. Stéphane Mallarmé, *Œuvres complètes,* ed. Henri Mondor and G.-Jean Aubry (Paris: Gallimard, Bibliothèque de la Pléiade, 1945), 645. Further references to page numbers in this edition will appear in parentheses; line numbers for Mallarmé poems given in my text also refer to this edition.

52. I am indebted here to Richard E. Goodkin for pointing out the correspondence between the italics and the poem's Italian setting.

53. See Roseline Crowley, "Toward the Poetics of Juxtaposition: *L'Après-Midi d'un Faune,*" *Yale French Studies* 54 (1977): 36. Crowley notes that "*pipeaux*" is a pun meaning either "pipe" or "trap." Arguing that only the latter definition makes sense in the context, she examines the resulting sound/sense disjunction and concludes that "the function of the pun is thus bound up with the failure of the narrative." I believe, however, that Crowley dismisses the first definition too quickly; she states only that a "pipe" in line 30 would violate "the logic of musical expression," without pausing to consider exactly what kinds of musical logic are set forth in the poem.

54. This quotation is taken from *Les Dieux antiques,* Mallarmé's adaptation of an English manual of mythology by George W. Cox; see *Œuvres complètes,* 1252.

55. Richard E. Goodkin, "Zeno's Paradox: Mallarmé, Valéry, and the Symbolist 'Movement,'" *Yale French Studies* 74 (1988): 143.

56. For more extensive discussion of Mallarmé's "thyrse plus complexe" and its relation to Baudelaire, see Barbara Johnson, *Défigurations du langage poétique* (Paris: Flammarion, 1979), 175–80.

57. William W. Austin gives these and other details in the introduction to his critical score of the *Prélude à "L'Après-Midi d'un Faune."* See Claude Debussy, *Prelude to "The Afternoon of a Faun,"* ed. William W. Austin (New York: W. W. Norton, 1970), 11.

58. In French: [C]ette musique prolonge l'émotion de mon poëme; votre illustration de *l'Après-Midi d'un Faune,* qui ne présenterait de dissonance avec mon texte, sinon qu'aller plus loin . . . ; Sylvain *d'haleine première* / Si ta flûte a réussi / Ouïs toute la lumière / Qu'y soufflera Debussy. The first quoted fragment is from a letter in which Debussy described Mallarmé's first reaction to his *Prélude;* the second is from a letter Mallarmé wrote to Debussy; the third is Mallarmé's dedication of a copy of his poem to Debussy (the italics emphasizing the poem's anterior/predominant status are mine). See *Œuvres complètes,* 1465 and 114.

59. The complete paragraph containing the sentence is of interest in this context: "Le remarquable est que, pour la première fois, au cours de l'histoire littéraire d'aucun peuple, concurremment aux grandes orgues générales et séculaires, où s'exalte, d'après un latent clavier, l'orthodoxie, quiconque avec son jeu et son ouïe individuels se peut composer un instrument, dès qu'il souffle, le frôle ou frappe avec science; en user à part et le dédier aussi à la Langue" (363).

60. In French: "Son sortilège, à lui [l'art littéraire], si ce n'est libérer, hors d'une poignée de poussière ou réalité sans l'enclore, au livre, même comme texte, la dispersion volatile soit l'esprit, qui n'a que faire de rien outre la musicalité de tout. . . . Cette visée, je la dis Transposition — Structure, une autre" (366). Mallarmé's subsequent uses of the word "transposition" (both of them famous) are as follows: (1) "[W]e are at the point, precisely, of seeking . . . an art of completing the transposition, in the Book, of the symphony or simply of taking back our own" [nous en sommes là, précisément, à rechercher . . . un art d'achever la transposition, au Livre, de la symphonie ou uniment de reprendre notre bien] (367); (2) "What good is the marvel of transposing a fact of nature into its vibratory near disappearance according to the play of the word, however; if it is not in order that there may emanate from it, without the trouble of a close or concrete reminder, the pure notion" [À quoi bon la merveille de transposer un fait de nature en sa presque disparition vibratoire selon le jeu de la parole, cependant; si ce n'est pour qu'en émane, sans la gêne d'un proche ou concret rappel, la notion pure] (368). Suggestively, Mallarmé "composed" "Crise de vers" mostly by "transposing" paragraphs from other works written for a variety of previous occasions.

61. See Barbara Johnson, "Les Fleurs du Mal Armé," in *A World of Difference* (Baltimore: Johns Hopkins University Press, 1987), 130. Although her context lies at some distance from my own, Johnson makes a similar point about the interpenetration of music and literature: "[S]uch nonlanguage [as music] is valued in Mallarmé's system not because it is outside, but because it is *within*, the poetic text. Both music and whiteness are extraordinarily privileged in Mallarmé's poetics precisely because they function as articulations *without content.*"

62. The whole paragraph begun by this quotation is pertinent here: "La Critique, en son intégrité, n'est, n'a de valeur ou n'égale presque la Poésie à qui apporter une noble opération complémentaire, que visant, directement et superbement, aussi les phénomènes ou l'univers: mais en dépit de cela, soit de sa qualité de primordial instinct placé au secret de nos replis (un malaise divin), cède-t-elle à l'attirance du théâtre qui montre seulement une représentation, pour ceux n'ayant point à voir les choses à même! de la pièce écrite au folio du ciel et mimée avec le geste de ses passions par l'Homme" (294).

63. Several important readings of "Hommage (à Richard Wagner)" focus on the clear division of the quatrains, which evoke the approaching ruin of traditional theater and literature, and the tercets, which suggest the renewal that these traditions owe to Wagner. See particularly Albert Thibaudet, *La Poésie de Stéphane Mallarmé*, 4th ed. (Paris: Gallimard, Nouvelle Revue Française, 1926), 307, and Robert Greer Cohn, *Toward the Poems of Mallarmé*, expanded ed. (Berkeley and Los Angeles: University of California Press, 1980), 177–88.

64. For further discussion on the resonance of "moire" in this and other poems by Mallarmé, see Cohn, *Toward the Poems of Mallarmé*, 177–78.

65. Mallarmé comes surprisingly close here to Adorno's analysis of *Phantasmagorie* in Wagner's operas. According to Adorno, Wagner's compositional technique, especially the priority he gives to "harmonic and instrumental sound," aims to conceal the artificial fabrication of his works by means of human labor, so that his "product presents itself as self-producing." Among Adorno's examples are the Venusberg music from *Tannhäuser* and the *Lohengrin* prelude, both of which create an effect of musical haze that appears to hover in midair. See Adorno, *Versuch über Wagner*, 80–81.

66. In French: Le Théâtre les appelle, non: pas de fixes, ni de séculaires et de notoires, mais un, dégagé de personnalité, car il compose notre aspect multiple (545).

67. In French: ces raréfactions et ces sommités naturelles que la Musique rend, arrière prolongement vibratoire de tout comme la Vie (545).

CHAPTER 5: *Breach of Genius*

1. Walter Benjamin, *Charles Baudelaire: Ein Lyriker im Zeitalter des Hochkapitalismus*, ed. Rolf Tiedemann (Frankfurt am Main: Suhrkamp, 1974), 133. This and all other translations, including the epigraph to this chapter, are my own unless otherwise indicated.

2. Marcel Proust, *À la recherche du temps perdu*, ed. Jean-Yves Tadié, 4 vols. (Paris: Gallimard, Bibliothèque de la Pléiade, 1987–89), 1:367. Further references to volume and page numbers from this edition of the *Recherche* will appear in parentheses. All translations from Proust are my own, although in making them I occasionally consulted the following: Marcel Proust, *Remembrance of Things Past*, trans. C. K. Scott Moncrieff and Terence Kilmartin, 3 vols. (New York: Random House, 1981), and Marcel Proust, *Marcel Proust on Art and Literature, 1896–1919*, trans. Sylvia Townsend Warner (London: Chatto and Windus, 1957; New York: Meridian Books, 1958).

3. Marcel Proust, *"Contre Sainte-Beuve," précédé de "Pastiches et mélanges" et suivi de Essais et articles*, ed. Pierre Clarac and Yves Sandre (Paris: Gallimard, Bibliothèque de la Pléiade, 1971), 623.

4. Proust, *Contre Sainte-Beuve*, 249.

5. See Appendix 1, ¶12. Further references to paragraphs in the present edition of *Richard Wagner et "Tannhäuser" à Paris* will be given parenthetically.

6. See chapter 2 above.

7. Georges Piroué, in *Proust et la musique du devenir* (Paris: Denoël, 1960), claims that Proust may have come into contact with some of Wagner's theoretical writings largely through French commentators, and particularly through Baudelaire; see p. 113, where Piroué discusses other echoes of Baudelaire's Wagner essay to be found in Proust. See also Émile Bedriomo, *Proust, Wagner, et la coïncidence des arts* (Tübingen: Gunter Narr; Paris: Éditions Jean-Michel Place, 1984). Basing part of his title on a quotation from Baudelaire's essay (¶6), Bedriomo explores a number of general relations between Baudelaire's and Proust's writing on Wagner. He examines in particular some connections between the *Recherche* and the letter that Baudelaire wrote to Wagner in 1860 (reprinted in Charles Baudelaire, *Œuvres complètes*, ed. Claude Pichois, 2 vols. [Paris: Gallimard, Bibliothèque de la Pléiade, 1983–85], 2:1452–53); Bedriomo concludes that "the content, indeed even the style, of the lines that Wagner inspires in Baudelaire are found again in *Du côté de chez Swann*" (47).

8. Proust, *Contre Sainte-Beuve*, 255.

9. Baudelaire, *Œuvres complètes*, 2:1452; Baudelaire's emphasis. This remark comes from the letter Baudelaire wrote to Wagner in 1860.

10. See Baudelaire, "À une passante," in *Œuvres complètes,* 1:92–93. The tercets run as follows:

Un éclair . . . puis la nuit!—Fugitive beauté
Dont le regard m'a fait soudainement renaître,
Ne te verrai-je plus que dans l'éternité?

Ailleurs, bien loin d'ici! trop tard! *jamais* peut-être!
Car j'ignore où tu fuis, tu ne sais où je vais,
O toi que j'eusse aimée, ô toi qui le savais!

[A lightning flash . . . then night!—Fugitive beauty
In whose gaze I was suddenly reborn,
Will I not see you again except in eternity?

Elsewhere, very far from here! too late! *never* perhaps!
For I do not know where you have fled, you do not know where I
    am going,
O you whom I might have loved, O you who knew it!]

11. Pierre Fontanier, *Les Figures du discours,* intro. Gérard Genette (Paris: Flammarion, 1977), 113; see chapter 3 above.

12. For a more detailed analysis of Odette's status as a work of art in Swann's life, see David Ellison, *The Reading of Proust* (Baltimore: Johns Hopkins University Press, 1984), 11–12. After explaining that "art is the mediating force that intervenes to complete and remedy the protagonist's original lack of passion," Ellison goes on to argue that the "little phrase" eventually "loses all intrinsic value, exists no longer as music" for Swann, who is unable to dissociate it from Odette. It is clear that the "little phrase" is rhetorically bound to Odette in Proust's text; but I would argue that it is precisely because of its specific character as music that the "little phrase" has the power to circulate between Swann and Odette, permeating and enlivening them both.

13. See chapter 3 above.

14. I owe a part of my argument here to Jacques Derrida, who in the context of a discussion on Descartes's *Discours de la méthode* analyzes the impossibility of ever entirely separating the concept of method from that of metaphor, both of which are also indissociable from the concept of a pathway [le chemin]. See "La Langue et le discours de la méthode," in *Recherches sur la philosophie et le langage,* vol. 3, *La Philosophie dans sa langue* (Grenoble: Cahier du groupe de recherches sur la philosophie et le langage, Département de Philosophie de l'Université de Grenoble II, 1983), 35–51.

15. See particularly the third section, "L'Artiste, homme du monde, homme des foules et enfant," in *Le Peintre de la vie moderne*. Baudelaire argues there that artistic genius may be compared to the familiar conditions of childhood or of convalescence following a critical illness, both of which involve excessively heightened intensity of observation and emotion; this intensity is essential to an artist such as Guys, whose passion is first "to see and to feel" the spectacle of contemporary living and then immediately to "extricate from fashion whatever it contains that is poetic and historic" (Baudelaire, *Œuvres complètes*, 2:687–94).

16. See Paul de Man's discussion of *Le Peintre de la vie moderne* in "Literary History and Literary Modernity," in *Blindness and Insight: Essays in the Rhetoric of Contemporary Criticism*, 2d ed., rev., Theory and History of Literature, vol. 7 (Minneapolis: University of Minnesota Press, 1983), 156–61. De Man emphasizes the "temporal ambivalence" that "prompts Baudelaire to couple any evocation of the present with terms such as 'représentation,' 'mémoire,' or even 'temps,' all opening perspective of distance and difference within the apparent uniqueness of the instant" (157). See also Susan Bernstein's commentary on part 4 of Baudelaire's Wagner essay in "Virtuosity of the Nineteenth Century: Music and Language in Heine, Liszt, and Baudelaire" (Ph.D. diss., Johns Hopkins University, 1991), 561–64. Bernstein argues that "Baudelaire's notion of *sui generis* gives a fair resumé of many of the paradoxical tensions, notable throughout his work, between history and the eternal ideal of poetry. . . . *Sui generis* thus functions as a critical category for that which cannot be subsumed within any given category; the cases amassed under the name of *sui generis*, therefore, cannot be understood as particular examples of a higher generality, for they are defined precisely as that which exceeds the logic of application and subsumption. That is, if the generality is said to originate in the particular, the unity of the category of *sui generis* can only be inductive and historical" (562).

17. For more background and analysis of the relations between excess, music, and melodrama, see Peter Brooks, *The Melodramatic Imagination: Balzac, Henry James, Melodrama, and the Mode of Excess* (New York: Columbia University Press, 1984), esp. 14 and 48–49. Brooks notes that apart from conventions such as ballet scenes, "further recourse to music is most evident at climactic moments and in scenes of rapid physical action, particularly mute action, which receive orchestral underlining" (48).

18. Among Wagner's operas, *Tristan* lends itself particularly well to this context, since its plot thematizes the sudden, unexpected blossoming of a love relationship between protagonists who ought to have remained, in a sense, "altogether foreign" to each other. For a discussion of relations between *Tristan* and the *Recherche* in a

broader context, see Richard E. Goodkin, "Proust and Wagner: The Climb to the Octave Above, or, The Scale of Love (and Death)," in *Around Proust* (Princeton: Princeton University Press, 1991), 103–26.

19. Jean-Jacques Nattiez furnishes a useful discussion of this passage from *La Prisonnière* in *Proust musicien* (Paris: Christian Bourgois, 1984), 36–45. Citing Robert Vigneron ("Structure de *Swann:* Balzac, Wagner, et Proust," *French Review* [May 1946]: 380), Nattiez confirms that Proust is incorrect when he claims that Wagner discovered the fundamental unity of his *Ring* tetralogy only after composing the four operas separately. But Nattiez also explains that Proust's reflections on motivic relations in *Tristan und Isolde,* as well as in *Parsifal,* are somewhat more historically accurate.

20. It is significant that the narrator later applies nearly the same terms to Vinteuil's septet: "A phrase of a painful character was opposed [to the mysterious appeal of the beginning], but [it was] so profound, so vague, so internal, almost so organic and visceral that one did not know, at each of its reprises, whether they were those of a theme or of a neuralgic attack" (3:764).

21. The narrator's whole meditation on the septet is permeated with allusions to paths, explicit "chemins" as well as other kinds of trails. Georges Poulet studies some of these in *L'Espace proustien* (Paris: Gallimard, 1963); see pp. 23–27, where he explores the relation between the beginning of the septet episode (when the narrator finds himself "in an unknown country") and one of the promenades recounted in "Combray."

22. This expression comes from Baudelaire's letter of February 10, 1861, to the publisher Bourdilliat and is quoted by Claude Pichois in his notes to Baudelaire, *Œuvres complètes,* 2:1458; see chapter 1 above.

APPENDIX I: *Richard Wagner et "Tannhäuser" à Paris*
by Charles Baudelaire

1. In *L'Art romantique:* "M'est-il permis à moi-même de raconter, de rendre avec des paroles la traduction inévitable que mon imagination fit du même morceau, . . ." [M. M.].

2. In *L'Art romantique:* "Wagner indique *une troupe d'anges qui apportent un vase sacré;* . . ." [M. M.].

3. In *L'Art romantique:* "Dès les premières mesures, les nerfs vivent à l'unisson de la mélodie; . . ." [M. M.].

4. La première partie de cette étude a paru à *la Revue Européenne,* où M. Perrin,

ancien directeur de l'Opéra-Comique, dont les sympathies pour Wagner sont bien connues, est chargé de la critique musicale [C. B.].

5. In *L'Art romantique: "Si le capitaine qui mettra pied à terre tous les sept ans y rencontre une femme fidèle, il sera sauvé"* [M. M.].

6. In *L'Art romantique: "*. . . et même à se munir de résignation pour l'avenir" [M. M.].

BIBLIOGRAPHY

Abbate, Carolyn. "Opera as Symphony, a Wagnerian Myth." In *Analyzing Opera: Verdi and Wagner,* edited by Carolyn Abbate and Roger Parker, 92–124. Berkeley and Los Angeles: University of California Press, 1989.

———. "The Parisian 'Vénus' and the 'Paris' *Tannhäuser.*" *Journal of the American Musicological Society* 36, no. 1 (1983): 73–123.

———. *Unsung Voices: Opera and Musical Narrative in the Nineteenth Century.* Princeton: Princeton University Press, 1991.

Adorno, Theodor W. *Versuch über Wagner.* 2d ed. Frankfurt am Main: Suhrkamp, 1981. Translated by Rodney Livingstone under the title *In Search of Wagner.* London: NLB, 1981.

Astruc, Zacharie. "Chronique musicale: Richard Wagner." *Revue internationale* 2 (Feb. 29, 1860): 464–67.

Baudelaire, Charles. *Baudelaire: Selected Writings on Art and Artists.* Translated with an introduction by P. E. Charvet. Harmondsworth, England: Penguin Books, 1972.

———. *Baudelaire: The Complete Verse.* Translated and edited by Francis Scarfe. 2 vols. London: Anvil Press Poetry, 1986.

———. *Baudelaire as a Literary Critic.* Translated and edited by Lois Boe Hyslop and Francis E. Hyslop Jr. University Park: Pennsylvania State University Press, 1964.

———. *Correspondance.* Edited by Claude Pichois and Jean Ziegler. 2 vols. Paris: Gallimard, Bibliothèque de la Pléiade, 1973.

———. *Œuvres complètes.* Edited by Claude Pichois. 2 vols. Paris: Gallimard, Bibliothèque de la Pléiade, 1983–85.

———. *The Painter of Modern Life and Other Essays.* Translated and edited by Jonathan Mayne. London: Phaidon Press, 1964; New York: Da Capo, 1986.

Beckett, Lucy. "Wagner and His Critics." In *The Wagner Companion,* edited by Peter Burbidge and Richard Sutton, 365–88. New York: Cambridge University Press, 1979.

Bedriomo, Émile. *Proust, Wagner, et la coïncidence des arts.* Tübingen: Gunter Narr; Paris: Éditions Jean-Michel Place, 1984.

Benjamin, Walter. *Charles Baudelaire: Ein Lyriker im Zeitalter des Hochkapitalismus.* Edited by Rolf Tiedemann. Frankfurt am Main: Suhrkamp, 1974. Translated by Harry Zohn under the title *Charles Baudelaire: A Lyric Poet in the Era of High Capitalism.* London: Verso, 1983.

———. *Ursprung des deutschen Trauerspiels.* Frankfurt am Main: Suhrkamp, 1963. Translated by John Osborne under the title *The Origin of German Tragic Drama.* London: NLB, 1977; London: Verso, 1985.

Benveniste, Emile. *Problèmes de linguistique générale.* 2 vols. Paris: Gallimard, 1966.

Berlioz, Hector. "Concerts de Richard Wagner: La Musique de l'avenir." In *À travers chants,* edited by Léon Guichard, 321–33. Paris: Gründ, 1971.

———. *Fantastic Symphony: An Authoritative Score, Historical Background, Analysis, Views, and Comments.* Edited by Edward T. Cone. New York: W. W. Norton, 1971.

Bermann, Sandra L. *The Sonnet over Time.* University of North Carolina Studies in Comparative Literature, no. 63. Chapel Hill: University of North Carolina Press, 1988.

Bernard, Élisabeth. *Le Chef d'orchestre.* Paris: Éditions La Découverte, 1989.

———. "La Vie symphonique à Paris entre 1861 et 1914 suivie d'une étude analytique des programmes des *Concerts Populaires de Musique Classique,* de l'*Association Artistique,* et de la *Société des Nouveaux-Concerts.*" Thèse de doctorat, 3ᵉ cycle, Université de Paris I, 1976.

Bernstein, Susan. "Virtuosity of the Nineteenth Century: Music and Language in Heine, Liszt, and Baudelaire." Ph.D. diss., Johns Hopkins University, 1991.

Blood, Susan. "The Ethical Imperative in Baudelaire's Aesthetics." Ph.D. diss., Johns Hopkins University, 1988.

Boiste, P. C. D. *Dictionnaire universel de la langue française, avec le latin et l'étymologie.* 5th ed. Paris: Firmin-Didot/Rey et Belhatte, 1866.

Boulez, Pierre. "De moi à moi." In *Penser la musique aujourd'hui.* Lausanne: Gonthier, 1963.

Brooks, Peter. *The Melodramatic Imagination: Balzac, Henry James, Melodrama, and the Mode of Excess.* New York: Columbia University Press, 1984.

Charlton, David. "Motive and Motif: Méhul before 1791." *Music and Letters* 57, no. 4 (1976): 362–69.

————. *The Overture in France, 1790–1810.* Ser. D, vol. 7 of *The Symphony, 1720–1840,* edited by Barry S. Brook. New York: Garland, 1983.

Chase, Cynthia. *Decomposing Figures: Rhetorical Readings in the Romantic Tradition.* Baltimore: Johns Hopkins University Press, 1986.

Cohen, H[enri]. "Concerts Populaires." *La Chronique musicale* 3, no. 15 (Feb. 1, 1874).

Cohn, Robert Greer. *Toward the Poems of Mallarmé.* Expanded ed. Berkeley and Los Angeles: University of California Press, 1980.

Compagnon, Antoine. *La Seconde Main, ou le travail de la citation.* Paris: Seuil, 1979.

Cooper, Jeffrey. *The Rise of Instrumental Music and Concert Series in Paris, 1828–1871.* Studies in Musicology, no. 65. Ann Arbor, Mich.: UMI, 1983.

Crowley, Roseline. "Toward the Poetics of Juxtaposition: *L'Après-Midi d'un Faune.*" *Yale French Studies* 54 (1977): 32–44.

Dahlhaus, Carl. *The Idea of Absolute Music.* Translated by Roger Lustig. Chicago: University of Chicago Press, 1989.

————. *Nineteenth-Century Music.* Translated by J. Bradford Robinson. Berkeley and Los Angeles: University of California Press, 1989.

————. "Wagner and Program Music." *Studies in Romanticism* 9, no. 1 (1970): 3–20.

Deane, Basil. "The French Operatic Overture from Grétry to Berlioz." *Proceedings of the Royal Music Association* 99 (1972–73): 67–80.

Deathridge, John, and Carl Dahlhaus. *The New Grove Wagner.* New York: W. W. Norton, 1984.

Debussy, Claude. *Prelude to "The Afternoon of a Faun."* Edited by William W. Austin. New York: W. W. Norton, 1970.

De Man, Paul. *Allegories of Reading: Figural Language in Rousseau, Nietzsche, Rilke, and Proust.* New Haven: Yale University Press, 1979.

————. "Anthropomorphism and Trope in the Lyric." In *The Rhetoric of Romanticism,* 239–62. New York: Columbia University Press, 1984.

————. *Blindness and Insight: Essays in the Rhetoric of Contemporary Criticism.* 2d ed., rev. Theory and History of Literature, vol. 7. Minneapolis: University of Minnesota Press, 1983.

————. "Pascal's Allegory of Persuasion." In *Allegory and Representation: Selected Papers from the English Institute, 1979–1980,* edited with preface by Stephen J. Greenblatt, 1–25. Baltimore: Johns Hopkins University Press, 1981.

Derrida, Jacques. *De la grammatologie.* Paris: Minuit, 1967.

————. *La Dissémination.* Paris: Seuil, 1972.

———. "Freud et la scène de l'écriture." In *L'Écriture et la différence,* 293–340. Paris: Seuil, 1967.

———. "La Langue et le discours de la méthode." In *Recherches sur la philosophie et le langage.* Vol. 3, *La Philosophie dans sa langue.* Grenoble: Cahier du groupe de recherches sur la philosophie et le langage, Département de Philosophie de l'Université de Grenoble II, 1983. 35–51.

———. "Signature événement contexte." In *Marges de la philosophie,* 365–93. Paris: Minuit, 1972.

Eigeldinger, Marc. "À propos de l'image du thyrse." *Revue d'histoire littéraire de la France* (Jan.–Feb. 1975): 110–12.

Ellison, David. *The Reading of Proust.* Baltimore: Johns Hopkins University Press, 1984.

Ernouf, Baron. "L'Œuvre de R. Wagner." *Revue comtemporaine* (Feb. 15, 1860).

Faure, Émile. "Le Premier Concert de Richard Wagner et la presse parisienne." *La Presse théâtrale et musicale* 7, no. 5 (Feb. 5, 1860).

———. "La Presse parisienne et les concerts Wagner." *La Presse théâtrale et musicale* 7, no. 6 (Feb. 12, 1860).

———. "La Presse parisienne et les concerts Wagner." *La Presse théâtrale et musicale* 7, no. 7 (Feb. 19, 1860).

Ferguson, Howard. "Prelude." In *The New Grove Dictionary of Music and Musicians,* edited by Stanley Sadie, 20 vols., 15:210–11. London: Macmillan, 1980.

Fétis, François-Joseph. "Richard Wagner." *Revue et Gazette musicale de Paris* 19, no. 23 (June 6, 1852): 185–87; no. 24 (June 13, 1852): 193–95; no. 25 (June 20, 1852): 201–3; no. 26 (June 27, 1852): 209–11; no. 28 (July 11, 1852): 225–27; no. 30 (July 25, 1852): 242–45; no. 32 (Aug. 8, 1852): 257–59.

Fontanier, Pierre. *Les Figures du discours.* With an introduction by Gérard Genette. Paris: Flammarion, 1977.

Gautier, Théophile. "Charles Baudelaire." Preface to *Œuvres complètes,* by Charles Baudelaire. 7 vols. Paris: Michel Lévy Frères, 1869.

Genette, Gérard. *Seuils.* Paris: Seuil, 1987.

Gilman, Margaret. *Baudelaire the Critic.* New York: Columbia University Press, 1943. New York: Octagon Press, 1971.

Glass, Frank W. *The Fertilizing Seed: Wagner's Concept of the Poetic Intent.* Ann Arbor, Mich.: UMI, 1983.

Goodkin, Richard E. "Proust and Wagner: The Climb to the Octave Above, or, The Scale of Love (and Death)." In *Around Proust,* 103–26. Princeton: Princeton University Press, 1991.

————. "Zeno's Paradox: Mallarmé, Valéry, and the Symbolist 'Movement.'" *Yale French Studies* 74 (1988): 133–56.

Grandmougin, Charles. *Esquisse sur Richard Wagner*. Paris: Durand, Schœnewerk, 1873.

Grey, Thomas S. "Wagner, the Overture, and the Aesthetics of Musical Form." *19th-Century Music* 12, no. 1 (1988): 3–22.

Grimm, Jacob. *Deutsche Mythologie*. Edited by Elard Hugo Meyer. 4th ed., 3 vols. Berlin: Ferd. Dümmler, 1876. Translated by James Steven Stallybrass under the title *Teutonic Mythology*. 4 vols. New York: George Bell, 1883; New York: Dover, 1966.

Guichard, Léon. *La Musique et les lettres en France au temps du wagnérisme*. Paris: Presses Universitaires de France, 1963.

Hannoosh, Michele. "Painting as Translation in Baudelaire's Art Criticism." *Forum for Modern Language Studies* 22, no. 1 (1986): 22–33.

Hartford, Robert, ed. *Bayreuth: The Early Years. An account of the Early Decades of the Wagner Festival as seen by the Celebrated Visitors & Participants*. Cambridge: Cambridge University Press, 1980.

Hassine, Juliette. *Essai sur Proust et Baudelaire*. Paris: Nizet, 1979.

Hoffmann, E[rnst] T[heodor] A[madeus]. *Contes fantastiques*. Translated by [Adolphe-François] Loève-Veimars, with an introduction and notes by José Lambert. 3 vols. Paris: Flammarion, 1979–82.

————. *Sämtliche Werke*. Edited by Hartmut Steinecke and Wulf Segebrecht. 6 vols. Frankfurt am Main: Deutscher Klassiker Verlag, 1993.

Hollander, John. *The Figure of Echo: A Mode of Allusion in Milton and After*. Berkeley and Los Angeles: University of California Press, 1981.

Johnson, Barbara. *Défigurations du langage poétique*. Paris: Flammarion, 1979.

————. *A World of Difference*. Baltimore: Johns Hopkins University Press, 1987.

Kivy, Peter. *Sound and Semblance: Reflections on Musical Representation*. Princeton: Princeton University Press, 1984.

Klein, Richard. "'Bénédiction'/'Perte d'auréole': Parables of Interpretation." *Modern Language Notes* 85, no. 4 (1970): 515–28.

La Cépède, Le Comte de. *La Poëtique de la musique*. 2 vols. Paris: L'Imprimerie de Monsieur, 1785.

Lacombe, Louis. "Richard Wagner." *La Presse théâtrale et musicale* 7, no. 10 (Mar. 11, 1860), no. 11 (Mar. 18, 1860), and no. 12 (Mar. 25, 1860).

Lacoue-Labarthe, Philippe. "Baudelaire *contra* Wagner." *Études françaises* 17, nos. 3–4 (1981): 23–52.

————. *Musica ficta (Figures de Wagner)*. Paris: Christian Bourgois, 1991.

Lavignac, Albert. *Le Voyage artistique à Bayreuth*. 4th ed. Paris: Delagrave, 1900.

Leprince, G. *Présence de Wagner*. Paris: Éditions du Vieux Colombier, 1963.

Le Sueur, Jean François. *Exposé d'une musique une, imitative, et propre à chaque solemnité, où l'on donne une Dissertation sur ses effets, & le Plan d'une Musique particulière à la Solemnité de la Pentecôte*. Paris: Veuve Hérissant, 1787.

Lévi-Strauss, Claude. *Le Cru et le cuit*. Paris: Plon, 1964.

Levy-Bloch, Mira. "La Traduction chez Baudelaire: Les Trois Imaginations du poète-traducteur." *Nineteenth-Century French Studies* 20, nos. 3–4 (1992): 361–79.

Liszt, Franz. "Berlioz und seine 'Harold-Symphonie.'" In *Gesammelte Schriften von Franz Liszt*, edited by L. Ramann, 6 vols., 4:3–102. Leipzig: Breitkopf und Härtel, 1882.

————. *"Lohengrin" et "Tannhäuser" de Richard Wagner*. Leipzig: F. A. Brockhaus, 1851. Paris: Adef-Albatros, 1980.

————. *Pages romantiques*. Edited by Jean Chantavoine. Paris: Éditions d'Aujourd'hui, 1985.

Loncke, Joycelynne. *Baudelaire et la musique*. Paris: Nizet, 1975.

Lorenz, Alfred. "Der musikalische Aufbau von Wagners *Lohengrin*." In *Bayreuther Festspielführer*, edited by Otto Strobel, 189–97. Bayreuth: Georg Niehrenheim, 1936.

Mallarmé, Stéphane. *Œuvres complètes*. Edited by Henri Mondor and G.-Jean Aubry. Paris: Gallimard, Bibliothèque de la Pléiade, 1945.

Marx, Adolf Bernhard. *Die Lehre von der musikalischen Komposition, praktisch theoretisch*. 4 vols. Leipzig: Breitkopf und Härtel, 1841–47.

Mather, Betty Bang, and David Lasocki. *The Art of Preluding, 1700–1830*. New York: McGinnis & Marx Music Publishers, 1984.

Maus, Fred Everett. "Music as Drama." *Music Theory Spectrum* 10 (1988): 56–73.

Moschelès, J.-P. "Revue de quinzaine." *La Chronique musicale* 4, no. 16 (Nov. 1, 1868).

Nattiez, Jean-Jacques. *Proust musicien*. Paris: Christian Bourgois, 1984.

————. *Wagner Androgyne: Essai sur l'interprétation*. Paris: Christian Bourgois, 1990. Translated by Stewart Spencer under the title *Wagner Androgyne: A Study in Interpretation*. Princeton: Princeton University Press, 1993.

Newman, Ernest. *The Life of Richard Wagner*. 4 vols. New York: Knopf, 1941.

————. *The Wagner Operas*. 2 vols. New York: Harper Colophon, 1983.

Nietzsche, Friedrich. *The Birth of Tragedy and The Case of Wagner*. Translated by Walter Kaufmann. New York: Random House, 1967.

————. *The Portable Nietzsche.* Translated and edited by Walter Kaufmann. New York: Viking, 1954.

————. *Sämtliche Werke: Kritische Studienausgabe in 15 Bänden.* Edited by Giorgio Colli and Mazzino Montinari. Munich: Deutscher Taschenbuch; Berlin: Walter de Gruyter, 1980.

————. *Werke in Drei Bänden.* Edited by Karl Schlechta. Munich: Carl Hanser, 1973.

Pichois, Claude. *Baudelaire, études et témoignages.* Neuchâtel: La Baconnière, 1982.

Piroué, Georges. *Proust et la musique du devenir.* Paris: Denoël, 1960.

Poulet, Georges. *La Distance intérieure.* Vol. 2 of *Études sur le temps humain.* 1952. Paris: Plon, Rocher, 1976.

————. *L'Espace proustien.* Paris: Gallimard, 1963.

Proust, Marcel. *À la recherche du temps perdu.* Edited by Jean-Yves Tadié. 4 vols. Paris: Gallimard, Bibliothèque de la Pléiade, 1987–89. Translated by C. K. Scott Moncrieff and Terence Kilmartin under the title *Remembrance of Things Past.* New York: Random House, 1981.

————. *"Contre Sainte-Beuve," précédé de "Pastiches et mélanges" et suivi de Essais et articles.* Edited by Pierre Clarac et Yves Sandre. Paris: Gallimard, Bibliothèque de la Pléiade, 1971.

————. *Marcel Proust on Art and Literature, 1896–1919.* Translated by Sylvia Townsend Warner. London: Chatto and Windus, 1957; New York: Meridian Books, 1958.

Raser, Timothy. "Reference and Citation in Baudelaire's Art Criticism." Paper presented at the Seventeenth Annual Colloquium in Nineteenth-Century French Studies. New Orleans, Oct. 18, 1991.

Reicha, Antoine. *Vollständiges Lehrbuch der musikalischen Composition.* Translated from the French in parallel columns and annotated by Carl Czerny. 4 vols. Vienna: Diabelli, 1832.

Richard, Jean-Pierre. "Profondeur de Baudelaire." In *Poésie et profondeur,* 91–162. Paris: Seuil, 1955.

Riemann, Hugo. *Beethovens Streichquartette erläutert.* Berlin: Schlesinger and Lienau, 1910.

————. *L. van Beethovens sämtliche Klavier-Solo-Sonaten.* 2 vols. Berlin: Hesse, 1917.

Robb, Graham. "Baudelaire and the Ghosts of Stone." *Romance Notes* 25, no. 2 (1984): 137–44.

Roche, Edmond. "Richard Wagner: Premier concert à grand orchestre donné, le 25 janvier 1860, au Théâtre Impérial Italien." *La Presse théâtrale et musicale* 7, no. 4 (Jan. 29, 1860).

Rousseau, Jean-Jacques. *Dictionnaire de la musique.* In vol. 4 of *Œuvres complètes.* 8 vols. Paris: Lefèvre, 1839.

————. *Les Rêveries du promeneur solitaire.* Paris: Garnier-Flammarion, 1964.

Sallis, John. *Crossings: Nietzsche and the Space of Tragedy.* Chicago: University of Chicago Press, 1991.

Saloman, Ora Frishberg. "La Cépède's *La Poétique de la musique* and Le Sueur." *Acta musicologica* 47 (Jan.–June 1975): 144–54.

Scruton, Roger. "Programme Music." In *The New Grove Dictionary of Music and Musicians,* edited by Stanley Sadie, 20 vols., 15:283–87. London: Macmillan, 1980.

————. "Representation in Music." *Journal of the Royal Institute of Philosophy* 51, no. 197 (July 1976): 273–87.

Scudo, Paul. *L'Année musicale, deuxième année.* Paris: Hachette, 1860.

Skelton, Geoffrey. "The Idea of Bayreuth." In *The Wagner Companion,* edited by Peter Burbidge and Richard Sutton, 389–411. New York: Cambridge University Press, 1979.

Société des Concerts du Conservatoire. Programs, 1828–1913. Bibliothèque Nationale, Département de la Musique, Paris.

Solie, Ruth A. "The Living Work: Organicism and Musical Analysis." *19th-Century Music* 4, no. 2 (1980): 147–56.

Stamelman, Richard. "The Shroud of Allegory: Death, Mourning, and Melancholy in Baudelaire's Work." *Texas Studies in Literature and Language* 25, no. 3 (1983): 390–409.

Steinbeck, Susanne. *Die Ouvertüre von Beethoven bis Wagner: Probleme und Lösungen.* Munich: Emil Katzbichler, 1973.

Strohm, Reinhard. "Gedanken zu Wagners Opernouvertüren." In *Wagnerliteratur-Wagnerforschung,* edited by Carl Dahlhaus and Egon Voss, 69–84. Mainz: B. Schott, 1985.

Subotnik, Rose Rosengard. *Developing Variations: Style and Idealogogy in Western Music.* Minneapolis: University of Minnesota Press, 1991.

Temperley, Nicholas. "Overture." In *The New Grove Dictionary of Music and Musicians,* edited by Stanley Sadie, 20 vols., 14:33–35. London: Macmillan, 1980.

Thibaudet, Albert. *La Poésie de Stéphane Mallarmé.* 4th ed. Paris: Gallimard, Nouvelle Revue Française, 1926.

Thomas, Henri. "Nietzsche et Baudelaire." In *La Chasse aux trésors,* 140–45. Paris: Gallimard, 1961.

Todorov, Tzvetan. "La Crise romantique." In *Théories du symbole,* 179–260. Paris: Seuil, 1977.

Treitler, Leo. "Mozart and the Idea of Absolute Music." In *Music and the Historical Imagination,* 176–214. Cambridge: Harvard University Press, 1989.

Turbow, Gerald Dale. "Art and Politics: Wagnerism in France." In *Wagnerism in European Culture and Politics,* edited by David C. Large and William Weber, 134–66. Ithaca, N.Y.: Cornell University Press, 1984.

————. "Wagnerism in France, 1839–1870: A Measure of a Social and Political Trend." Ph.D. diss., University of California, Los Angeles, 1965; Ann Arbor, Mich.: UMI, 1982.

Valéry, Paul. "Situation de Baudelaire." In *Œuvres complètes,* edited by Jean Hytier, 2 vols., 2:598–613. Paris: Gallimard, Bibliothèque de la Pléiade, 1957.

Wagner, Richard. "De l'ouverture." In *Œuvres en prose,* French translation by J.-G. Prod'homme, 13 vols., 1:231–49. Paris: Delagrave, 1907.

————. *Gesammelte Schriften und Dichtungen.* 4th ed. 10 vols. Leipzig: C. F. W. Siegel's Musikalienhandlung, 1907.

————. *Lohengrin.* Full Score. New York: Dover, 1982.

————. *Lohengrin.* Romantische Oper in 3 Akten. Klavierauszug mit Text von Theodor Uhlig. Leipzig: Breitkopf und Härtel, n.d. [1880–89?].

————. Program for concerts at the Théâtre-Italien, January 25, February 1, and February 8, 1860. Bound collection C.5065 (6). Bibliothèque de l'Opéra, Paris.

————. *Quatre poèmes d'opéras traduits en prose française, précédés d'une lettre sur la musique.* French translation by [Paul Amand] Challemel-Lacour. Paris: A. Bourdilliat, 1861.

————. *Richard Wagner's Prose Works.* Translated by William Ashton Ellis, 8 vols. New York: Broude Brothers, 1966.

————. *Tannhäuser.* Full Score. New York: Dover, 1984.

Warrack, John. "Leitmotif." In *The New Grove Dictionary of Music and Musicians,* edited by Stanley Sadie, 20 vols., 10:644–46. London: Macmillan, 1980.

Weber, William. "Wagner, Wagnerism, and Musical Idealism." In *Wagnerism in European Culture and Politics,* edited by David C. Large and William Weber, 28–71. Ithaca, N.Y.: Cornell University Press, 1984.

Wilner, Joshua. "Music without Rhythm: Incorporation and Intoxication in the Prose of Baudelaire and De Quincey." Ph.D. diss., Yale University, 1980.

Wing, Nathaniel. "The Danaides Vessel: On Reading Baudelaire's Allegories." In *The Limits of Narrative,* 8–18. Cambridge: Cambridge University Press, 1986.

Wyss, Beat. "*Ragnarök* of Illusion: Richard Wagner's 'Mystical Abyss' at Bayreuth." *October* 54 (1990): 57–78.

Zimmerman, Melvin. "La Genèse du symbole du thyrse chez Baudelaire." *Bulletin baudelairien* 2, no. 1 (1966): 8–11.

INDEX

Abbate, Carolyn, 207 (n. 26), 211
  (n. 14), 217 (n. 10), 226 (n. 13), 229
  (n. 36)
Abyss, 12, 208 (n. 34)
Admiration, 61–64, 65, 98
Adorno, Theodor, 52–54, 129–30, 214
  (nn. 38, 39), 233 (n. 65)
À la recherche du temps perdu, 144, 145,
  150, 156, 159, 163; "Un Amour de
  Swann," 144, 146–50; Vinteuil's
  music, 144, 146–50, 156–65, 235
  (n. 12); "Combray," 157, 163; La
  Prisonnière, 159–60; À l'ombre des
  jeunes filles en fleurs, 163
Allegory, 39–40, 47, 55, 60, 112, 114,
  212 (n. 21), 227 (n. 17); and
  narrative 54, 57–58, 214–15 (n. 41)
Anthropomorphism, 74, 91, 219 (n. 26)
"Après-Midi d'un Faune, L'"
  (Mallarmé), 132–35
"À propos de Baudelaire" (Proust),
  144
"Art philosophique, L'" (Baudelaire),
  39–40, 114
Astruc, Zacharie, 209 (n. 8), 210
  (n. 12), 221–22 (n. 38)

"À une passante" (Baudelaire), 146,
  235 (n. 10)

Banville, Théodore de, 39–40, 114
Bayreuth, 20–21, 153, 208 (n. 34)
Bedriomo, Emile, 234 (n. 7)
Beethoven, Ludwig van, 18, 30, 79,
  109–10, 119, 226 (n. 13), 230 (n. 44)
Benjamin, Walter, 28, 143
Benveniste, Émile, 208 (n. 3), 210–11
  (n. 13), 214 (n. 35)
Berlioz, Hector, 30, 36–40 passim, 119,
  207 (n. 29)
Bernstein, Susan, 203 (n. 1), 209
  (n. 3), 215 (n. 43), 217 (nn. 8, 9),
  222 (n. 39), 224 (n. 2), 225 (n. 8),
  236 (n. 16)
Birth of Tragedy, The (Nietzsche),
  89–93
Bizet, Georges, 95
Brooks, Peter, 236 (n. 17)
Boulez, Pierre, 143

Carmen (Bizet), 95
Case of Wagner, The (Nietzsche), 95–97

Chance, 27–28, 33, 40, 54, 60, 156. *See also* Gamble; Risk

Charlton, David, 228 (n. 27)

Chase, Cynthia, 219 (n. 26)

Chopin, Frédéric, 125, 230 (n. 40)

Cirque Napoléon, 20

Clairvoyance, 21, 72, 74

Compagnon, Antoine, 75, 220 (n. 28)

Concert: by Wagner (Paris, 1860), 5, 16–17, 18–19, 26, 28–29, 30, 35, 36, 62, 67, 72, 99, 122, 137, 209 (n. 5), 220 (n. 29), 221 (nn. 35, 38); reviews, 15–17; audience behavior and French press, 19–20. *See also* Journalism; Théâtre-Italien

Concerts Populaires de Musique Classique, 20, 207 (n. 30)

"Correspondances" (Baudelaire), 14, 48–49, 54, 107, 224 (n. 5)

"Crise de vers" (Mallarmé), 135–36, 232 (n. 60)

Crowley, Roseline, 231 (n. 53)

Czerny, Carl, 45

Debussy, Claude, 135–36

Delacroix, Eugène, 7–9, 155

"De l'ouverture" (Wagner), 78–79, 120, 221 (n. 32)

de Man, Paul, 54, 74, 91, 214 (nn. 33, 41), 225 (n. 6), 236 (n. 16)

De Quincey, Thomas, 124, 216 (n. 6), 219 (n. 19), 229 (n. 35)

Derrida, Jacques, 126, 208–9 (n. 3), 213 (n. 32), 216 (n. 45), 235 (n. 14)

Dictionnaire de la musique (Rousseau), 118

Diderot, Denis, 101, 229 (n. 35)

Digression, 23, 117, 124, 136, 229

(n. 35); in *Richard Wagner et "Tannhäuser" à Paris,* 102–8, 111–16, 142

Dionysus, 90, 92–93, 123, 223 (n. 54); Dionysian versus Apollinian, 89–94

Distance: between music and letters, 2, 16, 33, 38–39, 48, 60, 97–98, 148–49; between *Richard Wagner et "Tannhäuser" à Paris* and Wagner's music, 6–7, 9, 23–24, 47, 54, 57–58, 64, 98, 117, 156; aesthetic, 7, 14; critical, 7, 129–30, 231 (n. 50); linguistic, 8; between painting and music, 8–9; between the literal and the figurative, 8, 10, 15, 48, 166; between listeners and music, 19–21; temporal, 26–27; intersubjective, 27; between listening and writing, 33; between allegory and referent, 40, 54; between music and language, 65, 165; between art and criticism, 100–101, 116, 149; between opera and overture, 123–24

Echo, 100–102, 131, 135, 224 (n. 3)

Eigeldinger, Marc, 229 (n. 35)

Eine Mitteilung an meine Freunde (Wagner), 16

Ellison, David, 235 (n. 12)

Esquisse sur Richard Wagner (Grandmougin), 18

Exposition universelle (1855) (Baudelaire), 7–8

Fétis, François-Joseph, 16, 205 (n. 18)

Fliegende Holländer, Der (Wagner), 13–14

Fontanier, Pierre, 73–74, 147

Gamble, 27–28, 60, 156, 164, 165, 166.
    See also Chance; Risk
Gautier, Théophile, 215–16 (n. 44)
Genette, Gérard, 227 (n. 25), 228
    (n. 26)
Genius, 85–86, 104–5, 153–54, 159–60,
    162, 163–64; of Wagner, 25, 102–3,
    144, 150–56, 161; of Baudelaire,
    144–45, 166
Gesamtkunstwerk, 67
Glass, Frank W., 218 (n. 19)
Gluck, Christoph Willibald, 78–79, 155
Goodkin, Richard E., 231 (nn. 52, 55),
    236–37 (n. 18)
Grandmougin, Charles, 18–19
Greek drama, 67–72
Grimm, Jacob, 113
Guys, Constantin, 44, 87, 155, 236
    (n. 15)

Harmony, 7, 52–53, 214 (n. 39); and
    color, 9, 13
Hoffmann, E. T. A., 14–15, 205 (n. 16)
Hollander, John, 224 (n. 3)
Holy Grail, 34, 35, 37–38, 41, 126;
    temple of, 42–43, 44, 46–47, 48, 49,
    127; as musical motif, 45–46
"Hommage (à Wagner)" (Mallarmé),
    139–41, 233 (n. 63)
Hugo, Victor, 155
Huguenots, Les (Meyerbeer), 85

I (pronoun), 27–28, 51, 60, 65, 133, 151,
    156, 208–9 (n. 3)
Italicization, 23, 33, 54–60, 86, 88, 133,
    148, 155, 166, 215 (nn. 43, 44), 231
    (n. 52)

Jockey Club, 6
Johnson, Barbara, 204 (n. 8), 215
    (n. 43), 218 (n. 15), 232 (n. 56), 233
    (n. 61)
Journalism: and music criticism, 3, 16;
    Wagner and French press, 6, 16–17,
    19–20, 65–66, 99. *See also* Concert

Kivy, Peter, 211 (n. 14)
Klein, Richard, 212 (n. 21)
Kreisleriana (Hoffmann), 14–15
Kunst und die Revolution, Die (Wagner),
    16, 69
Kunstwerk der Zukunft, Das (Wagner),
    13, 16, 69

La Cépède, Comte de, 119, 227 (n. 25)
Lacombe, Louis, 35–36, 37, 38, 39, 43
Lacoue-Labarthe, Philippe, 209 (n. 3),
    215 (n. 43), 216 (nn. 3, 5), 218
    (n. 19), 220 (n. 31)
Landmark: as metaphor for
    Baudelaire's writing, 4–5, 21, 23; as
    metaphor for Wagner's genius, 153
Landscape: as metaphor for Wagner's
    music, 4, 6–9, 16–17, 18–19, 21–23,
    26, 40, 60, 166; painting, 204 (n. 10)
Lavignac, Albert, 22–23
Legend, 110–11, 112, 114, 227 (n. 17).
    See also Myth
Lemaître, Frédéric, 87
Le Sueur, Jean François, 213 (n. 27)
Lettre sur la musique (Wagner), 16, 68,
    76, 100, 108–11, 128, 155, 218 (nn. 17,
    19). *See also* Quotation
Lévi-Strauss, Claude, 227 (n. 19)
Levy-Bloch, Mira, 225 (n. 8)

Liszt, Franz, 1, 30, 33, 76, 77, 80, 85–
86, 96, 118, 120, 123, 124–27, 129, 230
(nn. 43, 44). *See also* Program
Lohengrin (Wagner), 64, 101, 107, 142,
231 (n. 50); premiere of, 85; Elsa
(character) in, 111, 112–13, 115, 128–
30, 227 (n. 18). *See also* Motif;
Program
*"Lohengrin" et "Tannhäuser" de Richard
Wagner* (Liszt), 76, 80, 85–86, 227
(n. 18)
Lorenz, Alfred, 45–46

Mallarmé, Stéphane, 1, 23, 102, 131–42
Mangeur d'opium, Un (Baudelaire), 216
(n. 6), 229 (n. 35)
Marx, Adolf Bernhard, 45
Maus, Fred Everett, 217 (n. 10)
Meistersinger, Die (Wagner), 16
Melodrama, 158, 236 (n. 17)
Melody, 7–8, 13, 44–45, 52–53, 214
(n. 39); motivic, 76–89, 96
Memory, 50–51, 142, 230 (n. 41);
"mnemonic echo," 100–101, 131;
motifs as mnemonic system, 124–25
Metaphor, 42, 46–47, 74, 91, 92, 166;
geographical, 1, 18; music as, 3;
spatial, 7; Baudelaire's search for,
23, 151–54
Metonymy, 42, 46–47, 74, 91
Meyerbeer, Giacomo, 85
Modernity, 155, 162
Mon Cœur mis à nu (Baudelaire), 220
(n. 30)
Monstrosity, 103, 105, 114–16
Monument as metaphor, 4–5, 18
Moreau, Gustave, 145
Motif: in *Lohengrin* prelude, 43–44, 45–

46, 55, 57, 124–25, 128–30; in music,
43–45, 76, 149, 160–61, 212 (n. 25),
213 (n. 27), 215 (n. 43), 220 (n. 29);
in painting, 44; versus theme, 45,
52–53; temple as, 49; in *Tannhäuser*
overture, 77, 121; and personification, 78; in *Lohengrin*, 81–85, 231
(n. 50). *See also* Melody
"Musique, La" (Baudelaire), 10–12, 14,
205 (n. 12)
"Musique et les Lettres, La"
(Mallarmé), 136–37, 142
Myth, 101, 102, 108, 112–16, 123–24,
131, 142, 225–26 (n. 9), 227 (nn. 18,
19); and opera, 70–72, 107, 117, 127,
129–30, 141

Napoléon III, 6
Nattiez, Jean-Jacques, 218–19 (n. 19),
237 (n. 19)
Nietzsche, Friedrich, 1, 23, 89–98, 222
(nn. 40, 41)
Nietzsche contra Wagner (Nietzsche), 98

*On Truth and Lie in an Extra-Moral
Sense* (Nietzsche), 91
Opéra: in Paris, 5–6, 19, 26, 63, 98
Oper und Drama (Wagner), 16, 69, 109,
217 (n. 7), 218 (n. 18)
Overture: and relation to opera, 29,
30, 101, 118–20, 228 (n. 27); to
Tannhäuser, 76–78, 79–80, 117–18,
120–24, 152, 229 (n. 36); to *Iphigénie
en Aulide*, 78; as a genre, 78, 221
(n. 32), 228 (nn. 27, 30); to *Don
Giovanni*, 79; to *Leonora* (third), 79;
to *Oberon*, 119; and sonata form, 120,
228 (n. 30). *See also* Motif; Program

Pages romantiques (Liszt), 230 (n. 44)

Painting, 7–9, 18, 31, 42, 44, 46, 50, 59, 86–87, 146, 166, 212 (n. 24)

Paralysis: and italicization, 58–59; and music, 84–85, 87, 96, 98, 148–49, 163; and metaphor, 91

Pasdeloup, Jules, 20

Pastoral Symphony (Beethoven), 30, 92, 209 (n. 6)

Peintre de la vie moderne, Le (Baudelaire), 87, 155, 224 (n. 4), 236 (nn. 15, 16)

Personification, 1, 23, 66, 69, 75, 147, 166, 217 (n. 10); defined by Fontanier, 73–74; versus incarnation, 73–75, 77–78, 79, 81, 84, 88, 89–98, 148; and *Tannhäuser*, 76–78; with musical motifs, 78–79, 84, 221 (n. 35); of music, 146–47, 152

"Phares, Les" (Baudelaire), 9

Pichois, Claude, 212 (n. 22), 220 (n. 30), 226 (n. 10)

Piroué, Georges, 234 (n. 7)

Poulet, Georges, 26, 236 (n. 21)

Prelude: to *Lohengrin*, 117, 124, 152; as a genre, 125, 229 (n. 38), 230 (n. 39). See also Motif; Program

Prélude à "L'Après-Midi d'un Faune" (Debussy), 135–36

Program: for 1860 concerts, 28–29, 209 (n. 5); definition of, 30–31; music, 30–32, 45, 126, 149, 209 (n. 7), 210 (n. 11), 211 (n. 14); by Liszt for *Lohengrin* prelude, 33, 40–47, 49, 54, 56–57, 126–28, 212 (n. 24); by Baudelaire for *Lohengrin* prelude, 33, 47–54, 58, 145; by Wagner for *Lohengrin* prelude, 33–40, 54, 56, 126–28; to *Tannhäuser* overture, 122, 229 (n. 32)

Prosopopoeia, 97, 217 (n. 10), 219–20 (n. 27)

Proust, Marcel, 1, 23, 143–50, 156–65

Quatre Poèmes d'opéras (Wagner), 68, 122, 205–6 (n. 18), 217–18 (n. 14)

Quotation, 23, 65, 66, 88–89, 98, 166, 217 (n. 9), 219–20 (n. 27); of Wagner's program for *Lohengrin* prelude, 38, 40; of Liszt's program for *Lohengrin* prelude, 41; misquotation of Wagner, 67, 73, 97; of Wagner's letter to Berlioz, 67–68, 73; of Wagner's *Lettre sur la musique*, 68–76, 107, 108; with ellipsis, 71–72, 85, 88, 226 (n. 14); of *"Lohengrin" et "Tannhäuser"*, 81–89; fictive, 97; of Baudelaire, 146

Raser, Timothy, 219–20 (n. 27)

Reicha, Antoine, 45, 212 (n. 25)

Rêveries du promeneur solitaire (Rousseau), 48, 145

Revue européenne, 6

Reyer, Ernest, 221 (n. 35)

Richard, Jean-Pierre, 204 (n. 10)

"Richard Wagner: Rêverie d'un poëte français" (Mallarmé), 138, 141

Rienzi (Wagner), 110

Ring des Nibelungen, Der (Wagner), 21, 152–53, 237 (n. 19); *Das Rheingold*, 21

Risk, 65, 76, 117, 136, 165. See also Chance; Gamble

Rousseau, Jean-Jacques, 48, 118, 145

"Sainte-Beuve et Baudelaire" (Proust), 144–45
Sallis, John, 223 (n. 47)
Salon de 1846 (Baudelaire), 7, 14, 86, 204 (n. 10)
Salon de 1859 (Baudelaire), 44, 87
Scudo, Paul, 63–64, 98, 207 (n. 29)
Sculpture, 86–87; as art of Apollo, 90–91, 94. *See also* Statue
Sea: as metaphor for music, 10–14
Serpent: and music, 82–84, 149; and Wagner, 95; and Eve, 112
Société des Concerts du Conservatoire, 30, 221 (n. 32)
Solie, Ruth, 222 (n. 38)
Stamelman, Richard, 212 (n. 21)
Statue, 64, 85–87, 88–89, 90–91, 94
Steinbeck, Susanne, 228 (n. 30), 230 (nn. 41, 47)
Subotnik, Rose Rosengard, 210 (n. 11)
Symphonie fantastique (Berlioz), 30, 209 (n. 6)

Tannhäuser (Wagner), 17, 101, 134, 137, 142; at Paris Opéra (1861), 5–6, 19, 24, 26, 63, 77, 99, 124, 156, 164, 229

(n. 36); libretto, 122–23. *See also* Overture
Tchaikovsky, Peter, 22
Temperley, Nicholas, 228 (n. 27)
Théâtre-Italien, 5, 26, 28–29, 35, 59, 207 (n. 29), 210 (n. 9)
Thomas, Henri, 89, 222 (n. 40)
Thyrsus, 123–24, 130, 135, 142, 164, 229 (nn. 33, 35), 232 (n. 56)
Translation, 31–33, 39–40, 48–51, 54–55, 57–60, 147, 162, 166, 213 (n. 32)
Treitler, Leo, 219 (n. 19)
Tristan und Isolde (Wagner), 13, 93, 148, 159–60, 236 (n. 18), 237 (n. 19)
Twilight of the Idols (Nietzsche), 94

Valéry, Paul, 225 (n. 7)
Venus, 77, 121
Villot, Frédéric, 68, 73
Voyage artistique à Bayreuth, Le (Lavignac), 22–23

Wing, Nathaniel, 212 (n. 21)
Wyss, Beat, 208 (n. 34)

Zimmerman, Melvin, 229 (n. 35)